A TEACHER'S RIGHT TO A PRIVATE LIFE

Also Available from Bloomsbury

Teachers as Intellectuals, Henry A. Giroux
Constructing Teacher Identities, Nicole Mockler
Teacher Agency, Mark Priestley, Gert Biesta and Sarah Robinson

A TEACHER'S RIGHT TO A PRIVATE LIFE

Community Control or Professional Autonomy

Todd A. DeMitchell and Richard Fossey

BLOOMSBURY ACADEMIC
LONDON • NEW YORK • OXFORD • NEW DELHI • SYDNEY

BLOOMSBURY ACADEMIC

Bloomsbury Publishing Plc, 50 Bedford Square, London, WC1B 3DP, UK
Bloomsbury Publishing Inc, 1359 Broadway, New York, NY 10018, USA
Bloomsbury Publishing Ireland, 29 Earlsfort Terrace, Dublin 2, D02 AY28, Ireland

BLOOMSBURY, BLOOMSBURY ACADEMIC and the Diana logo are trademarks of Bloomsbury Publishing Plc

First published in Great Britain 2026

Copyright © Todd A. DeMitchell and Richard Fossey, 2026

Todd A. DeMitchell and Richard Fossey have asserted their right under the Copyright, Designs and Patents Act, 1988, to be identified as Authors of this work.

Cover design: Paul Smith
Cover image © Nadzeya Pakhoma via Adobe Stock

All rights reserved. No part of this publication may be: i) reproduced or transmitted in any form, electronic or mechanical, including photocopying, recording or by means of any information storage or retrieval system without prior permission in writing from the publishers; or ii) used or reproduced in any way for the training, development or operation of artificial intelligence (AI) technologies, including generative AI technologies. The rights holders expressly reserve this publication from the text and data mining exception as per Article 4(3) of the Digital Single Market Directive (EU) 2019/790.

Bloomsbury Publishing Plc does not have any control over, or responsibility for, any third-party websites referred to or in this book. All internet addresses given in this book were correct at the time of going to press. The author and publisher regret any inconvenience caused if addresses have changed or sites have ceased to exist, but can accept no responsibility for any such changes.

A catalogue record for this book is available from the British Library.
A catalog record for this book is available from the Library of Congress.

ISBN: HB: 978-1-3505-3348-6
PB: 978-1-3505-3347-9
ePDF: 978-1-3505-3349-3
eBook: 978-1-3505-3350-9

Typeset by Newgen KnowledgeWorks Pvt. Ltd., Chennai, India
Printed and bound in Great Britain

For product safety related questions contact productsafety@bloomsbury.com.

To find out more about our authors and books visit www.bloomsbury.com and sign up for our newsletters.

CONTENTS

Front Piece	vii
Chapter 1 INTRODUCTION: THE PRIVATE LIVES OF AMERICAN TEACHERS. EXEMPLAR AND NEXUS	1
Chapter 2 THE EMERGENCE OF AMERICA'S COMMON SCHOOL AND THE ENDURING TENSION BETWEEN THE TEACHING PROFESSION AND THE COMMUNITY	27
Chapter 3 WHO DECIDES WHO WILL TEACH OUR CHILDREN? COMMUNITY CONTROL VERSUS PROFESSIONAL AUTONOMY: THE GUSFIELD MODEL OF OWNERSHIP OF PUBLIC PROBLEMS	61
Chapter 4 THE PROFESSIONAL TEACHER	75
Chapter 5 TEACHER AS A MANDATORY ROLE MODEL, COMMUNITY CONTROL: EXEMPLAR, ADVERSE NOTORIETY, AND COURT CASES	111
Chapter 6 *MORRISON* AND THE RISE OF PROFESSIONAL AUTONOMY: FINDING A NEXUS	145
Chapter 7 ONGOING TENSIONS ABOUT TEACHERS' OUT-OF-SCHOOL CONDUCT	175

Chapter 8
EXEMPLAR AND NEXUS: THE CONTINUING TENSION
OVER WHO SHALL TEACH OUR CHILDREN 205

Appendix A Rules for Teachers in Three Eras 213
Appendix B Efficiency Reports on Teachers from 1923 to 1928 216
Appendix C Table of Court Cases 217
Index 223
About the Authors 225

FRONT PIECE

We write this book on teacher out-of-school behavior based on the importance of education and educators to the students, parents, local community, and the broader society. The impact of educators on these actors is immense. The introductory sentence to the Anneberg Brown University *EdWorking* Paper succinctly captures the beginning point for our book. The authors write, "Few other occupations in the U.S. are as large or as important as the teaching profession."[1] The importance of the education profession may be understood by the concern about the private conduct of educators. Law professor John E. Rumel captures their level of scrutiny, writing:

> Seldom does a week pass without the popular press reporting on teacher off-duty conduct or speech that causes a stir in the local community and triggers adverse employment or licensure consequences for K-12 teachers.[2]

Notes

1 Matthew A. Kraft and Melissa Arnold Lyon, *The Rise and Fall of the Teaching Profession: Prestige, Interest, Preparation, and Satisfaction over the Last Half Century* Annenberg Brown University (EdWorkingPaper No. 22-679, November 2022), https://edworkingpapers.org/sites/default/files/Kraft%20Lyon%202022%20State%20of%20the%20Teaching%20Profession_0.pdf.
2 John E. Rumel, "Teacher Off-Duty Conduct and Speech in Adverse Employment and Licensure Proceedings," *University of Cincinnati Law Review* 83 (2015): 685–746, 685.

Chapter 1

INTRODUCTION: THE PRIVATE LIVES OF AMERICAN TEACHERS. EXEMPLAR AND NEXUS

The vexing question of whether a teacher bargained for an around-the-clock job as a role model has been posed with differing responses. Some would argue that the right to delve into the personal lives of teachers comes concomitantly with the job itself since [teachers] serve as role models to the students. On the other hand, others would argue that the right to limit a teacher's behavior should end when the teacher leaves the school grounds.[1]

As the Greek philosopher Diogenes (412 BC–322 BC) stated more than two thousand years ago, "The foundation of every state is the education of its youth."[2] The age-old question of "Who shall teach our children?" stems from that principle. Indeed, this was the core issue at Socrates' trial, when he was charged with corrupting the youth he taught.

The moral rectitude of teachers has been a topic of concern in American education since at least the beginning of the "one best system" and the rise of the common school in the early nineteenth century.[3] Willard Elsbree, in 1939, noted that the conduct of American schoolteachers has always been a matter of public concern,[4] including a teacher's conduct outside the schoolhouse. One teacher, reflecting on this phenomenon, remarked, "How I conduct my classes seems to be of no great interest to the school authorities, but what I do when school is not in session concerns them tremendously."[5] As the philosopher Josiah Royce observed in 1883, a teacher "may find of a sudden that his non-attendance at church or the fact that he drinks beer with his lunch, or rides a bicycle is considered of more moment than his power to instruct."[6]

Do public schoolteachers have a right to a private life when school is not in session? The US Supreme Court recognized an individual's right to privacy as early as the 1920s. Justice Brandeis argued that the US Constitution ensures that the government does not intrude into the "privacy of the individual."[7] He believed that an individual's private life should be free from government intrusion and that all individuals have "the right to be let alone."[8]

The Fourteenth Amendment requires that "no person be deprived of life, liberty or property without due process of law."[9] Although the US Constitution does not explicitly mention privacy, the Supreme Court has ruled that the right to privacy is implied in the concept of personal liberty as embodied in the Fourteenth Amendment.[10] Specifically, the substantive component of the Fourteenth Amendment Due Process Clause derives mainly from the Supreme Court's interpretation of the term "liberty."[11] As a result, an unreasonable denial of "liberty" may be found when certain governmental constraints on individual conduct unreasonably interfere with important individual rights, including the right to privacy.

As noted by Justice Anthony Kennedy: "there is a substantive component to the due process clause," and "the value of privacy is a very important part of that substantive component."[12] He consistently maintained that the right to privacy revolves around the concept of liberty. Accordingly, there are certain protected zones of privacy where the government should not interfere, regardless of the asserted governmental interest.

In his doctoral dissertation, Fred Eugene Harris implicitly explored the issue of a teacher's right to privacy when he examined judicial definitions of immorality in the context of a teacher's private life. "Conflicts arise out of a clash of rights," Harris wrote. "Teachers assert that their private lives are their own business, whereas school boards argue that teachers are models for their students and must meet the moral standards set by the community."[13]

Conflicts between school boards and educators over a teacher's off-duty conduct have been litigated in the Nation's courts for more than a century. Two core questions are at the heart of all this litigation. Does a teacher's interest in enjoying privacy away from public employment constitute a legally protected zone? Or is the nature of a teacher's work such that the government's compelling interest in educating the community's minors gives it the authority to regulate an educator's private life in accordance with community values and expectations?

This book examines the boundaries of a public school teacher's freedom to maintain a private life. Who has the ultimate authority to decide what areas are a protected zone of a teacher's privacy, and how is the size and contour of the zone to be determined? As we shall explain in the following chapters, two views have been articulated. One view holds that teachers' off-duty conduct must conform to community values and norms, even when they are not on duty. The other view, articulated by many state courts, is that a teacher's off-duty behavior cannot be regulated unless there is a causal connection or nexus showing that the teacher's private conduct negatively impacts their effectiveness in the classroom. Essentially, we address the perennial question: Who shall teach our children?

The Expectations for Teacher Behavior

Noted sociologist Dan C. Lortie emphasized the importance of public schools, writing in his seminal work that "Public schools shape our young and influence their lives."[14] Consequently, without question, who teaches in the Nation's schools is of grave importance. Parents are always anxious about who their children's teachers will be in the upcoming school year. Without data, they often rely on word-of-mouth information and perhaps their prior encounters with a particular teacher. Before the start of the school year, when classroom assignments are being developed, principals, particularly elementary school principals, are often pressured by parents who want their children placed with the "right" teacher.

Because of teachers' unique relationship with children, the community has long held that teachers must have appropriate pedagogical skills that engage students and that their actions, both on school grounds and in their private lives, reflect the community's moral and ethical expectations. Transgressions against a community's moral and ethical expectations are often met with charges of immorality. As a Florida appellate court defined it, immorality is "conduct inconsistent with the standards of public conscience and good morals."[15]

Because teachers play a critical role in our society's social fabric, they have historically been given limited protection for their private behavior. Teachers are expected to be exemplars or role models[16] for the larger community; thus, their private behavior can impact their public employment status. Statutes, court cases, and regulations require teachers to serve as role models because of their unique relationship with the community's youth.

> Teaching is not like driving rivets. It is not merely the rote, mechanical conveyance of factual information from one mind to another. It is the shaping of young minds, the cultivation of a precious resource. A teacher is the bailee of a parent's most valued possession [their] child. As such the teacher bears responsibilities far greater than those borne by most government employees.
>
> *Rogliano v. Fayette County Board of Education*, 347 S.E.2d 220, 226 (1986) (Neely, J., dissenting).

However, physicians, dentists, attorneys, and engineers are also role models who provide a service to patients and clients. These professions are expected to adhere to formalized ethical codes of conduct that structure the relationship between professionals and their clients or patients. In addition, a professional's relationship with the community is regulated by malpractice law, which can hold a professional person liable for negligent services. To date, however, educators have not been held liable for negligent teaching practices under malpractice concepts.[17] In addition to noting the difficulties of applying principles of tort liability to instructional practices, most courts have ruled that education malpractice lawsuits are contrary to public policy.

The control of public education has significant consequences for individuals, the community, and the Nation. The history of education in the United States chronicles the struggle over who decides which aspects of education are most important, including what, when, and how children should be taught, as well as who should teach them. This struggle is rooted in the formation of the American public education system[18] and has assumed particular salience in the second decade of the twenty-first century.[19]

The Community's Exemplar and the Nexus Between Private Behavior and Harm to the Education Process

Maintaining an appropriate balance between the right of parents to control their children's education and the community's obligation to create future citizens has been a persistent conundrum. Parents seek to mold their children in ways consistent with their ideals, social understandings, and aspirations, while communities and the state seeks to form the ideal citizen through discourse and the democratic process. It is not surprising that these visions often collide.[20]

Exemplar

The personal lives of American teachers have long been the subject of scrutiny by both local communities and school authorities. As we previously stated, two theories of teacher out-of-school conduct have defined the controversy over the contours of a teacher's out-of-school behavior. The exemplar theory emerged from the common school movement, which coincided with the push to professionalize teaching and secure the state's role in educating its citizens. For example, an Illinois court in 1885 wrote the following about a teacher's private life: "If suspicion of vice or immorality be once entertained against a teacher, his [or her] influence for good is gone. The parents become distrustful, the pupils contemptuous, and the school discipline essential to success are at an end."[21]

Teachers have long been held to a higher standard of conduct than the typical citizen due to their unique relationship with the community's children.[22] Parents are obliged to entrust their children to teachers for extended periods by the authority of compulsory education laws. For example, in a dissenting opinion regarding the revocation of a medical license for immoral conduct, a California court of appeals judge wrote, "Parents may expect a teacher who, after all, stands in their place for several hours a day, to be an 'exemplar.'"[23]

No other professional activity outside of teaching has such extended control and influence over minors. As Clifford P. Hooker, a noted school law scholar, wrote three decades ago:

> Historically, parents and school officials have maintained that a teacher cannot lead two lives—one as a role model in the school and another as a private citizen. It was assumed that one who chose a career in teaching surrendered a substantial measure of individual privacy.[24]

Referring to the development of the concept of exemplar, one of this volume's authors wrote that historically, "the community's control over teachers was pervasive. Not only were the teacher's classroom conduct and skill keenly evaluated, almost all facets of the teacher's personal life were scrutinized. The watch kept over a teacher's private life was taken up [by] many with a diligence surpassed by few."[25]

For example, a 2014 court opinion ruled that a teacher's personal blog formed the legal basis for her dismissal. Natalie Munroe, a high school English teacher in Doylestown, Pennsylvania, complained on several occasions about her students' lack of motivation, calling them "jerk," "ratlike," "dunderheads," "whiny," and "simpering grade-grubber with an unrealistically high perception of own ability level."[26] She wrote that parents were "breeding a disgusting brood of insolent, unappreciative, selfish brats."[27]

Additionally, Ms. Munroe expressed concerns about the administration. While she claimed to have only nine subscribed readers, two of whom were her husband and herself, the administration became aware of her blogs when approached by a reporter for comment. The district subsequently dismissed Munroe, and she sued the school district for violating her constitutional right to free speech.

At trial, both sides agreed that Munroe wrote as a private citizen.[28] She did not reveal her identity as a teacher and did not name the students. However, her blogs gained widespread recognition throughout the school community, mainly due to media coverage. The district court ruled that while she may have occasionally written as a private citizen on matters of public interest, "she chose to do so in an opprobrious tone likely to generate a strong reaction from anyone connected with the school who read it."[29]

The court found that Munroe's off-campus speech did not merit constitutional protection. The court observed that she used "gratuitously demeaning and insulting language" toward her students.[30] The court weighed Munroe's role as a teacher heavily when balancing her right to express her views on her blog site and the interests of the school. The court concluded that public school teachers need a degree of the public's "trust not found in many other positions of public employment."[31]

Similarly, a New York hearing panel on teacher dismissals wrote of teachers as role models:

> A person who accepts a teaching position willingly places himself and his conduct in the arena of public attention. What may be acceptable in other walks of life takes on an entirely different aspect when engaged in by a teacher. A teacher's influence and effect on students extends beyond the classroom and the school. A teacher stands *in loco parentis*. A teacher is a role model for students to emulate. A teacher is a purveyor of community values. A teacher is

responsible for the well-being of all students. A teacher is all of these things and more.³²

> [T]he teacher's interest in exercising her rights must be balanced against the state's interest in promoting the efficiency of the public services it performs through its employees.
>
> *Ponton v. Newport News School Board*, 632 F. Supp 1056, 1062 (E.D. Va. 1986).

Nexus

However, in the latter half of the twentieth century, public school educators have been "afforded some protections with regard to their out-of-school conduct."³³ Nexus arose as a counterbalance to some of the exemplar standard's inflexible and overly restrictive applications.³⁴ Writing in 1970, McGhehey observed,

> The developments in the case law during the last 10 years or so suggest that neither immoral behavior nor criminal convictions may provide the automatic basis for dismissal commonly assumed by school board members and school administrators. Instead, the courts appear to be fashioning a requirement that the public employer show a causal connection, a nexus, between illegal or immoral behavior and performance on the job.³⁵

For example, in an Oregon case regarding sexual orientation, a school board dismissed Peggy Burton, a high school teacher, for dereliction of her duties due to her sexual orientation, even though she made no sexual advances toward any of her students. When questioned, she confirmed to the school authorities that she was a practicing homosexual. In her second year of teaching, the school district terminated her employment during the second month of her contract due to allegations of immorality, which were deemed to be a violation of state law. The resolution adopted by the school board on October 18, 1971, read, "Peggy Burton be dismissed and the contract terminated as a teacher in the district because of her immorality of being a practicing homosexual."³⁶

Immorality is a commonly stated cause for adverse employment actions regarding sexual orientation, and the exemplar standard is often applied in these dismissal cases. However, in the *Burton* case, the district court judge found that the statutory morality provision was unconstitutionally vague. Judge Solomon wrote,

> Immorality means different things to different people, and its definition depends on the idiosyncrasies of the individual school board members. It may be applied so broadly that every teacher in the state could be subject to discipline. The potential for arbitrary and discriminatory enforcement is inherent in such a statute.
>
> A statute so broad makes those charged with its enforcement the arbiters of morality for the entire community. In doing so, it subjects the livelihood of every teacher in the state to the irrationality and irregularity of such judgments. The statute is vague because it fails to give fair warning of what conduct is prohibited and because it permits erratic and prejudiced exercises of authority.[37]

In the 1960s and 1970s, other courts expressed similar concerns about the subjectivity and arbitrary nature of the exemplary standard for assessing teachers' off-duty behavior. Labor law professor James A. Gross commented on the fluidity of the exemplar standard, writing that it could foreseeably lead to employment decisions "based on the idiosyncratic mores of communities, school administrators, and quasi-judicial decision-makers, rather than professional job-related standards of conduct."[38] Professor Gross asserted that the holding of the Oregon federal court cited above underscored the need for an "objective evidentiary nexus between the alleged misconduct and a teacher's job performance."[39]

A nexus is a connection. When applied to an educator's out-of-school behavior, a nexus analysis seeks to determine whether the questionable behavior (illegal or immoral) affects a teacher's job performance or harms the learning environment. The most cited watershed case adopting the nexus standard is *Morrison v. State Board of Education*, in which California's highest court ruled that private behavior of a teacher can only result in employment sanctions if the conduct affects the teacher's ability to teach or harms the education process.[40]

This theory posits that school authorities must demonstrate that the teacher's behavior has an adverse impact on the school or diminishes the teacher's effectiveness in the classroom. "The profession now had a theory it could assert as it struggled to remove the weight of exemplar from its shoulders."[41] School law scholars have identified *Morrison* as the seminal judicial decision establishing that the nexus standard is the appropriate framework for analyzing off-duty conduct by teachers.[42]

Is the teaching profession similar to other professions and occupations? Do other occupations or professions assume the role of *in loco parentis* or function in "custodial and tutelary" capacities? Does the legally compelled nature of placing children with adults away from home for extended periods justify a greater degree of scrutiny than for other professionals who only have sporadic contact and limited time with children? The answers to these questions help explain why adverse notoriety within the community[43] and exemplar are factors that help define the work of teachers and place upon them, at times unfairly, the burden of being mandatory role models even when they are off duty.

Under the exemplar or role-model theory, a teacher's private life is subject to review and discipline, regardless of whether the teacher is on duty. The exemplar standard requires the teacher to be a role model and never a mere citizen. However, the requirements of exemplar have been relaxed over the last half century through court decisions, most notably the California Supreme Court's 1969 decision in *Morrison v. State Board of Education*[44] (see Chapter 6 for a detailed discussion of *Morrison*), in which California's highest court held that a teacher cannot be dismissed for private conduct that has nothing to do with his status as a teacher.

Morrison articulated a nexus standard in which a school district must show that a teacher's out-of-school conduct adversely affects the school or reduces the teacher's effectiveness in the classroom to justify dismissal or other discipline.[45] "Nevertheless, a teacher's private life is still held to an exemplar standard to a marked degree not found in other professions, although the concept continues to evolve."[46]

However, some commentators have argued against the role model theory. For example, Kristin D. Shotwell asserts, "Simply because teachers hold a position of trust, does not mean their private morality should be subject to closer scrutiny than other members of the community."[47] Furthermore, Wayne Martino questions the role model framework of a teacher's life "and their impact on student learning in schools."[48] Nexus has become the predominant standard for assessing a teacher's out-of-school behavior, but the exemplar standard has not been completely extinguished, as will be discussed later.

An International Perspective

The United States is not alone in holding public school educators to the status of exemplar. For example, Stuart Foxman, writing about Canadian educators, stated that teachers' off-duty conduct—even when it's not directly related to students—is relevant to their suitability to teach. He wrote:

> While other regulated professions have an expectation of professionalism, the teaching profession is seen as particularly important in society. Why are teachers different? The [Canadian] Supreme Court noted the special position of responsibility and influence that they occupy. That comes with high expectations. Breaches of those expectations can cause widespread damage.[49]

While this book focuses on the American experience regarding teachers' private lives, questions about community expectations for teachers concerning their out-of-school behavior cross national boundaries.[50] In his study of teacher misconduct in five Canadian provinces, Canadian professor Paul W. Bennett wrote that "teacher misconduct and regulating the teaching profession has become a critical public policy issue, especially in the wake of national reports on child sexual assault and the spread of online sexual harassment."[51]

The Manitoba Teachers' Society reflects Professor Bennett's observation in their statement "that teachers occupy a position of trust, confidence, and considerable influence with children."[52] Their document titled *Professional Regulation and Teacher Misconduct* states in relevant part, "The Manitoba Teachers' Society believes that: teachers are trusted by the public and others in the profession to act ethically and responsibly."[53]

Similarly, American school law scholar Charles J. Russo offered:

> Regardless of whether they wish to be regarded as such, there can be little doubt that most teachers and parents in Australia, New Zealand, and the United States, and elsewhere agree that teachers, in particular, serve as role models for their students regardless of whether educators act in or out of school.[54]

For example, in New Zealand, referenced by Professor Russo above, the New Zealand Education Act of 1989 states as a criterion for reporting serious misconduct breach of the Code of Professional Responsibility is defined as, "(k) an act or omission that brings or is likely to bring, the teaching profession into disrepute."[55] The test for establishing disrepute is an objective test that "requires consideration of whether reasonable members of the public informed of the acts and circumstances, could reasonably conclude that the reputation and good standing of the profession is lowered by the respondent's actions."[56]

For example, a New Zealand teacher was censured for "'misleading' school authorities about his use of Classroom Release Time and drinking excessively" at a conference. The principal refused to sign the censure letter, and the matter of an appropriate response was referred to the Disciplinary Tribunal for possible misconduct under the applicable statutes. Despite conceding at the earlier Complaints Assessment Committee that his behavior constituted misconduct and signing a letter of censure, the Tribunal concluded that the incident was "trivial and does not warrant a disciplinary response."[57] Thus, the Tribunal did not impose discipline, finding that the conduct did not amount to misconduct.[58] The Tribunal considered the case a close call but was swayed by mitigating factors.

Nevertheless, it wrote that its decision is "not to meant to condone or endorse the respondent's conduct ... Misleading your employer is inappropriate and undermines the relationship of trust between an employer and employee."[59] Furthermore, the tribunal held, "While the drunkenness occurred at a work conference, the conduct did not occur in a school setting and did not have any tendency to affect the learning of children."[60]

This test, as articulated in the New Zealand tribunal's opinion, acknowledges that the public's perception is a crucial factor in determining who can best serve as a role model for students. New Zealand and the United States recognize the importance of the educator as exemplar, through the community pressure of adverse notoriety (discussed in Chapter 5), balanced with the nexus between conduct and harm to the educational experience.

A last example of the international adoption can be found in the United Kingdom. The Department of Education's *Teachers' Standards* states that "A teacher is expected to demonstrate consistently high standards of personal and professional conduct." The first standard of conduct states, "Teachers uphold public trust in the profession and maintain high standards of ethics and behaviour, within and outside school."[61] Clearly, teachers in the United Kingdom are held to a high standard of conduct both inside and outside their school. This is similar to the exemplar standard in the US public schools.

For example, a 2018 article by the British Broadcasting Corporation (BBC) explored the 450 staff members across England who were banned from 2013 to 2018 ("The National Education Union said the number of bans was 'tiny' compared with 500,000 teachers in schools").[62] An example of violations of the "Teachers' Standards" for out-of-school conduct follows.

A primary teacher was banned indefinitely from teaching in England.[63] The panel found her behavior to be unacceptable professional conduct and conduct that brings the profession into disrepute. The panel reviewed the allegations and facts from the position of a teacher's influence on pupils, parents, and community members. They write, "The panel has taken account of the uniquely influential role that teachers can hold in pupils' lives and that pupils must be able to view teachers as role models in the way they behave."[64] Upon reviewing the panel's advice, the Secretary of State for Education instituted the ban.

The specifics of the teacher's behavior that formed the basis for the ban follow:

> These behaviours include fraud and/or serious dishonesty, violence and serious sexual misconduct. In relation to fraud, the panel found that Miss Black's actions in obtaining paid compassionate leave as a result of false representations is analogous to fraud. The panel found that Miss Black was violent towards Parent A. The panel has found that Miss Black has been responsible for serious dishonesty in the elaborate lies that she told to the school and Parent A. The panel also noted that there had been sexual misconduct in Miss Black's unsolicited sexual advances towards Parent A.[65]

These three examples from Canada, New Zealand, and the United Kingdom demonstrate a similar position to America's exemplar and nexus of the critical, serving as a role model that characterizes the profession. While they demonstrate the commitment and responsibility to the community and its children, there is also a tension with educators ability to lead private lives. Our initial question is who should define not only the expectations for teacher conduct and what standard should be used to decide who shall teach our children—exemplar or nexus? We approach this brief exploration with caution, as it is a small sample of countries that share a common heritage and legal system. A more definitive comparative study is left to other scholars.

We next turn to our study of the private lives of teachers and the tension over who controls the expectations for their out-of-school conduct. The following is an overview of the book.

The Book: Exemplar and Nexus, the Enduring Tension

This book examines who controls the dialogue surrounding teachers' private lives as a factor in determining who shall teach our children—the community through the exemplar concept or the profession—using the concept of nexus. The community's expectation that teachers act as exemplary role models has been consistent since the rise of the common school movement. However, in the late 1960s, a competing analysis of teacher private conduct arose in the California courts: the nexus standard.

The Drag Queen

While many may think that school authorities can no longer regulate educators' private lives, the tension between the exemplar standard and the nexus standard endures. For example, in 2024, Shane Murnan, an elementary school principal in Oklahoma and a veteran educator, resigned rather than face being fired.

Murnan worked as an educator during the day and as a drag queen, "Shantel Mandalay," on nights and weekends in clubs. Initially, his night and weekend activities were not a concern for his employer. Murnan did not hide his off-duty activities, although he acknowledged, "I've never put it out there to make it an issue."[66]

However, Murnan's "drag queen" performances became controversial within the community and beyond, attracting adverse notoriety. Supporters of Murnan spoke at board meetings and wore shirts that read "#StandWithMurnan." Protestors gathered outside the school, including street preachers, to protest against Murnan's continued employment as a school administrator. Extra police patrolled the school, and school officials received death threats and bomb threats. Emails were sent to the school district from various states.

Libs of TikTok posted information on Murnan's side activity as well as notification of Murnan's arrest for possession of child pornography in 2001 when he was a fifth-grade teacher. Two judges dismissed the charges against him, and the cases were expunged. Following that incident, Oklahoma renewed Murnan's teaching credential. His current school district did a background check before hiring him, and the district was aware of the past court cases. In a twist, the state superintendent, Ryan Walters, who had publicly called for Murnan's dismissal "because of his participation in drag performances," signed off on the renewal of Murnan's teaching license in April 2013, following a felony background check.[67]

Murnan had an "outstanding reputation" and came "highly recommended" by his previous colleagues. During the early days of the controversy, one of the elementary school teachers in his school commented:

> Teachers come to work smiling ... Students are happy. They are loved. They are cared for. They are supported, but most importantly because of his consistency, his visibility and his willingness to allow mistakes for the sake of growth, we are now thriving and our students are learning.[68]

There was no evidence to suggest that Murnan acted in an unprofessional or harmful manner toward his students. Even so, a parent "questioned whether he was the right hire, given the accusation he faced."[69]

The Oklahoma Department of Education accused Murnan of being unfit to teach because he performed as a drag queen in his private life. Consequently, the Department proposed a rule to address the issue. Superintendent Walters said in a statement that he had "proposed the most aggressive model in the nation for identifying and uprooting these folks from our schools." He posted a social media post entitled, "Drag queens don't belong in the classroom. This is common sense."[70]

The Rule's Impact Statement stated in pertinent part:

> a. What is the purpose of the proposed rule change?
> The purpose of this rule change is to allow for dismissal of a certified teacher for sexual acts, acts that appeal to the prurient interest in sex, or acts that excessively promote sexuality either in the presence of a minor or in a manner available to a minor online.
> b. Will the rule change impact the public health, safety, and environment, and is the change designed to reduce significant risks to the public health, safety, and environment? If so, explain [the] nature of [the] risk and to what extent the proposed rule change will reduce the risk.

> The rule change concerns public health and safety because teachers who participate in certain sexualized conduct in the presence of minors or in a manner accessible to minors online are also likely to behave inappropriately in the presence of minors in a classroom. The proposed amendment removes that risk.[71]

Murnan was not allowed to return to his school for an extended period and eventually resigned under pressure from school district authorities. The school district superintendent asserted that it was not Murnan's out-of-school behavior that was problematic so much as the disruption caused by demonstrators and the threats that school officials received. These disruptions and threats required the school district to incur the costs of a substitute principal and additional school security.[72]

This case illustrates that the exemplar standard still plays a role in the decisions of some school officials regarding who shall teach our children. There was no showing that Murnan's private, out-of-school conduct caused actual harm to the education of children apart from the responses from some individuals who sought disruption as a means of expressing their views. And many of these individuals were not from the local community. Consequently, were the school's community standards, expectations, and values, which the educator was not upholding, driving Murnan out of his job, or was it a case of a heckler's veto at work?

At the time of this publication, we do not know whether exemplar or nexus will determine whether an Oklahoma educator has the right to a private life that includes performing as a drag queen. Whose concept of what constitutes a community standard should prevail in controversies like the one that engulfed Mr. Murnan? Is it the local community that decides what constitutes unacceptable private behavior? Can we, as a community, allow the loudest, most strident, and threatening voice to become the standard? Or are there certain behaviors that, in and of themselves, render a public-school educator unfit to teach our children?

The current moral panic over the public schools' curriculum, library books, and teacher selection has gripped the Nation's attention.[73] Issues regarding the Nation's public schools have been brought before the bar of reason. The question of who shall teach our children is one of enduring tension and of the utmost importance to the community.

> Emphasis has been placed upon the peculiar nature of the vocation of teaching—the fashioning of human lives—and upon the importance of exemplary conduct on the part of teachers, both within and without the classroom. At no time in our history have lawyers, doctors, and other professional workers been expected to maintain a comparable level of righteousness with that required of schoolteachers.
>
> Willard S. Elsbree, *The American Teacher* (New York: American Book Company, 1939), 535.

Organization of the Book

Counting this introductory chapter, the book has eight chapters. Chapter 2 explores the emergence of the common school movement in America and its impact on the question of who shall teach our children. Following the War of 1812 and the emergence of Republican ideals, American school reformers focused on transforming America's locally controlled schools into statewide public school systems, primarily controlled by professional educators. The shift in the locus of power over public schooling created tension between the community and the emerging common school, as it challenged the community's hold over what should be taught, how it should be taught, and who should teach it. History professor Neem, writing on the struggle to implement the common school, wrote, "Americans rightly struggle to find the balance between popular control and professional authority."[74]

David Tyack's seminal work, *The One Best System: A History of Urban Education*, traced the consolidation and transformation of the rural school. Tyack identified the tension between the community and a bureaucratic and professional education system. Professor Tyack wrote:

> The movement to take control of the rural common school away from the local community and to turn it over to the professionals was part of a more general organizational evolution in American education in which laypeople lost much of their direct control over the schools.[75]

Chapter 3 continues the discussion of this tension, analyzing the argument within the conceptual framework of the Gusfield Model.

Chapter 4 focuses on the ethics of the teaching profession. It explores codes of professional ethics and concludes with an analysis of the ethical issues pertaining to the sexual abuse of students. Chapter 5 discusses the early cases that form the framework for the concept of exemplar, including adverse notoriety. Chapter 6 traces the development of nexus, starting with the California *Morrison* decision. Chapter 7 reviews the current challenges created by educators' out-of-school behavior, such as sexual orientation, marijuana legalization, alcohol related offenses, sexual behavior, and the perils of technology. Chapter 8 discusses the ongoing tension between exemplar and nexus, as well as the role of adverse notoriety.

The legal concepts of exemplar and nexus have both been used as standards for disciplining teachers for their off-duty conduct. Exemplar holds that teachers are mandatory role models because of their unique influence on the community's children. In the not-so-distant past, school boards and the courts have applied the exemplar standard to teachers' off-duty behavior, smothering the private lives of teachers and reducing them to mere appendages of the community.

Law professor John Rumel, in a study of teacher out-of-school behavior, wrote that judicial decisions "substantially favored the schools and their constituents over the teachers whom they employed. In other words, very little weight was placed on the teachers' side of the scale."[76] However, a counterbalance to the excesses of exemplar arose in the later part of the 1960s during the push for advancing civil rights. In the *Morrison* decision, the California Supreme Court articulated the concept of nexus, ruling that a school board cannot dismiss a teacher for private conduct unless the behavior negatively impacts the teacher's ability to be effective as an educator. *Morrison* has been cited as persuasive authority in many jurisdictions and is one of the "strongest 'pro-nexus' cases."[77]

Morrison recognized that not all out-of-school conduct negatively impacts the education of students, which would justify disciplinary action. While nexus has protected teachers from many unreasonable applications of the exemplar standard, it has not relieved teachers of the burden of becoming mandatory role models when they are off duty. Herein lies the challenge: who decides who is fit to teach the nation's children, and what aspects of teachers' private lives are acceptable to the community and consistent with professional expectations?

The tension between exemplar and nexus began with the rise of the American common school, which David B. Tyack characterized as the emergence of American schooling as *The One Best System*.[78] The tension over who should teach our children began with the emergence of a major transformation, forging a state-controlled, free system of education for white children, supported through a bureaucracy, and the establishment of a training program for teachers through the creation of normal schools. The strict local control of schools gave way to state-level control, and the haphazard, laissez-faire approach to public education was replaced by organized systems of education. At the heart of the common school movement was the belief that free, common schooling dedicated to good citizenship and moral education would produce citizens capable of addressing the various challenges facing the new republic.[79]

However, strong forces pushed against the rising tide of state-supported, universal public education. Religious objections to the Protestant slant of the curriculum, opposition to taxation, the demands for local control, and the erosion of parental rights provoked opposition.

The common school used education to achieve civic interests and was an institutional response to cultural and social changes. "Schools were seen as a means of turning Americans—whether 'native' or 'foreign-born,' rural or urban—into patriotic and law-abiding citizens, thereby achieving the Jeffersonian goal of securing the republic."[80]

Control over the community's schools was wrested from the community during the common school movement. The tension between the community and the emerging education profession began in the nineteenth century, as the common school movement became the prevailing model for American public education. The issue of control over who is fit to teach the nation's children emerged from the transition of power over education in the early decades of the 1800s—a shift from community control to the profession's autonomy.

This conflict between parents' wishes and the decisions of school authorities has historically occurred in several areas; compulsory education, placement in special education classes, and most notably in curriculum decisions, to name a few. The tension between the purposes of majoritarian government and the desires of individuals to live their life unrestricted readily clash in the area of education. For example, a federal district court held in an issue over whether the public schools could establish a mandatory community service program over the wishes of parents. The court observed, "where our nation has enjoyed a long history of encouraging families to take responsibility for the instruction of their own children, while at the same time, making school attendance compulsory and granting control of the curriculum to state and local officials."[81] However, the court upheld the right of the school district to establish its curriculum. The court wrote, "Plaintiff parents may not use this Court to interpose their own way of life or their own philosophy, however laudable, as a barrier to reasonable state and local regulation of the educational curriculum."[82]

> The following quote has been attributed to President Abraham Lincoln, "the philosophy of the classroom in one generation will be the philosophy of government in the next."
>
> Abraham Lincoln, https://www.brainyquote.com/quotes/abraham_lincoln_133687/.

NEXT: The next chapter explores the early tension between a community's response to the development of the early public system of education and the emergence of professional efforts to build a system of education support by the state. Following the War of 1812, tension built between the local community and education reformers who sought control of the new state-supported institution not only in the burgeoning urban centers but spreading it to the rural towns. And, the conflict between the community and profession over who shall teach our children and what shall be taught became flashpoints in the contest over what should be the goal, the values, and the role of this new public education. It also explores the impact of the feminization of education.

Notes

1. Marka B. Fleming, Amanda Harmon Cooley, and Gwendolyn Mc-Fadden-Wade, "Morals Clauses for Educators in Secondary and Postsecondary Schools: Legal Applications and Constitutional Concerns," *Brigham Young University Education & Law Journal* 2009(1) (2009): 67, 102.
2. Author, Diogenes Quotes, Brainy Quote (n.d.), https://www.brainyquote.com/quotes/diogenes_100801.
3. David B. Tyack, *The One Best System: A History of American Urban Education* (Cambridge, MA: Harvard University Press, 1974).
4. Willard S. Elsbree, *The American Teacher* (New York: The American Book Company, 1939).

5. Howard K. Beale, *Are American Teachers Free? An Analysis Restraints Upon the Freedom of Teaching in American Schools* (New York: Charles Scribner's Sons, 1936), 395.
6. Josiah Royce, "The Freedom of Teaching," *Overland Monthly* (1883): 235–9.
7. John Trebilcock, "Off Campus: School Board Control Over Teacher Conduct," *Tulsa Law Journal* 35, no. 2 (2000): 445–65, 450.
8. *Olmstead v. United States*, 277 U.S. 438, 478 (1928).
9. U.S. Const. Amend. XIV.
10. *Planned Parenthood v. Casey*, 505 U.S. 833 (1992) (reaffirming *Roe v. Wade* and emphasizing the importance of a right to control one's body and life) However, see the recent Supreme Court abortion case, *Dobbs v. Jackson Women's Health Organization*, No. 19-1392, 597 US ___ (2022), in which the majority overturned *Roe v. Ward*. Is a constitutional right to liberty and privacy in jeopardy?
11. The United States Supreme Court, in a tenure case, defined liberty as,

    > It denotes not merely freedom from bodily restraint but also the right of the individual to contract, to engage in any of the common occupations of life, to acquire useful knowledge, to marry, establish a home, bring up children, to worship God according to the dictates of his own conscience, and generally to enjoy those privileges long recognized as essential to the orderly pursuit of happiness by free men. *Board of Regents v. Roth*, 408 U.S. 564, 572 (1972).

12. Lisa Parshall, "Redefining Due Process Analysis: Justice Anthony M. Kennedy and the Concept of Emergent Rights," *Albany Law Review* 69, no. 1 (2005): 237–98, 238.
13. Fred Eugene Harris, *A Judicial Definition of Immorality as Cause for Teacher Dismissal: A Comparison of Two Eras.* Unpublished doctoral dissertation, University of North Carolina at Greensboro (1989), http://libres.uncg.edu/ir/uncg/f/Harris_uncg_9005819.pdf, 1.
14. Dan C. Lortie, *Schoolteacher: A Sociological Study* (Chicago: University of Chicago Press, 1975), vii. See also, "Education provides the basic tools by which individuals might lead economically productive lives to the benefit of us all. In sum, education has a fundamental role in maintaining the fabric of our society." *Plyler v. Doe*, 457 U.S. 202, 221 (1982).
15. *Clark v. School Board of Lake County*, 596 So.2d 735, 738 (Fla. Dist. Ct. App. 1992) ("It is conduct sufficiently notorious to bring the individual concerned or the education profession into public disgrace or disrespect and impair the individual's service in the community").
16. Theodore D. Kemper, an author of a number of social power and status papers, describes a role model as a person who "possesses skills and displays techniques which [an] actor lacks ... and from whom, by observation and comparison with his own performance the actor can learn."

Theodore D. Kemper, "Reference Groups, Socialization and Achievement," *American Sociological Review* 33, no. 1 (February 1968): 31–45, 33.
17 For an exploration of educational malpractice, see Todd A. DeMitchell, Richard Fossey, and Terri A. DeMitchell, *Raising a Cautionary Flag: Educational Malpractice and the Professional Teacher* (Lanham, MD: Rowman & Littlefield, 2022).
18 Todd A. DeMitchell and Joseph J. Onosko, "A Parent's Child and the State's Future Citizen: Judicial and Legislative Responses to the Tension Over the Right to Direct an Education," *University of Southern California Interdisciplinary Law Journal* 22, no. 3 (2013): 591–636, 595.
19 For a discussion of the current moral panic over what is taught and who teaches it, see Todd A. DeMitchell, Richard Fossey, and Terri A. DeMitchell, "A Moral Panic, Banning Books, and the Constitution: The Right to Direct the Upbringing and the Right to Receive in a Time of Inflection," *Education Law Reporter* 905, no. 3 (2022): 905–28, 909. They write, "There are times and issues in which the relationship between school and community and parents are sorely tested, and this is one of those times."
20 Ibid, 915.
21 *Tingley v. Vaughn*, 17 Ill. App. 347, 351 (1885).
22 For example, see *Reitmeyer v. Unemployment Comp. Board of Education*, 145 Pa. Commw. 177 (1992) in which a Pennsylvania middle school teacher's distribution of copies of a racist "joke sheet" to his colleagues, several complained to the superintendent, constituted an act considered to be immoral and willful misconduct. Knowledge of the sharing of the joke sheet spread to the community. Members of the community demanded that the school board take action. The court agreed with the school board that the behavior served as a poor role model and upheld the school board's decision to terminate. The court held that "Reitmeyer's act of distributing the hate sheet at school was a horrible example for his students and did not command the respect and good will of the community." Ibid., 181.
23 *McLaughlin v. Board of Medical Examiners*, 35 Cal. App. 3d 1010, 1020 (Cal. Ct. App. 1973) (Kraus, P.J. dissenting).
24 Clifford P. Hooker, "Terminating Teachers and Revoking Their Licensure for Conduct beyond the Schoolhouse Gate," *Education Law Reporter* 96 (1994): 1–15, 2.
25 Todd A. DeMitchell, "Private Lives: Community Control v. Professional Autonomy," *Education Law Reporter* 78 (1993): 187–97, 190.
26 *Munroe v. Central Bucks School Dist*rict, 34 F. Supp. 3d 532, 534 (E.D. Pa. 2014). For a discussion of *Munroe*, see Charles J. Russo and Allan G. Osborne, "Warning to Educators: Disruptive Online Posts Can, and May be Used Against You," *Education Law Reporter* 308 (2014): 580–7.
27 Ibid.

28 The court found, over the objections of the school district, that several of Munroe's posts were on matters of public concern such as academic integrity and the value of honor. However, the court asserted that these blogs touching on matters of public concern, were done so to discuss personal issues. ibid., 537–8.
29 Ibid., 538.
30 Ibid., 540.
31 Ibid., 539.
32 *Community School Board. District 25 v. Ronald Drew*, N.Y.S. Ed. Dept. at 9–10 (1980).
33 Suzanne E. Eckes, "Strippers, Beer, and Bachelorette Parties: Regulating Teachers Out-of-School Conduct," *Principal Leadership* 14, no. 1 (September 2013): 8–10, 8.
34 See generally *Gover v. Stovall*, 237 Ky. 172 (Ky. Ct. App. 1931). Gover, a teacher, was in the school between eight and nine o'clock at night with another man and three young ladies, one of whom was a pupil in the school. The group kept the lights off and kept the meeting a secret for several days. Even though no immoral act was perpetrated or attempted, Gover was dismissed because his conduct invited criticism and produced suspicions of immorality.
35 Marion A. McGhehey, "Illegal or Immoral Behavior and Performance in the Classroom: The Necessary Nexus," New Directions in School Law, National Organization of Legal Problems in Education (Conference Colorado Springs, CO, 1976). Cited in Harris, supra note 13, 29.
36 *Burton v. Cascade School District Union High School No. 5*, 512 F. 2d 850, 851 (9th Cir. 1975). Ms. Burton appealed the district court's decision refusing to order reinstatement and instead awarding her the balance of her salary for termination and one-half of her salary for the following year. The circuit court in a two–one decision upheld the judgment of the court. The dissent argued the issue was not whether the remedy imposed on the school district would deter it form similar action in the future. Instead, Judge Lumbard argued "The real issue is how best to vindicate Ms. Burton's rights." Ibid., 856 (Lumbard, J., dissenting).
37 *Burton v. Cascade School District Union High School No. 5*, 353 F. Supp. 254, 255 (D. Oregon 1973).
38 James A. Gross, *Teachers on Trial: Values, Standards, & Equity in Judging Conduct and Competence* (Ithaca, NY: ILR Press, Cornell University, 1988): 24–5.
39 Ibid., 26.
40 See W. VA. CODE § 18A-3-6, which reads in pertinent part, "there must be a rational nexus between the conduct of the teacher and the performance of his or her job." This code section was applied to a teacher who was convicted, under a plea agreement, to one count of a

misdemeanor offense for domestic battery for beating his son with a belt. *Powell v. Paine*, 655 S.E.2d 204 (W. Va. 2007).
41 Todd A. DeMitchell, "Teacher Conduct Outside the Schoolhouse Gate: Exemplar or Nexus?" *International Journal of Educational Reform* 6, no. 1 (1997): 91–6, 94.
42 John E. Rumel, "Teacher Off-Duty Conduct and Speech in Adverse Employment and Licensure Proceedings," *University of Cincinnati Law Review* 83 (2015): 685–746, 698.
43 See, e.g., *Pettit v. State Board. of Educ*ation (1973) 10 Cal. 3d 29, 35, n. 5 (writing, "Various cases have emphasized the significance of the public nature of a teacher's misconduct, or the notoriety and publicity accorded it."
44 461 P.2d 375 (Cal. 1969).
45 Ibid., 391.
46 Leslie Robert Stellman, *Teacher Terminations: Is the "Role Model" Concept a Thing of the Past?* Paper Presentation, Education Law Association 11 (November 2011).
47 Kristin D. Shotwell, "Secretly Falling in Love: America's Love Affair with Controlling the Hearts and Minds of Public School Teachers," *Journal of Law & Education* 39 (2010): 37, 69.
48 Wayne Martino, "Teachers as Role Models," in *International Handbook of Research on Teachers and Teaching*, ed. Lawrence J. Saha and A. Gary Dworkin. *Springer International Handbooks of Education*, vol 21. (Boston, MA: Springer, 2009), 755–68, 755.
49 Stuart Foxman, "Off-duty Conduct," *Professionally Speaking* (2018), https://professionallyspeaking.oct.ca/2018-09/2018-09-Feat ure-Story-2-PS.asp.
50 Canada also places legal limits on a teacher's right to a private life. See *John Shewan and Lize Shewan v. The Board of School Trustees School District 34 (Abbotsford)*, 2 British Columbia Court of Appeal (1987). John and Lize were high school teachers. John submitted a picture of his wife reclining on a bed in an alluring pose wearing a garter belt, stockings, and high heels while naked from the waist up. The picture was published in a widely circulated magazine featuring erotic pictures of women. Lize was dismissed for "misconduct." The Court of Appeal found the posting of the picture constituted misconduct. The court held that misconduct is not "confined to the actions in the schoolroom." Ibid. Furthermore, the court wrote,

> "Improper" conduct, even off the job, can lead to a loss of confidence towards not only the teacher involved but towards teachers generally and the public school system as a whole. Furthermore, the judgment suggests, that when it is sufficiently controversial, off-duty conduct on the part of a teacher can lead to avoidable disruption to the normalfunctioning of the school and the education system.

Ibid., 6. The court stated that a teacher's off-duty conduct is a legitimate subject to "special standards."
For a review of *Shewan* see, Bruce Maxwell, "When Teachers' Off-Duty Creative Pursuits Conflict with Role Model Expectations: A Critical Analysis of Shewan," *Interchange* 49, no. 3 (May 2018): 161–78.
51 Paul W. Bennett, "Lifting the Veil and Closing the Loopholes: Teacher Misconduct, Professional Standards and Regulatory Reform," *Education and Law Journal* 32, no. 2 (November 2023): 97–120, 97.
52 The Manitoba Teachers' Society, "Professional Regulation and Teacher Misconduct: What you Need to Know," (n.d.), https://www.mbteach.org/mtscms/wp-content/uploads/2022/09/MTS_Professional_Regulation_Teacher_Misconduct_2022.pdf.
53 Ibid.
54 Charles J. Russo, "Regulating the Boundaries between the Public Lives of Teachers in Changing Cultural Contexts: An American Perspective," *International Journal of Law and Education* 16, no. 2 (2012): 43–53, 43, https://ecommons.udayton.edu/eda_fac_pub/137/.
55 New Zealand Education Act 1989, s 401(9)(1)(k).
56 *CAC v. Teacher*, NZTDT 2022/11 (19 April 2023), Para. #10. See, *Collie v. Nursing Council of New Zealand* [2001] NZAR 74.
57 Ibid., Para. #16.
58 Ibid., Para. #2.
59 Ibid., Para. #23.
60 Ibid., Para. #24(v).
61 Department of Education, "Teachers' Standards," (n.d.), https://assets.publishing.service.gov.uk/media/5a750668ed915d3c7d529cad/Teachers_standard_information.pdf.
62 Lawrence Cawley, "Teacher Bans: Sexually Motivated Conduct is Most Common Cause," *BBC* (July 25, 2018), https://www.bbc.com/news/uk-england-44643267.
63 National College for Teaching and Leadership, "Miss Sarah Black: Professional Conduct Panel Outcome," (September 13, 2016): 24, https://assets.publishing.service.gov.uk/government/uploads/system/uploads/attachment_data/file/554535/Black__Sarah__14411_-_WEB_Decision.pdf.
64 Ibid., 20.
65 Ibid., 22–3.
66 Tyler Kingdade, "Principal with drag queen side gig resigns under pressure from Oklahoma schools official," *NBC NEWS* (February 12, 2024), https://www.nbcnews.com/news/oklahoma-principal-drag-queen-resigns-ryan-walters-pressure-rcna138132.
67 Nuria Martinez-Keel, "Controversy over principal, drag shows pulls Oklahoma district into national spotlight," *The Oklahoman* (September

12, 2023), https://www.oklahoman.com/story/news/2023/09/12/western-heights-public-schools-oklahoma-libsoftiktok-drag-show-principal/70832065007/.
68 Ibid.
69 Ibid.
70 Superintendent Ryan Walters, "Drag Queens don't belong in the classroom. This is common sense," X (5:08 PM February 2, 2024), https://twitter.com/RyanWaltersSupt/status/1753541049140543803.
71 Oklahoma State Department of Education, "Rule Impact Statement: 210:20–29–5 Principle III [AMENDED] (January 22, 2024), https://sde.ok.gov/sites/default/files/RIS%20210.20.29.5.pdf (emphasis in original).
72 Bennett Brinkman, "'Forced' out after drag drama, Shane Murnan rejects Western Heights' confidentiality agreement," *NonDoc* (February 2, 2024), https://nondoc.com/2024/02/02/shane-murnan-resignation-from-western-heights-drag-drama/.
73 Todd A. DeMitchell, Richard Fossey, and Terri A. DeMitchell, "A Moral Panic, Banning Books, and the Constitution: The Right to Direct the Upbringing and the Right to Receive Information in a Time of Inflection," *Education Law Reporter* 397, no. 3 (2022): 905–28. See. Also Jaweed Kaleem, "How drag queen story hour became a battle over gender, sexuality and kids," *Los Angeles Times* (February 22, 2023), https://www.latimes.com/world-nation/story/2023-02-22/drag-queen-story-hour; Ian Millhiser, "The lawsuits seeking to keep drag queens legal, explained," *Vox* (September 7, 2023), https://www.vox.com/2023/9/7/23860447/supreme-court-drag-shows-ban-tennessee-montana-texas-florida-queens.
74 Johann N. Neem, "State of the Field: What is the Legacy of the Common Schools Movement? Revisiting Carl Kaestle's 1983 Pillars of the Republic," *History Faculty and Staff Publications* (2016): 342–55, 347, https://cedar.wwu.edu/cgi/viewcontent.cgi?article=1077&context=history_facpubs.
75 Tyack, *supra* note 3, 25.
76 Rumel, *supra* note 42, 693.
77 *Hainline v. Bond*, 250 Kan. 217, 223 (1992).
78 See Tyack, *supra*, note 3.
79 Barbara Winslow, "Education Reform in Antebellum America," The Gilder Lehrman Institute of American History (n.d.), https://ap.gilderlehrman.org/history-by-era/first-age-reform/essays/education-reform-antebellum-america. Ms. Winslow further described the reform impetus, writing, "A desire to reform and expand education accompanied and informed many of the political, social, and economic impulses toward reform." Ibid.
80 Jennings L. Wagoner and William Haarlow, "Common School Movement: Colonial and Republican Schooling, Changes in the Antebellum Era, the Rise of the Common School," *Stateuniversity.com*

(2023), https://education.stateuniversity.com/pages/1871/Common-School-Movement.html.
81 *Immediato by Immediato v. Rye Neck School District*, 873 F.Supp. 846, 849 (S.D.N.Y. 1995).
82 Ibid., 853.

Chapter 2

THE EMERGENCE OF AMERICA'S COMMON SCHOOL AND THE ENDURING TENSION BETWEEN THE TEACHING PROFESSION AND THE COMMUNITY

> The common school, however humble its surroundings or deficient its curriculum, is the most valuable public institution in the state.[1]

The control of public education has great consequences for individual Americans, their local communities, and the Nation as a whole. A preeminent historian of American education, Lawrence A. Cremin, asserted that important questions in education go "to the heart of the kind of society we want to live in and the kind of society we want our children to live in."[2] The history of education in the United States chronicles the struggle over who has the power to decide which aspects of education are of the greatest worth, including where, when, and what children shall be taught. This issue has its roots in the development of the American public education system.

The early European colonists brought the traditional view that a child's education is a family responsibility involving private, nongovernmental, and often religious-based entities staffed by private tutors. According to Cremin, the family carried the greatest educational burden, followed by the church, with formal schooling occupying a marginal third place. During this time, few children attended school,[3] and formal schooling was not the primary method of educating the young.[4]

Jamestown and the Southern colonies followed the model of assigning full responsibility for education to individual families. However, the Massachusetts Bay Colony charted a new course, one that required local communities to assume responsibility for educating children and youth. Thus, the Puritans introduced the concept that government had a role to play in establishing and maintaining local schools.

Indeed, the roots of our current system of public education emerged from the rocky soil of the Massachusetts Bay Colony.[5] It was not the secular institution of today, with the First Amendment's prohibition against the government establishing a religion and protecting the rights of students, albeit not as robust as those of adults. However, in 1642, religion and state were intertwined, and the twin education taproot served both religion and the state—a novel concept at the time.

"Although religion was central to the governance of Massachusetts, it was not a theocracy."[6] The community was bound by a covenant with God, which affected the community's well-being but not necessarily that of the individual. God could reward society with prosperity for following the covenant but could also visit punishment upon the community for failure to follow His will. This served as a means of unifying individuals within the community, as well as vertically, to God.

Thus, elected officials, who were not clergy, enacted and enforced laws while the clergy preached and met the spiritual needs of the community members. They were separate but linked. Magistrates were responsible for monitoring the community for signs of God's displeasure so as to make changes (laws) to gain His pleasure. Consequently, "national covenants required good works on the part of the citizens."[7] Magisterial duty served the society's responsibilities to meet God's will by ensuring that the community would become a "city upon a hill."[8]

Education in colonial New England was highly valued, primarily for white males. "Literacy took on a religious element," as Edward Janak, an educational historian and professor at the University of Toledo, explained. "If you look at the New England colonies," Janak pointed out, "the construction of schools outpaced all other types of buildings. That tells you the value they placed on reading."[9]

The foundational education laws of the Puritans embraced the need for teachers. While the teaching force was not yet professionally trained, they were necessary. "In early America, the Puritans embraced the role model theory."[10] For example, in the various colonies, the employment of teachers typically included an examination of the prospective teachers' religious and moral rectitude.[11] The table is now set for the Commonwealth to graft the requirements of community good works with education.

Colonial Education

The Puritans passed the first direct school act in 1647. The law was known as the Old Deluder Satan Act based on the opening line: "It being one chief project of that old deluder, Satan, to keep men from the knowledge of the Scriptures."[12]

Protestant influence on education during the colonial period was found in legislation such as the Massachusetts School Law of 1642. This law stated that a good education was important to the Commonwealth and required heads of households to provide for the education of children living under their roof to be taught to read and understand the scriptures and the laws of the Commonwealth. Reading and understanding the scriptures and the colony's laws was necessary for their adherence. Thus, education helped preserve the status quo in a largely homogenous and religion-centered society. Although the 1642 law did not mandate school attendance, it endorsed the idea that education was a community good that local governments could regulate.

Five years later, the Massachusetts General Court enacted the "Old Deluder Satan Act." The General Court, concerned "by what it perceived as persistent parental negligence," passed a more comprehensive education law.[13] This law did not compel attendance, but it provided the prototype for a state-mandated education system that would one day require parents to send their children to the local schools. The law required households to provide a "petty school" (basically an elementary school) and towns having more than ten households to establish both a petty school and a grammar school—the equivalent of a secondary school. The schooling requirement was "accomplished through parental initiative and informal, local control of institutions."[14]

The petty schools were one-room schools. Students attended when they could. Children were primarily taught to read and spell through rote learning, as well as to grasp the fundamental rules of grammar and arithmetic, alongside instruction in religion and morality. Dame schools, where women provided instruction in reading and rudimentary math, often in their kitchens, were established for children typically aged five to seven. This schooling was similar to today's kindergarten curriculum and educational experiences. Young children were given a "hornbook," which was a printed copy of the alphabet and a short prayer mounted on wood and covered with transparent cow horn. Older children read the

New England Primer, which primarily consisted of religious materials, including the Lord's Prayer. Most schooling was closely linked to the Protestant Bible. Arithmetic instruction concentrated mainly on addition and subtraction rather than higher mathematics.

The informal "dame schools" served both girls and boys. However, only boys had the option, typically based on family wealth or status, to attend grammar schools. "Girls received little formal education in the colonized United States during the 17th and 18th centuries."[15] Latin grammar schools were typically reserved for boys from wealthy families, where they were taught Latin and Greek in preparation for Harvard College or the seminary. Attendance at the petty schools was irregular and haphazardly supported, primarily by parents and, to a lesser degree, churches. Some students attended a grammar school for up to seven years.

Education in colonial New England was primarily a two-track system. The primary schools provided basic literacy for lower-class children, with only a few completing primary school and advancing to Latin grammar schools. The sons of the wealthy were tutored at home and then attended a Latin grammar school in preparation for attendance at Harvard College.

Schooling was not extensive; it was either controlled by parents hiring tutors or coordinated by groups of parents who established subscription schools or voted in town meetings to employ a teacher and support a school on a year-to-year basis. Schools were locally funded through a hodgepodge of financial schemes, and school curricula were as varied as the teachers who delivered them. However, overall, schools and the curriculum were conservative in nature, seeking to preserve religious and cultural heritage.[16]

Laws mandating schooling in New England were not necessarily the template for the other colonies. The Massachusetts Bay Colony's link between literacy, primarily Biblical literacy, and the government's interests were not replicated in the other colonies. "Outside New England, colonial governments largely left the burden of children's education to fall on families, churches, and a few privately endowed schools for the poor."[17]

Schooling in most colonies varied due to the wide range of religious groups, social class differences, and diverse countries of origin. Gender-segregated and gender-differentiated education was typical everywhere. While the proportion of male teachers varied by region during the country's colonial period, formal teaching was dominated by men throughout the colonies.[18] "Teachers were poorly paid, transient, and inexperienced, some were undereducated themselves. In no state was education compulsory or fully supported by taxes."[19]

For example, in the Middle Colonies, a variety of religions existed, unlike New England, where Puritanism was predominant. The presence of different faiths and diverse cultural groups led to a diversity of schooling options. Additionally, there was no established legal tradition that viewed education as a community responsibility. In addition, the Middle Colonies were more influenced by the Enlightenment; thus, the curriculum leaned more toward philosophy than religion. Apprenticeships and practical education were also emphasized.

In the Southern colonies, geographical differences impacted the development of schooling. The farms and plantations were spread out, thus making the establishment of a schoolhouse more problematic. Consequently, wealthy plantation owners often hired tutors for their children or sent them to Europe for their education. Sir William Berkeley, governor of Virginia, wrote in 1671 that in his colony, education, like in many other colonies, was essentially a private matter. He described education in Virginia as following "the same course that is taken in England out of towns; every man according to his own ability in instructing his children."[20] And in the Southern colonies, it would take a civil war for the children of enslaved people to receive an education.[21]

Furthermore, one commentator noted, "Schooling and teaching were neither uniform nor institutionalized during the first century and a half of Europeanized life on the American continent."[22] The schools were not institutions with rigid, formal structures. Instead, as one education historian noted, colonial education often relied on "informal" modes of instruction.[23] Michael S. Katz wrote that it was difficult to generalize about schooling during this period; there was enormous diversity in how youth were educated. "However," he wrote, "it is clear that education was not conceived of solely as schooling activities nor restricted to the special province of the schools."[24]

However, by 1787, the importance of formal education in America was becoming broadly recognized, as reflected in the Northwest Ordinance of 1787, Article 3, which declared, "Religion, morality, and knowledge, being necessary to good government and the happiness of mankind, schools and the means of education shall forever be encouraged."[25] "As education assumed a role in creating the American Republic, it inevitably became involved in defining the American people."[26]

In the early nineteenth century, a new vision of education emerged out of New England. Horace Mann of Massachusetts and other education reformers recognized that education was more than a private good that benefited an individual. America needed educated citizens to meet their civic responsibilities in a democratic society. In the view of these reformers, every child deserved a basic education regardless of family wealth and position.

Mann advocated for universally available, publicly funded, free schools for all children. He, and other reformers, emphasized the civic and economic benefits to society—education for citizenship and for work. His advocacy for the school stemmed from his belief that political stability and political harmony relied on an education universally available. School reformers saw common schools "as a means of turning Americans—whether 'native' or 'foreign born', rural or urban—into patriotic and law-abiding citizens, thereby achieving the Jeffersonian goal of securing the republic."[27]

Colonists believed that educating the citizenry was important, but they had not yet established a well-organized and comprehensive educational system. The children's educational experience was not directed toward the enlightenment of the individual but rather to the duties that the citizen owed to the government. The primary schools, which educated a broad portion of the community's children, delivered an education consisting of basic reading, some writing, and rudimentary arithmetic, all delivered through content that was religious, moral, and authoritarian.

In contrast to colonial philosophy, the common school movement was rooted in the idea that the American Republic needed an intelligent and virtuous citizenry. Thus, the educational reformers of the 1830s and 1840s developed an ambitious agenda of educational change; common schools were crafted as an instrument of government to create informed citizens and sound public policies that addressed social, economic, and political problems, not just to maintain order and improve the general conditions of the public.[28] "The movement of free public schools was part of a widespread humanitarian crusade characterized by a faith in the perfectibility of humankind."[29] Horace Mann, the chief architect of the common school movement, sought to create a common school experience for all people, regardless of social class.[30] According to Mann, schooling was necessary to "preserve republican institutions."[31] A cornerstone of the common school was universal schooling, in which all children were required to attend a tax-supported school and learn a common curriculum.

Common school advocates asserted that universal schooling with standardized textbooks, secure funding, and a prepared teaching force would have a leveling effect, allowing merit, rather than social status, to be the critical factor in success. The common school would teach immigrants the attitudes and values as well as appreciation and understanding of American institutions.[32]

Interestingly, Horace Mann also advocated that the benches on which students sat for their lessons be replaced with chairs with backs. The common school, like the school finance reform litigation of the twentieth century, was founded on the belief that wealth, family status, and geography should not be limiting factors in determining an individual's life prospects.

As public demand and support for a system of schooling grew from the Puritan template through the common school movement, the seeds of tension between the community's needs and desires, primarily voiced by parents, and the state's and its emerging educational establishment's interests began to take hold. A legal commentator wrote of this emerging tension:

> Parents who previously had a great deal of control over their child's education and upbringing soon found themselves transferring some of this power to the government, as states selected curricula and required attendance. Some parents, who believed that it was their right to determine how their child was raised, fought to protect their rights as parents.[33]

Below, we discuss the rise of the common school movement in the nineteenth century, which remains the template for American public education today. The political push for establishing common schools throughout the Nation was a paradigm shift in education, truly a watershed event. Whereas the colonial education system reinforced social status, a common education sought to confer status through learning rather than birth. This shift likely strengthened the emerging middle class, as it provided more individuals with a ladder to a higher social and economic status.

The American Common School Movement

> The actions of local people coming together "to run their schoolhouses, to hire teachers, and to collect taxes helped forge a sense of community and made people invested in their schools."[34]

Schooling in the Republic's early days was predominantly rural and overseen by a lay board rather than the clergy. The schools were considered extensions of the community, unbureaucratic, and lacking a professional core of teachers. David B. Tyack asserted that these haphazard, informal arrangements fostered a close relationship between school and community. There was a sense that the schools belonged to the community, not necessarily in a legal sense, but rather in a social sense.

The schools in the early years of the American Republic were financed through a hodgepodge of financial schemes. Community members exerted significant control over their schools, believing that the schools belonged to them, not to professional teachers.[35] The system of boarding teachers around the community provided a mechanism for subordinating the teacher to the community, as well as monitoring the teacher's personal life.[36] Schooling was primarily a local initiative and was firmly embedded in the community. These structures and notions would be challenged and transformed through the rise of the common school movement.

Following the American Revolution, several political leaders advocated for creating a more formal, unified system of publicly funded, free schools. Many asserted that education was to have a dominant place in the new order.[37] "It was an age of exuberant faith in the power and possibility of education."[38] The Republic required an intelligent and virtuous citizenry; thus, public schools were designed as an instrument of government, serving as a lever for government policies that addressed a wide range of social, economic, and political problems.

Following the War of 1812, education gained new significance. The transformation of America from colonies to a new Republic was dominated by the Nation's search to find its place on the world stage while seeking to define what it meant to be an American. What we are as a nation and who we are as a people were the dominant questions. America's republican form of government was strengthened when the United States survived its first major war, the War of 1812. America was taking its place among the nations of the world.

By the 1840s, significant changes had occurred.[39] The emergence of the Industrial Revolution, centered primarily in the Northeast in the 1840s, dramatically reshaped America. The emergence of charity schools accompanied the rise of large urban centers. Increased and efficient modes of transportation opened new areas for development. A surge in immigration from Western Europe, followed by migration from Eastern Europe, brought significant cultural changes. Demographics and technology were the inexorable forces that created changes in their wake.

The Nation essentially turned to education to resolve its social and economic problems, just as the New England Puritans had turned to education to support their fledgling society.[40] In other words, schools were intended to serve as an instrument of governmental policy to address social, economic, and political issues.

American society assigned three major challenges to the schools for resolution:

1. Preserving the Republic by inculcating republican values in all American citizens,
2. Ridding the urban centers of poverty and crime, and
3. Americanizing the immigrant population to appreciate and embrace democratic values, the English language, and the Nation's predominantly Protestant religious beliefs.

Professor Kaestle perceived the common school movement as a cultural response to the transformative effects of industrialization, capitalism, urbanization, and immigration on America. Crime, poverty, and a diversifying population were the effects of the cultural changes to which the common school reformers responded. They believed moral education and good citizenship would foster greater cultural conformity and best address the urgent social problems besetting the Nation.[41]

Public education in the early nineteenth century was rudimentary, irregularly attended, haphazardly supported, and locally controlled. School funding was a hodgepodge of property taxes, tuition payments, fuel contributions, and some state taxes, with no uniform or stable financial scheme. Most education ended at the primary level, with few students continuing to higher levels. Education was neither universal nor compulsory throughout the states. Dana Goldstein characterized the early years around the time of the War of 1812 as generally organized by town councils, local churches, urban charitable societies, or—in more remote parts of the country—ad hoc groups of neighbors. A mix of tuition payments and local tax dollars supported schools. Two-thirds of American students attended one-room schoolhouses, where as many as seventy children from age five through sixteen were educated together, usually by just one overwhelmed schoolteacher, who was nearly always male. Many communities held school only twelve weeks per year, six in the summer and six in the winter. There were rarely any textbooks, and the most frequent assignment was to memorize and recite Bible passages. Teachers whipped naughty children or made them sit in the corner wearing a dunce cap.[42]

There was no uniform or articulated curriculum, and teaching lacked any professional anchor involving a body of knowledge gained through extended, systematic study. There was no professional training that provided standards of teaching practice. Teachers were, in large part, transitory and male. To many, teaching was a way station, a stopover on the path to another vocational destination. Due partly to poor pay, teaching "was crowded with the very dregs, the down-and-outers of society."[43] "In the South and Pennsylvania, itinerant schoolmasters were often portrayed as drunken, foreign, and ignorant."[44] Teaching was a short-lived occupation that was far from being considered a calling or a profession. In addition, there was no professional training that provided standards of teaching practice.

Most communities in the nineteenth century had schools. Still, a system of free public schools supporting the public good had not been operationalized or fully conceptualized in the early 1800s. Since the population was predominantly rural, there was a noticeable lack of uniformity between schools in the various towns and locales.

In response to the hodge-podge approach to educating the citizenry for participation in the emerging Republic, common school reformers, like Horace Mann, worked to institute the following measures:

1. Providing a common educational experience for all students
2. Providing clear-cut, stable financial support for public education
3. Controlling public education at the state level
4. Professionalizing teaching
5. Using education to fight poverty and crime
6. Americanizing the Nation's immigrants[45]

In these rural communities, the local school was typically owned by the community and managed as it saw fit. The rural district schools were in many ways idiosyncratic, reflecting the individual communities rather than a recognized institution. Local control of the schools was firmly entrenched, with parents exerting influence over who was hired and who was retained. There was no buffer of professionalism between the teacher and the community that could blunt quixotic and rash actions against teachers. Teachers were considered to be merely faithful public servants, subservient to the interests of parents and the community.

The control and influence of the local community members were felt sharply, if not oppressively, by the schoolteachers of this period. For example, as part of their wages, teachers were often boarded around staying in their students' homes. Not only did the community control teachers' work lives, but it also controlled their private lives. David Tyack and Elisabeth Hansot commented, "Evidence abounds that townspeople kept a vigilant eye on the out-of-class behavior of educators, and that moral 'lapses' resulted in firings more often than did incompetence in the classroom."[46] Education historian Willard S. Elsbree in 1939 asserted that the subordination of teachers was greatest during the 1920s and 1930s.[47]

Feminization of Teaching

As the common school movement spread and states passed legislation compelling school attendance, the local, often one-room school changed the organization of schooling. These changes were more than just organizational changes; they were social changes. First, teaching, once male-dominated, became overwhelmingly female by the late 1800s. Another change was the increasing practice of boarding teachers with multiple parents and community members, often for only a week at a time, thus giving the teachers an itinerant feel to their lives. The practice was extensive, especially in rural communities, but less common in urban school districts. For example, in 1862, the number of teachers in Vermont subjected to this mode of life was about 3,352 teachers— approximately 68 percent of the state's teaching force.[48]

The immediate effect of this practice was the loss of a teacher's private life. Living with families allowed their hosts to scrutinize the intimate details and the minutia of a teacher's life. During the colonial period, the moral character of teachers was not necessarily a prized characteristic. Instead, the ability to control students was more highly valued.

The common school movement aimed to educate as many children as possible to achieve its goals. Advocates viewed universal education as a means to alleviate poverty, reduce crime, and address other social issues.[49] Educational leaders needed more teachers, a particularly inexpensive source of labor to teach the influx of students. Horace Mann and Catherine Beecher, leaders in the movement, lobbied in support of women teachers, arguing that they had purer morals, were natural teachers and nurturers, and were endowed with a sort of missionary zeal: in other words, "women were ideally suited for teaching."[50] Mann wanted an education "to match women's gentle manners, rather than the severity of male teachers, with innocent children."[51] And female teachers were paid significantly less than their male counterparts.

Women soon dominated the teaching profession, especially in the lower grades.[52] Male teachers gravitated toward administrative positions, such as principal, superintendent, and educational experts, as schooling became more bureaucratized and the Industrial Revolution created more job opportunities for men. As men left the classroom, females filled the void. The "feminization of teaching"[53] also coincided with the rise of the cult of domesticity and true womanhood, a white-middle-and upper-class ideology built on clear gender roles.[54] Grumet asserted, "The ideal ... teacher was one who could control the children and be controlled by her superiors."[55]

The emergence of the feminization of teaching was influenced by the push for compulsory education, which swelled the student population and required a significant need for more teachers. At the same time, the bureaucratization of schools into systems created a hierarchy of positions, with men almost universally filling administrative positions. The community's search for a new cadre of teachers shifted to female applicants who had limited employment opportunities and could thus fill teaching positions at a significantly lower wage than male teachers would require. Changing perceptions of women, along with a push to use education for achieving governmental goals, combined to create a new perception of the teacher. "The aspects of teaching that seemed appropriate to women were emphasized: nurturance and morality."[56]

The feminization of teaching, we assert, contributed to the concomitant rise of the exemplar standard. Men were being replaced by women in the classrooms, particularly in the lower grades. Republican virtues were consistent with the perception of females as moral examples and nurturers. Boarding teachers provided the opportunity for scrutiny of the private lives of teachers. Appendix A underscores this proposition in that the private lives of female teachers were closely watched and circumscribed.

The rules become more specific in 1915 than in 1872, with more of a focus on female teachers (e.g., #2, You are not to keep company with men; #6 You may not ride in a carriage or automobile with any man unless he is your father or brother; and #10 You must wear at least two petticoats.) However, the 1872 rules allow men to date (#4 Men teachers may take one evening each week for courting purposes, or two evenings a week if they go to church regularly.), but female teachers who marry will be dismissed (#6 Women teachers who marry or engage in unseemly conduct will be dismissed.). This prohibition for female teachers to marry is also found in a 1915 rule, which states, "You will not marry during the term of your contract."

The carry-over to the 1936 contract shows a continuation of many of the restrictions on female teachers that were common in the nineteenth century. For instance, teachers must promise not to fall in love, become engaged, or secretly marry. They were restricted to their dormitory or the school and to the type of clothing that must be worn, not just in the schoolhouse but in any public setting. The prohibition on going out with young men, except to support Sunday school work, reinforced the view of female teachers as adolescents with restrictions from their parents rather than as employees under a work contract between adult educators and their employers.

Some rules restricted both male and female private behaviors. Actions deemed normal if taken by other adult community members were considered inappropriate for teachers. In some ways, these strictures were reminiscent of restrictions that parents placed on their minor children. Examples from the 1915 rules include: "#3 You must be home between the hours of 8 p.m. and 6 a.m. unless attending a school function; #4 You may not loiter downtown in ice cream stores"; and from the 1872 rules: "#8 Any teacher who smokes, uses liquor in any form, frequents pool or public halls, or gets shaved in a barber shop will give good reason to suspect his worth, intention, integrity and honesty").

Teachers were expected to uphold and adhere closely to the community's standards of thought and action. They were expected to participate in all community events. Beale, writing from the perspective of the 1930s and 1940s, commented, "The teacher is still 'only a teacher,' not entitled to vigorous views on things that matter in the community if his views differ from those generally accepted."[57] The teacher was a public servant. The role model requirements attached to them reinforced the concept of selfless service to the community, including giving up large swaths of their private lives to the community's control.

The scrutiny over teachers' private lives was not a central feature of colonial times. Private conduct arose as an expectation and requirement for teachers with the rise of the common school movement and the significant changes to the structure and functions of education and to the central position that education had assumed. The focus of the moral life of the teacher sharpened by the early twentieth century with ardent calls from educational philosophers such as John Dewey and William Hutchins for moral development and character education in public schools.[58] As the twentieth century progressed, these calls were heeded by state legislatures, which passed character education and educator employment statutes requiring moral conduct among teachers.[59] The public expectation that teachers lead morally upright lives remained essentially unchanged throughout the nineteenth and twentieth centuries.

Opposition to the Common School Movement

The idea of a publicly supported education system was not universally accepted. For example, Kaestle wrote that "in the South there was less enthusiasm for local common schooling and more successful resistance to the creation of state systems."[60]

Many believed that education was a luxury to be paid for by the family if they so desired and had the means. Many asserted that education was a private and not a public matter. Another common belief was that the masses, especially in the growing urban centers, would not benefit from a free public education because they were neither morally nor intellectually fit for education.

Opponents also argued that the "thrifty" should not have to pay for the "shiftless" and that free public schools rewarded the poor.[61] The editor of the *Philadelphia National Gazette* argued in the 1830s that free universal education was nothing more than a harebrained scheme of social radicals, claiming that it was absolutely illegal and immoral to tax one part of the community to educate the children of another.[62] One New York opponent of free state-supported schools said that he "would fill the belly or 'cover the back' of a pauper, but he would never send him to school."[63]

There was great skepticism among some members of the populace about the value of education and even greater skepticism about state-supported education; "they did not want more government involvement" in education.[64] The push for centralizing education was denounced as "Prussian." In short, the idea of a publicly supported education was not universally accepted. Many believed that education was a frill and a luxury to be paid for by the family if they so desired and had the means. Many asserted that education was a private and not a public matter.

The Common Schools as Nonsectarian Schools? The Catholic Response

Many Roman Catholics (and some Protestant sects) strenuously objected to the supposedly 'nonsectarian' schools. Many Catholics agreed with New York City Bishop John Hughes, who argued that the public schools were anti-Catholic and unacceptable to his flock. When repeated pleas for a share of public funds dedicated to the support of religious schools failed to win legislative approval in New York and elsewhere, many Catholics rejected the nondenominational public school compromise, a situation that eventually led to the creation of a separate and parallel system of parochial schools.[65]

In the broadest sense, Catholic education commenced with the missionary activities of the Catholic powers (France and Spain) that explored and settled the regions that later became the United States beginning in the sixteenth century. But Catholic parochial schools, which played a major role in educating American children from the post-Civil War period through the 1960s, developed in response to the Protestant character of nineteenth-century public schools, the anti-Catholic prejudices that permeated American culture throughout the nineteenth century, and the urgent educational needs of Catholic immigrants who came to the United States in large numbers during the nineteenth and early twentieth centuries.

In the English colonies, most settlers were Protestants. Before the American Revolution, the British colonies contained only about 25,000 Catholics in a population of nearly two million, mainly concentrated in Pennsylvania and Maryland. According to Walch, no documentary evidence exists of a Catholic school operating in Pennsylvania before the 1780s. Only two Catholic schools in Maryland were established before the American Revolution: Newton Manor, founded in 1640, and Bohemia Manor, established in 1745.[66] Laws discriminating against Catholics were common in the English colonies, and a Maryland law passed in the early eighteenth century banished "any Catholic involved in the education of children."[67]

Beginning in the late 1820s, the Catholic hierarchy in the United States began to recognize the need for formal Catholic education to protect Catholic children from the influence of the predominant Protestant culture. However, Catholic schools were not a fixture in educational institutions, except for the establishment of Georgetown University. During this time, the movement to establish common schools began. As historian Carl Kaestle observed, the ideology of the Common Schools Movement centered on "republicanism, Protestantism and capitalism, three sources of social belief that were intertwined and mutually supporting."[68] Common school advocates believed that public education should include moral training based on nonsectarian Protestant principles, and they favored the inclusion of nondenominational Protestant religious instruction for all children, regardless of their religious affiliation—both Protestants and Catholics.

Thus, from the start, the common schools included religious instruction "on the pieties of generic Protestantism" and Bible reading from the King James Version of the Bible.[69] Textbooks also promoted Protestant religious values and often were openly anti-Catholic. Indeed, the Catholic bishops noted in their 1829 pastoral letter to the laity that "the school-boy can scarcely find a book in which some one or more of our institutions or practices is not exhibited far otherwise that it really is, and greatly to our disadvantage."[70]

Understandably, many Catholics were deeply suspicious of the public schools. Catholic parents resented paying taxes for schools that were openly hostile to Catholicism, and they protested against having their children exposed to the King James Version of the Bible. Urban Catholics complained about the Protestant biases of the fledgling public schools, providing yet another source of opposition and a reproach to the reformers' claims that public schools were "common" to all.[71]

Bishop John Hughes, an Irish immigrant and prelate of the New York Catholic Diocese, launched a protest in reaction to the curricular materials and classroom instruction that often had a decidedly anti-Irish and anti-Catholic message. Described as fierce and uncompromising, Hughes proclaimed, "We are unwilling to pay taxes for the purpose of destroying our religion in the minds of our children. That such books should be put into [their] hands is unjust, unnatural, and intolerable."[72] Bishop Hughes asserted that Catholic children deserved their own schools and called on New York's civic leaders to make funds available for Catholic schools. In the great school debate of 1840, he rebutted ministers from different denominations, hour after hour. He exclaimed to the crowds who would flock to these debates, "We will not send our children where they will be trained up without religion, lose respect for their parents and the faith of their fathers, and come out turning up their noses at the name of Catholic … In a word, give us our just proportion of the common school fund!"[73]

The debate about public funding for Catholic schools continued in the press, with many taking a position against using public funds to support religious education. An editorial writer for the *New York Herald* wrote in November 1841, "Once we admit that the Catholics have a right to a portion of the school fund, every other sect will have the same right … We shall be convulsed with endless jarrings and quarrels about the distribution of it and little left for the public schools."[74]

A reader responded in the same vein: "The Catholics have a right to think and worship in their own way: but have no right to claim one cent of the public money to propagate their own faith."[75] This nineteenth-century debate over public funds for religious education foreshadowed the current controversy over the parental choice movement, which has manifested itself in vouchers, educational savings accounts, and the establishment of religiously related charter schools.[76]

In some communities, tensions between Catholics and Protestants were resolved through curriculum changes that limited instruction to strictly secular subjects. However, in many cities with large Catholic populations, Protestant authorities refused to recognize the religious sensibilities of Catholic families.

In addition, the common school movement gained momentum during a time of intense nativist prejudice toward Catholic immigrants, who were mostly Germans and Irish. Occasionally, this prejudice led to violence. In 1834, rioters, stirred up by the anti-Catholic preaching of Lyman Beecher, burned the Ursuline Convent in Charlestown, Massachusetts.[77]

In the early days of the fight to establish the common school, the content of the common curriculum became a matter of great debate and a spark for the Philadelphia Bible Riots in 1844.[78] The nativists and Irish immigrants clashed after the Catholic bishop of Philadelphia wrote a letter to the local school board, asking that Catholic children be excused from reading from the King James Version of the Bible. Several people were killed in these riots, and two Catholic churches were burned. Public authorities called out the First Brigade of the Pennsylvania Militia to restore public order.

The Catholic hierarchy became increasingly alarmed about the pervasively Protestant and often openly anti-Catholic character of the public schools. Through a series of three plenary sessions starting in 1852, the Catholic bishops emphasized their support for Catholic schools as a counterbalance to the growing influence of the common schools, which the bishops saw as an attack and slander on their sacred religion and teachings. At the Third Plenary Council, the bishops adopted legislation to strengthen Catholic schools. Critically, they required all Catholic parishes to establish parochial schools within two years unless the local bishop granted a postponement, and the Plenary Council obligated Catholic parents to send their children to parochial schools unless they homeschooled their children or sent them to other Catholic schools.[79]

The decrees issued by the American bishops at the Third Plenary Council of Baltimore accelerated the construction of Catholic schools in the United States. Together, the parochial school and the parish church became the centerpiece of Catholic culture in the United States in the late nineteenth and early twentieth century, as Catholic immigrants flocked to ethnic parishes for mutual support against the prejudices they experienced from the dominant Protestant culture.

In many ways, the implementation of a system of Catholic parish schools arose in response to the common school movement. These nonpublic schools formed the foundation of private schools that sought to educate their children in accordance with their parents' religious beliefs and values.

Despite the pushback against the common schools, there was great hope for the Republic and a fiery faith among the common school reformers "in the power and possibility of education."[80] Political leaders were concerned about the Nation's educational needs. They were skeptical about the effectiveness and the efficiency of the patchwork of schools that dotted the Republic. They argued for more schools organized within systems that could standardize education within their jurisdictions and maintain quality standards.

The Rise of Bureaucratic Schooling

The public school as we know it was born in the mid-nineteenth century. Its founders called it the "common" school. Common schools were funded by local property taxes, charged no tuition, were open to all white children, were governed by local school committees, and were subject to a modest amount of state regulation. They arose through two decades of debate prior to the Civil War in the Northeast and the Midwest of what is now the United States, and later in the nineteenth century in the South and the West.[81]

The common school reformers eventually prevailed, upsetting the current power structure by establishing a state-regulated school system supported by public funds for the school, nudging schools toward a longer school year, and encouraging professional development, mainly by establishing normal schools for teacher preparation. Local control was previously firmly vested in the parents, and in most communities, there has been no system of publicly supported schools. "Not until education was viewed as a government function, as opposed to a family function, did organized systems of schooling appear."[82] This new state function sowed the seeds of tension between parents and the state over who should direct children's education.

During the rise of the common school in America, Canada experienced a similar increasing interest in the assertion of professional influence over education. Dr. Paul Bennet, in a study of the teaching profession in Novia Scotia, Canada stated, "Throughout the one-room schoolhouse era from the 1820s until the 1950s, teachers prized their autonomy."[83]

Compulsory education of children in public schools became a standard of the common school movement. As one noted education historian wrote, "The effort to professionalize, homogenize, and organize common schooling threatened highly prized local control."[84] The result was a shift in the locus of educational decision-making as schooling evolved into a government function with a professional teaching force, a more centralized curriculum, and a reliable funding source through a uniform tax base, primarily on property. "The common school movement brought education more fully into the public sphere and made it amenable to public policy."[85]

It is important to note that the expansion of access to education was not evenly distributed to the Nation's children. Females and Blacks did not have full access to a public education, and enslaved people had no access to an education whatsoever. Indeed, in some jurisdictions, it was against the law to educate enslaved people. The concern for the children of free Blacks or the children of slaves was not at the forefront of the argument for a common school. Nor was it in the background. It was largely missing from the conversation.

Neither race nor marginal populations were a central concern of the common school equation reform agenda. Instead, "opportunity, not equality, ranked high among the goals of early school reform."[86] Thus, although Black children suffered from deplorable conditions in segregated schools, the Supreme Court ruled that racial segregation was not unconstitutional under the "separate but equal" doctrine. It would take the Court until the middle of the twentieth century to cast racially segregated schools into the dustbin of history.

Thus, thanks to the common school movement, education became seen as a public good in which the government at the state level invested in public education that moved from decentralized, loosely structured village schools to a more standardized system managed by a centralized professional bureaucracy.[87] Education historian Lawrence A. Cremin identified the politicization of public education as a means of addressing significant, pressing social problems. The common school movement forged a direct link between education and governmental policies regarding social, economic, and political issues.

Education became the indirect means for addressing specific social issues rather than through the direct political process.[88] Politicians frequently turned to the schools to address public problems. Stanford University professor David F. Labaree called this tendency the "educationalizing social problems," in which education is tasked with addressing social issues. For example, he wrote:

> We ask education to ameliorate race and class inequality through school desegregation, compensatory coursework, programs to reduce prejudice and free lunches ... We ask it to promote sexual responsibility through sex education, traffic safety through driver education, healthy eating through nutritional education, and preservation of natural resources through environmental education. American society asks its system of education to take responsibility for remediating all of these social problems, and for the most part educators have been eager to assume the burden.[89]

The fact that much is expected of education underscores the critical role that public education plays in the rhythm of the community through the impact of its processes, such as the time allocated to academic schedules and activities. The response to the ravages of Covid-19 and its impact on schools was felt nationwide, with a major controversy centering on the schools. Specifically, many public school systems moved instruction online and mandated masks when students, faculty, and staff were on campus. And potentially, as a response to the reactions to the pandemic, public schools were the target of a moral panic.[90] The political push for legislating parent rights to direct the upbringing of their children focused on the long tension between educating the child and educating the citizen.

The Tension: The Parents' Right to Direct the Upbringing of Their Children and the State's Duty to Educate Its Citizens

In the early days of our Republic, the local community had considerable power over the rural district school. The patrons of the school had little doubt that the school was theirs to control and not the property of the professional educator. But things were changing. "These communities controlled their schools in ways that would become impossible as regulations became more centralized and teachers more professional." Regulations centralized and bureaucratized the schools and as educators became more professional they wanted to assert the privilege of that status by seeking greater autonomy.[91]

The success of the common school movement caused a seismic shift in power from the child's parents to a "a more standardized, centralized, professional bureaucracy and away from decentralized, loosely structured village schools." Professor Tyack asserted that the "ambiguity of authority and diffusion of control" that characterized the rural district schools as education was transformed into a bureaucratized, government-run education system.[92] The development of the common school as a public benefit and an instrument of public policy conflicted with parents' desire to control their children's education. This tension, which first arose with the rise of the common school movement in the nineteenth century, became a recurring theme in public education.

This tension has often played out in judicial and legislative venues. Kristin Shotwell wrote, "the nineteenth century idea of the teacher as a public figure and role model eventually became codified in statutes and administrative codes."[93] Furthermore, two education professors commented:

> Public education became an instrument of government initiatives and policies. It also became a public good, not just a private benefit of the fortunate. As the Nation grew and cities and states asserted more control over the form and function of public schooling, challenges to government power in the arena of public education were brought to the courts by concerned parents.[94]

A transfer of authority from parents to the newly institutionalized and bureaucratized school occurred when the common school template was adopted. A school official in the 1880s captured this sea change, writing, "one might trust 'parental instinct' to educate an individual child, but the state required homogeneity; 'the right of preservation of the body politic' took precedence over all other rights."[95] The broad education reform goal of a state supported education to address social and policy issues was supported by various state courts.

For example, the Indiana Supreme Court upheld the state's compulsory education law, holding that parents have a natural obligation to educate their child; however, "this duty owes not to the child only, but to the commonwealth."[96] Similarly, the New Hampshire Supreme

Court held the primary purpose of maintaining a public school system is "the promotion of the general intelligence of the people constituting the body politic."[97]

However, in 1877, the Illinois Supreme Court reflected a presumption in favor of parents' control over the education of the children, stating that even if parental decisions resulted in misfortune for the child, the parent's decision would be upheld if it did not "affect the government of the school or incommode the other students or the teachers."[98] And a Nebraska court asked and answered the question of control of a child's education, writing, "Who is to determine what studies she shall pursue in school—a teacher who has a mere temporary interest in her welfare, or her father, who may reasonably be supposed to be desirous of pursuing such course as will promote the happiness of his child?"[99]

In the new century, however, the courts moved from supporting parents' rights to control their children's education to upholding educators' policy decisions, even when those decisions overrode parental objections. The linchpin of the modern education system is dependent upon a professional teaching force, and tensions have often arisen between the parent and the state over a child's education. A trade-off has been made in which parents relinquish authority over discipline and work of the school in exchange for the school's "promise to confer opportunity and status" to their children.[100]

Nevertheless, the Supreme Court ruled more than a century ago that parents have a fundamental right to direct the upbringing of their children, and that right can, in certain circumstances, override the authority of the schools. According to the US Supreme Court in the seminal case of *Pierce v. Society of Sisters*, "The child is not the mere creature of the state; those who nurture him and direct his destiny have the right, coupled with the high duty, to recognize and prepare him for additional obligations."[101] Eleven years before the Oregon decision in *Pierce*, a Nebraska court stated that the parent's duty to educate is "owed not only to the child but to the commonwealth."[102]

The tension between parental rights and bureaucratic authority persists to this day.[103] However, courts have never ruled that parents have a legal right to veto curricular decisions made by school authorities. Allan Osborne and Charles Russo, two noted school law commentators, succinctly wrote, "Parents do have substantial rights to direct their children's education in terms of being able to choose where their offspring will attend school even if they cannot necessarily dictate the curricula within those venues."[104]

Similarly, Brooke Schultz, commenting on the political environment surrounding public education, observed:

> In politics today, many U.S. parents have joined a conservative movement pushing for state legislation giving parents more oversight of schools. At issue are library books and course material, transgender students' use of school bathrooms and the instruction of topics related to race, sexual orientation and gender identity.[105]

The tension over who controls a child's education is not new; it has endured. Professor Tyack recognized the tension between local control and expert guidance in his analysis of the common school movement. He commented that too often, communities were "oblivious of possible local tyranny and parochialism," and reformers did not always understand the "fragility" of the voluntary community.[106] Professor Martha M. McCarthy, writing about conflicts about the school curriculum, observed that challenges to school offerings were initiated primarily by individual parents or conservative groups without legislative backing until recently.[107] Recent legislation banning certain books in public school libraries and classrooms is part of widespread concerns about teaching "divisive concepts,"[108] and the increased legislative interest in passing "parental rights" legislation[109] is reflective of this continued tension.

NEXT: The common school movement set the stage for the tension between the community and the teaching profession as a public system of schooling emerged. The reform movement established a bureaucratic approach to the state-supported education system, started a movement toward the professionalization of the teaching force, and provided a major new career path for women. The next chapter explores Gusfield's model for identifying who owns public problems and applies this model to the tension between the community and the education profession regarding who will teach our children.

Notes

1 *Williams v. Stanton Common School District*, 173 Ky 708, 708 (1893).
2 Lawrence Cremin, *Public Education* (New York: Basic Books, 1976), 74–5.
3 Lawrence A, Cremin, *Traditions of American Education* (New York: Basic Books, 1977), 12–13. Dame Schools are an example of primary or petty schools, in which women provided instruction in reading and

rudimentary math, often in their kitchens, and were one of the ways by which an elementary education was delivered to students. Boys who could afford to pay continued their education in Latin grammar schools.

4 Ibid., 28.
5 In 1875 Francis Adams wrote:

> More than one of the United States claim the honor of having first introduced the free school in America. On behalf of New York, it is said that the Dutch who colonized that state, took it there from Holland. Hartford (Conn.) appears to be the first town which established a free school, but there can be little doubt that Massachusetts was the first state to make laws providing for a regular system of education.

Francis Adams, *The Free School System of the United States* (New York: Arno Press, 1875), 46.

6 Vincent Stine, "A Church-State Partnership in Defense of the Puritan National Covenant," *Journal of Church and State* 56, no. 3 (Summer 2014): 486–502, 487. In 1635, the Boston Latin School, the oldest publicly funded school, was created by the Boston Town Meeting and not by a church. The voters agreed to use rents from Deer, Long, and Spectacle Islands to support the school and pay the schoolmaster.
Author, "April 1642: Massachusetts Passes First Education Law," *Massmoments* (n.d.), https://www.massmoments.org/moment-details/massachusetts-passes-first-education-law.html.

7 Harry S. Stout, *The New England Soul: Preaching and Religious Culture in Colonial New England* (New York: Oxford University Press, 1986), 24.

8 John Winthrop in his well-known speech in 1630, articulated "A Model of Christian Charity" aboard the *Arbella* prior to reaching the shore of Massachusetts as an inspiration for the English colonists' new community. Winthrop stated in part about the Articles of their Covenant: "The lord make it like that of New England: for wee must Consider that wee shall be as a Citty upon a Hill, the eies of all people are uppon us."
Author, "City Upon a Hill," *Digital History* (n.d.), https://www.digitalhistory.uh.edu/disp_textbook.cfm?smtID=3&psid=3918.

9 Daniel Roos, "What School Was Like in the 13 Colonies," *History* (September 7, 2022), https://www.history.com/news/13-colonies-school. "For Puritans, Reading Was a Religious Duty" (Article Heading, emphasis deleted).

10 Ruth L. Davison, John L. Strope, and Donald F. Uerling, "The Personal Lives and Professional Responsibilities of P-12 Educators: Off-Duty Conduct as Grounds for Adverse Employment Action," *Education Law Reporter* 171 (2003): 691–714, 692.

11 Michael Imber, "Morality and Teacher Effectiveness," *American School Board Journal* 188, no. 4 (April 2001): 64–6, Johann N.64.

12 *The Laws and Liberties of Massachusetts*, Reprinted from the Copy of the 1648 Edition in the Henry E. Huntington Library, with an introduction by Max Farrand. Harvard University Press, 1929, https://www.mass.gov/doc/old-deluder-satan-law/download.
13 Massmoments, *supra* note 6.
14 Carl F. Kaestle, *Pillars of the Republic: Common Schools and American Society, 1780–1860* (New York: Hill and Wang, 1983), 3.
15 Michele Kahn and Paul C. Gorski, "The Gendered Heterosexist Evolution of the Teacher Exemplar in the United States: Equity Implications for LGBTQ and Gender Nonconforming Teachers," *International Journal of Multicultural Education* 18, no. 2 (2016):15–38, 17. The authors drew the connection that "the lack of widespread education for women naturally contributed to the lack of female teachers." Ibid.
16 James Shuls, "Papists and Pluralists: The Founding of America's First Grassroots School Choice Organization," *Journal of School Choice* (July 3, 2022): 5, https://www.tandfonline.com/loi/wjsc20.
17 Roos, *supra* note 9.
18 Kahn and Gorski, *supra* note 15, ibid.
19 Nancy Kober, "History and Evolution of Public Education in the US," *Center on Education Policy* (George Washington University) (2020): 1–8, 2.
20 Wayne J. Urban and Jennings L. Wagoner, Jr., *American Education: A History* (2nd ed.) (New York: McGraw Hill), 22–3.
21 For additional readings on the education struggle of African Americans, see, Andrea Williams, *Self-Taught: African American Education in Slavery and Freedom* (Chapel Hill, NC: The University of Carolina Press, 2015) and Hilary Moss, *Schooling Citizens: The Struggle for African American Education in Antebellum America* (Chicago: University of Chicago Press, 2009).
22 Dan C. Lortie, *School Teacher: A Sociological Study* (Chicago: University of Chicago Press, 1975), 2.
23 Kaestle, *supra* note 14, 5.
24 Michael S. Katz, *A History of Compulsory Education Laws* (Bloomington, IN: Phi Delta Kappa, 1976), 13.
25 Ordinance of 1787: The Northwest Territorial Government art. III, *reprinted in* 1 U.S.C. at LV, LVII (2006).
26 Lawrence A. Cremin, *American Education: The National Experience 1783–1876* (New York: Harper Collins, 1980), 7.
27 Author, "Common School Movement: Colonial and Republican Schooling, Changes in the Antebellum Era, The Rise of the Common School," https://education.stateuniversity.com/pages/1871/Common-School-Movement.html.
28 Todd A. DeMitchell and Joseph J. Onosko, "A Parent's Child and the State's Future Citizen: Judicial and Legislative Responses to the Tension Over the

Right to Direct an Education," *Southern California Interdisciplinary Law Journal* 22, no. 3 (2013): 591–636, 597–8.

29 Alexander Rippa, *Education in a Free Society: An American History* (8th Ed.) (New York: Longman, 1996), 87.

30 Lawrence A. Cremin, *The Transformation of the School: Progressivism in American Education, 1876–1957* (New York: Alfred A. Knopf, 1961), 8–10.

31 Rosemary C. Salomone, "Common Schools, Uncommon Values: Listening to the Voices of Dissent," *Yale Law & Policy Review* 14 (1996): 169–235, 174.

32 Ibid.

33 Samantha R. Foran, "Parents' Rights or Parents' Wrongs: The Political Weaponization of Parental Rights to Control Public Education," *Wisconsin Law Review* 2022, no. 6 (2022): 1513–48, 1517. Professor Glenn notes the move of the locus of decision making, writing that the common school was defined, "largely in terms of the creation of convictions and loyalties of shaping a common mind or soul for the nation." (Charles Leslie Glenn, *The Myth of the Common School* (Amherst, MA: The University of Massachusetts Press, 1987), 261.

34 Karl F. Kaestle, *Pillars of the Republic: Common Schools and American Society, 1780-1860* (New York: Hill and Wang, 1983), 185.

35 David B. Tyack, *The One Best System: A History of American Urban Education* (Cambridge, MA: Harvard University Press, 1974).

36 Todd A. DeMitchell, "Private Lives: Community Control vs. Professional Autonomy," *Education Law Reporter* 78 (1993): 187–97, 190. For a fictional account of boarding around and life as a school teacher during the common school movement, see Edward Eggleston, The *Hoosier School-Master* (Bloomington, Indiana: Indiana University Press, 1984, reprint from the original 1871 edition). (When Ralph Hartsook, the new schoolmaster moved to Pete Jones's house, Pete described his accommodations in the following way: "P'rhaps you'd like [a] bed. Well just climb up the ladder on the outside of the house … You'll find a bed in the furdest corner. My Pete's already got half of it, and you can take t'other half."). Ibid., 66.

37 Cremin, *supra* note 26, 5. ("The task of erecting and maintaining that foundation became the task of American education.") Ibid.

38 Ibid.

39 Carl K. Kaestle, "Introduction," in Sarah Mondale and Sarah B. Patton, *School: The Story of American Public Education* (Boston: Beacon Press, 2002), 13. Professor Kaestle wrote:

> The states of the Northeast were undergoing an industrial revolution. 'The number of cities in the region with a population of more than 10.000 increased from three in 1800 to forty- two by 1850. Textile production shot up. Canals and then railroads crisscrossed the area

and the nation. Immigration swelled. bringing large numbers of Roman Catholics to a predominant p Protestant nation. These factors formed the necessary preconditions for the creation of public schools. The pace of change and the urgency of new social problems fostered the development of new institutions.

Ibid.
40 Todd A. DeMitchell, "Educating America: The Nineteenth-Century Common School Promise in the Twentieth Century, A Personal Essay," *International Journal of Educational Reform* 9, no. 1 (January 2000): 79–86, 80.
41 Kaestle, *supra* note 14, 71–5.
42 Dana Goldstein, *The Teacher Wars: A History of America's Embattled Profession* (New York: Doubleday, 2014), 13.
43 Ruskin Teeter, *The Opening Up of American Education: A Sampler* (New York:
University Press of America, 1983), 50.
44 Kaestle, *supra* note 14, 20.
45 DeMitchell, *supra* note 36, 82–5.
46 David B. Tyack and Elisabeth Hansot, *Managers of Virtue: Public School Leadership in America, 1820–1980* (New York: Basic Books, 1982), 174.
47 Willard S. Elsbree, *The American Teacher* (New York: The American Book Company, 1939), 71.
48 Fred Eugene Harris, *A Judicial Definition of Immorality as Cause for Teacher Dismissal: A Comparison of Two Eras.* Unpublished doctoral dissertation, University of North Carolina at Greensboro (1989), http://libres.uncg.edu/ir/uncg/f/Harris_uncg_9005819.pdf, 20.
49 Nancy Kober, "History and Evolution of Public Education," *Center on Education Policy*, George Washington University (2020), https://files.eric.ed.gov/fulltext/ED606970.pdf.
50 Michele Kahn and Paul C. Gorski, "The Gendered and Heterosexist Evolution of Teacher Exemplar in the United States: Equity Implications for LGBTQ and Gender Nonconforming Teachers," *International Journal of Multicultural Education* 18, no. 2 (2016): 15–38, 18.
51 Elizabeth Boyle, "The Feminization of Teaching in America," *MIT Program in Women's and Gender Studies – Kampf Prize* (2004), https://stuff.mit.edu/afs/athena.mit.edu/org/w/wgs/prize/eb04.html#:~:text=Different%20states%20and%20different%20areas,increased%20from%201850%20to%201900. She continued, "It was only after a child's mind had become tough that it should be subject to the 'firm grasp of the masculine hand' of society at age twenty-one." Ibid. (internal citation omitted).
The feminization of education, especially in the primary grades, is not just an American phenomenon; it is a global trend. Sheelagh Drudy found that women make 84 percent of the elementary school teaching force in North

America and Europe, in Latin America and the Caribbean 77 percent, and in the Pacific and Asia 60 percent.
Sheelagh Drudy, "Gender balance/gender bias: the teaching profession and the impact of feminization," Gender and Education 20, no. 4: 309–23.

52 Previously, women did not stay in the classroom for extended periods of time. Around the middle of the twentieth century, about the time of the start of the emergence of the concept of nexus which loosened some of the more restrictive bonds of exemplar, the career status of women changed. Harvard education professor, Susan Moore Johnson, said, "The career opened up so women could actually make a lifetime commitment to teaching." "Nursing and teaching, those were the two professions" that a college-educated woman could choose, "and it's not incidental that they are caring professions." Greater career options for women have continued to expand.
Alyson Klein, "Public Schools Rely on Underpaid Female Labor. It's Not Sustainable," *Education Week* (August 31, 2023), https://www.edweek.org/teaching-learning/public-schools-rely-on-underpaid-female-labor-its-not-sustainable/2023/08.

53 "In occupational studies, feminization refers to 'a process in which the number of women in an occupation increases until the occupation switches from being predominantly male to predominantly female.'" (internal citation omitted)
Yayan Rahayani, "Feminization of Teaching," *Journal of English and Education* 4, no. 2 (December 2010): 13–24, 13.

54 Kahn and Gorski, *supra* note 50, Ibid.
55 Madeline R. Grumet, *Bitter Milk: Women and Teaching* (Amherst, MA: University of Massachusetts Press, 1988), 43.
56 Kahn and Gorski, *supra* note 50, Ibid.
57 Howard K. Beale, *A History of Freedom of Teaching in American Schools* (New York: Charles Scribner's Sons, 1941), 244.
58 Marka B. Fleming, Amanda Harmon-Cooley, and Gwendolyn Mcfadden-Wade, "Morals Clauses for Education in Secondary and Post-Secondary Schools: Legal Applications and Constitutional Concerns," *Brigham Young University Education and Law Journal* 2009, no. 1 (Spring 2009): 67–102, 71.
59 Ibid.
60 Kaestle, *supra* note 14, 192.
61 Elsbree, *supra* note 47, 71.
62 Lawrence Cremin, *Popular Education and Its Discontents* (New York: Harper Collins, 1989), 3.
63 Teeter, *supra* note 43, 59–60.
64 Kaestle, *supra* note 39, 13.

65 Jennings L. Wagoner and William N. Harlow, "Common School Movement: Colonial and Republican Schooling, Changes in the Antebellum Era, The Rise of the Common School" (n.d.), https://education.stateuniversity.com/pages/1871/Common-School-Movement.html.
66 Timothy Walch, *Parish School: American Catholic Parochial Education from Colonial Times to the Present* (Washington, DC: National Catholic Education Association, 2003).
67 Jay P. Dolan, *The American Catholic Experience: A History from Colonial Times to the Present* (Garden City, NY: Doubleday & Co., 1985), 85.
68 Kaestle, *supra* note 14, 76.
69 Jon Gjerde, *Catholicism and the Shaping of Nineteenth-Century America*. S. Deborah Kang (ed.) (New York: Cambridge University Press, 2012), 143.
70 Peter Keenan Guilday, *The National Pastorals of the American Hierarchy (1792–1919)* (Washington D.C.: National Catholic Welfare Council, 1923), 28.
71 Kaestle, *supra* note 38, 15.
72 Carl F. Kaestle, "The Educated Citizen." In Sarah Mondale and Sarah B. Patton, *School: The Story of American Public Education* (Boston: Beacon Press, 2001), 19–50, 33.
73 Ibid., 36.
74 Ibid.
75 Ibid.
76 See Author, The Issue of Religious Public Charter Schools, NPR (August 7, 2023), https://www.npr.org/2023/08/07/1192491029/the-issue-of-religious-public-charter-schools.

> In June, a state board voted three-to-two to approve plans for St. Isidore of Seville Virtual Catholic School. [The school] is named after the seventh-century patron saint of the internet. And it would be the first publicly funded religious charter school in the country.
>
> Is the separation of church and state narrowing when it comes to public education? What could St. Isidore's approval mean for other schools around the country?

Ibid.
77 Nancy Luisgnan Schultz, *Fire and Roses: The Burning of the Charlestown Convent, 1834* (New York: Free Press, 2000).
78 Bruce Dorsey, *Freedom of Religion: Bibles, Public Schools, and Philadelphia's Bloody Riots of 1844*, Historical Society of Pennsylvania (n.d.), http://hspapp06.hsp.org/node/2911. See also Zachary M. Schrag, "Nativist Riots of 1844," *The Encyclopedia of Greater Philadelphia* (2013), https://philadelphiaencyclopedia.org/essays/nativist-riots-of-1844/. "In February, Hugh Clark (1796–1862), a Catholic school director there, suggested suspending Bible reading until the school board could devise a policy acceptable to Catholics and Protestants alike. Nativists saw this as a

threat to their liberty and as a chance to mobilize voters, and they rallied by the thousands in Independence Square." Ibid. The first serious violence broke out on May 6, 1844, resulting in several deaths.

79   Bernard Julius. Meiring, *Educational Aspects of the Legislation of the Councils of Baltimore 1829-1884* (Berkeley: University of California, 1963), 231.
80   Cremin, *supra* note 26, 5.
81   Kaestle, *supra* note 39, 11.
82   Joel Spring, *The American School: From the Puritans to No Child Left Behind* (New York: McGraw-Hill Humanities/Social Sciences/Language, 7th ed. 2007), 11.
83   Paul W. Bennett and Karen Mitchell, *"Maintaining "Spotless Records": Professional Standards, Teacher Misconduct and the Teaching Profession* (Policy Paper) (Halifax, Nova Scotia, Canada: Atlantic Institute for Market, March 2014), 1–31, 11.
84   Kaestle, *supra* note 14, 158.
85   Kaestle, *supra* note 39, 17.
86   Michael B. Katz, *Reconstructing American Education* (Cambridge, MA: Harvard University Press, 1987), 117.
87   See Tyack, *supra* note 35.
88   Cremin, *supra* note 26 (vi–vii).
89   David F. Labaree, "The Winning Ways of a Losing Strategy: Educationalizing Social Problems in the United States," *Educational Theory* 58, no. 4 (2008): 447–60, 447.
90   See Todd A. DeMitchell, Richard Fossey, and Terri A. DeMitchell, "A Moral Panic, Banning Books, and the Constitution: The Right to Direct the Upbringing and the Right to Receive Information in a Time of Inflection," *Education Law Reporter* 397 (2022): 905–28, 928. "Educators and school board members have a high duty to safeguard their students' constitutional rights and to respond to parental concerns in an orderly fashion that best serves all students. Parents rightly advocate for their children while educators must advocate for all children. Both duties are legitimate, and both are necessary."
91   Kaestle, *supra* note 13, 22.
92   Tyack, *supra* note 35, 34.
93   Kristin Shotwell, "Secretly Falling in Love: America's Love Affair with Controlling the Hearts and Minds of Public School Teachers," *Journal of Law & Education* 39 (2010): 37–55, 54.
94   DeMitchell and Onosko, *supra* note 26, 600.
95   Tyack, *supra* note 42, 75. Elizabeth Boyle in her MIT lecture on the feminization of teaching characterized colonial education as "Casual, sporadic, and unregulated." Boyle, *supra* note 51.
96   *State v. Bailey*, 61 N.E. 730, 732 (Ind. 1901) (further writing, "The welfare of the child, and the best interests of society require that the state shall

exert its sovereign authority to secure to the child the opportunity to acquire an education."). Ibid.

97 *Fogg v. Board of Education*, 82 A. 173, 174–5 (N.H. 1912). Thirty-three years earlier, the New Hampshire wrote:

> The power of each parent to decide the question what studies the scholars should pursue, or what exercises they should perform, would be a power of disorganizing the school, and practically rendering it substantially useless. However judicious it may be to consult the wishes of parents, the disintegrating principle of parental authority to prevent all classification and destroy all system in any school, public or private, is unknown to the law.

98 *Trustees of School Board v. People ex rel. Van Allen*, 87 Ill. 303, 309 (1877). Generally, see *Prince v. Massachusetts*, 321 U.S. 158, 166 (1944) writing, "It is cardinal with us that the custody, care, and nurture of the child reside first in the parents, whose primary function and freedom include preparation for obligations the state can neither supply nor hinder."

99 *State ex rel. Sheibley v. School District No.1*, 48 N.W. 393, 395 (Neb. 1891).

100 Kaestle, *supra* note 14, 161.

101 268 U.S. 510, 535 (1925).

102 *Kelley v. Ferguson*, 95 Neb. 63, 72, 144 N.W. 1039, 1044 (Neb. 1914). An earlier New York court added support to the Nebraska court regarding the relationship between parents and the state, writing, "There is no parental authority independent of the supreme power of the state." *Mercein v. People ex rel. Barry*, 25 Wend. 64, 103 (N.Y. 1840).

103 For a discussion of the tension between parents and the state, see Jeffrey Shulman "The Parent as (Mere) Educational Trustee: Whose Education is it, Anyway?" *Nebraska Law Review* 89 (2010): 290–357 (writing, "However, to those parents who want their children untouched by other points of view, the state must say that the rights of parents, while profound, are circumscribed—contingent, as the Supreme Court has always noted, on preparing the young for the additional obligations they will take on as members of a pluralistic society.") Ibid., 298. See also, Melissa Moschella, "Defending the Fundamental Right of Parents: A Response to Recent Attacks," *Notre Dame Journal of Law, Ethics and Public Policy* 37, no. 2 (Spring 2023, forthcoming): 10 (asserting, parental rights are essentially a recognition of parents' authority to make decisions on behalf of or affecting their children, even when others (including state authorities) may disagree with those decisions.), https://ssrn.com/abstract=4109271. In addition, see DeMitchell and Onosko, *supra* note 25, 608 writing, "The cases that followed Meyer and Pierce underscored the broad right of the public school to establish the curriculum for all

children in contrast to the very limited right of parents to demand a replacement curriculum of their choosing."

104 Allan G. Osborne and Charles J. Russo, "Educational Decision-Making in K-12 Schools When Divorced Parents Disagree: What is in the Best Interests of the Child?" *Education Law Reporter* 273 (2011): 1–20, 7.

105 Brooke Schultz, "Explainer: The history behind 'parents' rights' in schools." *Associated Press* (November 14, 2022), https://apnews.com/article/religion-education-gender-identity-0e2ca2cf0ef7d7bc6ef5b125f1ee0969.

106 Johann N. Neem, "State of the Field: What is the Legacy of the Common Schools Movement? Revisiting Carl Kaestle's 1983 *Pillars of the Republic*," *History Faculty and Staff Publications* (2016): 342–55, 347, https://cedar.wwu.edu/cgi/viewcontent.cgi?article=1077&context=history_facpubs.

107 Martha M. McCarthy, "Challenges to and Restrictions on What Is Taught in Schools: Changes Over Time and Implications of Recent Developments," *Education Law Reporter* 413, no. 2 (2023): 521–34, 534. She continues, writing, "The current legislated censorship is much more dangerous in terms of threatening our democracy by limiting access to information and the free exchange of ideas. Afterall, what students learn in school today will have significant implications for how they function in adulthood." Ibid., 534.

108 For a discussion of divisive concepts legislation and the judicial pushback in New Hampshire, see Jacob A. Bennett and Todd A. DeMitchell, "Federal District Finds Plausible Claims Against 'Divisive Concepts' Law: *Local 8027, AFT-NH, AFL-CIO v. Edelblut*," *Education Law Reporter* (in press). They wrote of this topic:

> Divisive concepts laws arose within and possibly helped to fuel the current moral panic and culture war which has gripped public schools nationwide. The proliferation of laws that restrict topics that teachers can address in their classrooms and the fear of reprisal through legal and punitive employment actions have chilled professional practice and may have induced a surge in teacher churn creating a shortage of teachers to staff classrooms. One response has been to turn to the courts for a redress of the divisive concepts laws that infringe on constitutional rights.

Ibid. 12 (internal citations omitted).

109 An independent analysis by Bella DiMarco writing for Future*Ed*, writes:

> Parents' rights bills continue to circulate through state legislatures this year, with many once again focusing on parents' right to know what their children are learning in classrooms, particularly around issues of race and gender. Future*Ed* identified 62 parental-rights bills in 24 states that were introduced or pre-filed by March 2023, mostly

by Republican lawmakers. In 2022, 85 bills were introduced in 26 states with six bills signed into law.

Bella DiMaco, "Legislative Tracker: 2023 Parent-Rights Bills in the States," *FutureEd* (March 16, 2023), https://www.future-ed.org/legislative-tracker-2023-parent-rights-bills-in-the-states/.

Jonathan Friedman, director of free expression and education for Pen America critiques the rise of parental rights legislation starting in 2021, writing:

> Rather than protecting the rights of all parents to engage in their children's education, these bills empower a vocal minority to intimidate teachers, librarians and school districts, while ignoring the views of the majority of families ... Rather than directly prohibiting specific concepts or materials, these bills impose vaguely defined standards on curricula and create burdensome mechanisms for public review, fostering a system where teachers and schools are forced to self-censor in order to avoid legal repercussions and public vitriol. These bills represent a growing national effort to impose new ideological constraints on public education. They are frequently being advanced as technical solutions to increase school transparency, but the impact will be to tilt schools in favor of local ideologues.
>
> They also stand to damage the constructive partnership between parents and teachers that is necessary for public schools to function.

Jonathan Friedman, "Education intimidation bills are the opposite of parents' rights," *The Hill* (September 1, 2023), https://apple.news/AmQyUEH6KQAG2JKCbnwugjQ.

Chapter 3

WHO DECIDES WHO WILL TEACH OUR CHILDREN? COMMUNITY CONTROL VERSUS PROFESSIONAL AUTONOMY: THE GUSFIELD MODEL OF OWNERSHIP OF PUBLIC PROBLEMS

> A teacher works in a sensitive area in a schoolroom. There he[/she] shapes the attitude of young minds toward the society in which they live. In this, the state has a vital concern. That the school authorities have the right and duty to screen the officials, teachers, and employees as to their fitness to maintain the integrity of the schools as a part of ordered society, cannot be doubted.[1]

As stated in Chapter 1, society has long debated about the proper qualifications of teachers when they are on or off duty. From the trial of Socrates for corrupting the youth of ancient Athens to the second decade of the twenty-first century, parents, community leaders, and educational leaders have consistently been concerned about the pedagogical skills and moral quality of classroom teachers.

Education is important because, as Tyack and Cuban write, the goals of public education are a "potent means for defining the present and shaping the future"; it is "one way that Americans make sense of their lives."[2]

The US Supreme Court has also recognized the importance of public education. In *Brown v. Board of Education*, the Court's seminal education decision of 1954, the Court wrote:

> Today, education is perhaps the most important function of state and local governments … In these days, it is doubtful that any child may reasonably be expected to succeed in life if he [or she] is denied the opportunity of an education. Such an opportunity, where the state

has undertaken to provide it, is a right, which must be made available to all on equal terms.³

Twenty-eight years later, in *Plyler v. Doe*, the Supreme Court emphasized the importance of education in a democratic society, writing, "We have recognized the public schools as a most vital civic institution for the preservation of a democratic system of government and as the primary vehicle for transmitting the values on which our society rests."⁴

Lawrence Cremin, a preeminent American education historian, asserted that the important questions in education go "to the heart of the kind of society we want our children to live in."⁵ The following quote has been attributed to President Abraham Lincoln, "the philosophy of the classroom in one generation will be the philosophy of government in the next."⁶

Therefore, the control of public education has great consequences for families, communities, and the nation. "The history of education in the United States chronicles the struggle over who has the power to decide which aspects of education are of the greatest worth, including where, when, and what children shall be taught."⁷ And most importantly, who shall teach our children.

> Schools reflect society and societies reflect the schooling of their citizens.
>
> Maura Sellars & Scott Imig, "Mirror, Mirror on the Wall? Is There Anything Fair in Here at All? Examining the Current Relationship of School and Society," *Discourse Studies in the Cultural Politics of Education* 44, no. 3 (September 2022): 1–14, 1.

Parents are always anxious about who their children will have as teachers in the upcoming school year. We primarily judge our selection of an attorney, dentist, physician, plumber, car mechanic, and carpenter based on what we know about the person's skills and abilities to get the job done right, regardless of the specific task at hand. In some respects, parents assess their teachers like they assess other professions. They believe that teachers must possess appropriate teaching skills that engage students in ways that enhance learning; in other words, parents expect their teachers to be pedagogically competent.

Because of their unique relationship with children, however, parents and the larger community also expect teachers to embody the morals and ethics of the highest order. The community expects, backed up by legislation and judicial decisions, educators to serve as role models for children entrusted into their care. As one legal scholar stated:

> To put it simply, teachers are expected to act differently than other people. Thus, teaching is a curious profession. Communities feel very comfortable with telling teachers how to do their jobs and live their lives, and likely no other job occupies the minds of the American public as does teaching.[8]

Indeed, Chief Justice Neely of Virginia's Supreme Court of Appeals expresses this view in a 1986 dissenting opinion:

> If the state may require parents to relinquish their children to the influence of public school teachers on a daily basis, then surely it is reasonable for parents to demand that public school teachers adhere to standards of conduct consonant with the moral standards of the community, especially when such conduct is required by law.[9]

Thus, it is universally agreed that teachers occupy a pivotal position in schools. They stand at the crossroads of education; the "centrality of quality teachers to educational outcomes is intuitive."[10] It is largely through their efforts that the goals of education are achieved or thwarted. At the core of their work, teachers provide instruction, structure learning activities, and assess students' work.[11] All other activities at the school are primarily designed to support, augment, and extend the primacy of the essential teacher–student instructional interaction.

"It is well established that teacher quality makes a difference in student learning."[12] For example, Senior Fellow at the Hoover Institution of Stanford University Eric A. Hanushek states, "First, teachers are very important; no other measured aspect of schools is nearly as important in determining student achievement."[13] For educators, parents, and the community, this is an article of faith.

In short, teachers working with students is the core of a school's activities. Most of what is of sustained value that happens in a school occurs in interactions between students and educators. As Joseph M. Carroll observed, "Nothing, absolutely nothing has happened in education until it has happened to a student."[14]

Of course, a teacher's influence over students can be either positive or negative. An effective teacher makes a positive impact on a student's learning, and an ineffective teacher also makes a difference, albeit a negative one.[15]

Teachers as Mandatory Role Models: The Concept of Exemplar

Communities assert that teachers because of their role as guide and preceptor of their children must possess and exhibit the qualities of "high character." Their obligations to the community can be paid only in terms of character for their knowledge and skill in instruction have no value when divorced from sound principles of conduct. In fact, character is the irreducible minimum of the teacher's equipment. It is a part of the professional outfit that cannot be measured in tangible terms other than conduct.[16]

Teachers have long been considered holders of a special position of trust and responsibility because of their relationship with the community's children. "Since the early history of this country, the public has been far more restrictive in its expectations for the conduct of teachers than for the conduct of the average citizen."[17] This unique position has ultimately been translated into a legal concept termed "exemplar."[18] Teachers, as exemplars, are held to a higher standard of personal conduct than the average citizen.[19]

The US Supreme Court captured the mandatory role model expectation writing, "A teacher serves as a role model for [his/her] students, exerting a subtle but important influence over their values and perceptions. Thus, through both the presentation of course materials and the example he sets, a teacher has an opportunity to influence the attitudes of students toward government, the political process, and a citizen's social responsibilities. This influence is crucial to the continued good health of a democracy."[20]

Because of their relationship with students, teachers have always been considered role models due to the reasonable belief that teachers' off-duty conduct sets an example for how students should act.

An early example of the influence of teachers is found in the early stage of the common school movement. The 1841 Report of the *Boston Board of Education* (p. 57) stated:

If then, manners of the teacher are to be imitated by the pupils, if he is the glass, at which they 'do dress themselves,' how strong is the necessity, that he should understand those nameless and innumerable practices, in regard to deportment, dress, conversation, and all personable habits, that constitute the difference between a gentleman and a clown. We can bear some oddity, or eccentricity in a friend whom we admire for his talents, or revere for his virtues, but it becomes quite a different thing, when oddity, or the eccentricity, is to be a pattern or model from which fifty or a hundred are to form their manners.[21]

Thus, in an 1898 court case, a school superintendent was dismissed because of an indictment for adultery.[22] The superintendent's private conduct was deemed to have a negative impact on his effectiveness as an educator.

As educational historians David B. Tyack and Elisabeth Hansot wrote, "evidence abounds that townspeople kept a vigilant eye on the out-of-class behavior of educators, and that the moral 'lapses' resulted in firings more often than did incompetence in the classroom."[23] Howard K. Beale, writing in 1936, warned that a teacher's controversial off-duty conduct likely caused more trouble for the teacher than conduct in school.[24] Further, Beale noted, "The teacher's relations with the community may entail some of the most irksome restraints upon his freedom."[25]

In the early days of our Republic, the local community had considerable power over the rural district school. The patrons of the school had little doubt that the school was theirs to control and not the property of the professional educator. But times were changing. "These communities controlled their schools in ways that would become impossible as regulations became more centralized and teachers more professional."[26] Regulations were enacted that centralized and bureaucratized the schools, and educators became more professional and wanted to assert the privilege of their professional status by seeking autonomy.

The next section discusses the pushback response to the onerous oversight of teachers' private lives and the community dictate that teachers be held to the standard of exemplar. For example, under the exemplar standard, an unwed pregnant teacher was dismissed under the following rationale: (1) that unwed parenthood is prima facie proof of immorality; (2) that unwed parents are unfit role models; (3) that employment of an unwed parent in a scholastic environment materially contributes to the problem of school-girl pregnancies.[27]

The Fifth Circuit Court of Appeals in *Andrew v. Drew Municipal Separate School District* invalidated the school board's decision, holding that the school district's automatic decision that an unwed employee who is pregnant is disqualified from employment violates equal protection. The court wrote, "Insofar as the rule inextricably binds unwed parental status to irredeemable immorality, it violates both due process and equal protection."[28]

As an indication that times were changing, courts became increasingly willing to question "the community's ability to police the private lives of teachers."[29] For example, the Fifth Circuit Court of Appeals followed the *Andrews* case with another ruling on the dismissal of a teacher based on an unwed pregnancy. Avery, an elementary school reading instructor, was dismissed after she became pregnant and failed to notify the superintendent by the fourth month of her pregnancy as required by board policy. The school board dismissed her for insubordination, neglect of duty and failure to give timely notice, and also for immorality for her pregnancy out of wedlock. The federal district court upheld the dismissal based on her failure to follow the notice rule, asserting that it was not necessary to reach the constitutional issue, even though the judge stated that the discharge for immorality could be unconstitutional. On appeal, the Fifth Circuit vacated the judgment and directed an entry of judgment for the plaintiff. The court rejected the proposition as it did in *Andrews* seven years earlier that unwed parenthood is *per se* proof of immorality and thus "is an unfit role model."[30]

Nexus: The Connection Between Behavior and Negative Effect on Education

> There is a growing tendency everywhere to treat the teacher as another normally acceptable citizen who has certain professional skills used in teaching. With the exception of a few communities a teacher no longer lives in a fishbowl. As long as a teacher manifests some discretion in his choice of friends, his behavior, and his attitudes, he can live a perfectly normal life.[31]

The teachers of the early nineteenth century had little to no connection to other educators. There was no real community of educators.

"There were no professional organizations or unions to counterbalance the power of the local community over the personal lives of local school teachers."[32]

By the mid-nineteenth century, however, local and autonomous schools began being replaced by school districts with bureaucratized administrative leadership. In addition, teachers began organizing professional organizations to support their teaching, and they formed unions to give them a voice in school policy and working conditions independent of the community.

Teachers' drive for more autonomy and greater control over their private lives was part of a broader cultural push by individual Americans for greater individual rights and freedom. "All Americans, teachers included, began to expect greater latitude in their freedoms of action and speech."[33]

The education profession asserted that teachers should have the right to a private life and that their privacy should be respected unless it could be shown that an educator's behavior directly and negatively impacted their teaching or the school. Thus, the private acts of a teacher were considered just that, private.

By the twenty-first century, American courts generally recognized that teachers enjoyed a right to privacy, although that right was not unlimited. For example, in a 2007 Virginia case, an art teacher was fired when he appeared, without his consent, in a YouTube clip where he painted pictures using his buttocks. The paintings were produced at the teacher's expense and created during his private time away from school. The school board fired the teacher, asserting that the conduct constituted conduct unbecoming of a teacher and demonstrated that he could no longer serve as a role model for his students.[34]

The teacher sued in federal district court, alleging that there was no evidence to suggest that the video negatively reflected on his teaching ability. In the video, the teacher was wearing a thong and a Groucho Marx disguise and identified himself by a pseudonym. The teacher and the school district ultimately settled the case for $65,000, equal approximately to two years of service.[35]

The mandatory role model of exemplar measures teacher conduct against the yardstick of community expectations, whereas nexus grounds its analysis more in the expected standards of the teaching profession. Law professor John Rumel wrote that courts gradually moved away from examining teachers' out-of-school behavior under the exemplar standard. "[T]he vast majority of courts," Rummel observed, "when faced with a choice between evaluating teacher off-duty conduct under a role model standard derived from a statutory morals provision or under a nexus standard, has opted for the nexus standard."[36] However, when "an educator's conduct involves students, the educator can much more easily be disciplined because the showing of adverse effects [(exemplar)] is more likely to be inferred and not required."[37]

Nevertheless, although courts were becoming increasingly sympathetic to the notion that teachers enjoy a sphere of privacy when they are off the clock, controversies continued to arise when school authorities became aware of a teacher's off-duty behavior that the school board and the larger community found unacceptable. The tension between the community (exemplar) and the profession (nexus) over control of who shall teach our children lends itself to an analysis using a construct developed by Joseph R. Gusfield in his work *The Culture of Public Problems*.[38]

The Gusfield Model: Contested Meanings

This chapter tightens the focus on the tension between exemplar and nexus by using the sociological model developed by Joseph R. Gusfield. This theory provides an explanation for the contest over who decides the ownership of a public problem. We apply the Gusfield model to the tension between the community's tendency to define teacher out-of-school behavior in terms of the role model theory and the profession's assertion of a finding of a nexus, an objective measure, of the impact of the disputed behavior.

Sociology professor Joseph R. Gusfield asserts that there are often conflicting and changing ways in which society defines social problems. The Gusfield model, although developed through an analysis of drinking, driving, and the formation of a public problem, can inform our discussion about the struggle between the community and the profession as to who decides who is fit to be a classroom teacher. The model has three components: ownership, causation, and political responsibility.

According to Gusfield's theory, ownership is the power to define and describe a problem. Ownership does not mean responsibility to solve the problem. Owners "create and influence the public definition of a problem."[39] Gusfield uses the metaphor of property to describe ownership. The owner of a problem creates and influences the public definition of a problem.

The history of the control of alcohol problems helps to illustrate this concept of ownership. During the nineteenth and early twentieth centuries in the United States, the Protestant churches, with the cooperation of the Women's Christian Temperance Union and the Anti-Saloon League, "defined the legitimate cognitive and moral approaches toward alcohol use."[40] When these groups spoke about alcohol use, many listened. Whereas, when other groups spoke, such as the medical profession or the universities, they were unable to gain a loud voice in suggesting alternative perspectives to the problem of drinking.[41] The dialogue was essentially controlled by the churches.

With the repeal of prohibition, the churches lost ownership of the discussion of alcoholism. They were no longer the authoritative voice. "Ownership passed to the universities, the medical profession, and the problem drinkers themselves."[42] Ownership, like property, can be transferred.

Also, like property, ownership can be contested. Several groups can compete for the ownership of a problem—struggling to be the authoritative voice that defines and structures the dialogue about a controversial social issue. The ownership of the problem of who shall be permitted to teach our children is contested. The two groups competing for ownership are the community, including parents, business leaders, civic organizations, the press, and their elected officials, and the profession, which includes teachers, professional associations, and the educational bureaucracy. These two groups have basically polarized around the issue of a teacher's right to a private life. What role the private conduct of a teacher should play when deciding who shall teach our children or who shall continue to teach our children is the problem being contested by the two groups trying to assert ownership.

The second component of Gusfield's model is causation. Causation "is a matter of belief or cognition, an assertion about the sequence that accounts for the existence of a problem."[43] In our discussion of the private lives of teachers, the community defends the theory of the exemplar status of teachers while the profession advances the belief that the concept of nexus should be used when viewing the private life of a teacher as it impacts employment.

The third element of Gusfield's theoretical model is political responsibility or obligation, terms which Gusfield uses interchangeably. This element assigns a person. office, or organization with the responsibility of controlling a situation or solving a problem. Gusfield, by way of illustration, discusses how government officials are assigned the responsibility to solve the problem of inflation.[44] In the issue before us, both the community and the profession assign responsibility for addressing the problem to the courts and quasi-judicial agencies, which are tasked with determining whether a teacher's personal conduct renders them unable to continue teaching our children.

The Gusfield model provided us with two groups that struggle over what private conduct renders a teacher unfit to teach. Both groups assert different theories of causation—the exemplar status of the teacher versus the nexus standard for judging a teacher's private conduct. Both groups assign the responsibility for reviewing a teacher's private conduct to the courts. The courts or quasi-judicial state agencies are ultimately assigned responsibility for determining whether a teacher's off-duty behavior warrants termination whenever school boards and teachers—usually represented by their unions—disagree about whether a teacher's conduct justifies a school board's firing a teacher.

Two theories of causation regarding the problem of what role a teacher's private life plays in employment decisions have been advanced by two parties competing for ownership of the problem. The first party, the community, asserts the theory of exemplar. The schoolteacher has traditionally been regarded as a moral role model for students.[45] The concept of exemplar is still vibrant and very much alive today in many communities.

The second party to the contested ownership is the profession. John Trebilcock, discussing the changing control of the community over education and teachers, wrote, "An increasing professionalism in the teaching community has led to more bureaucratization in schools and less direct control from the community."[46] The theory advanced by the profession is nexus. M. Chester Nolte, noted school law commentator, has described nexus thus: "A school employee cannot be penalized for misbehavior unless a school board can prove that such misbehavior diminishes his/her ability to perform the job."[47]

Both parties are claiming ownership over the problem of a teacher's private life and employment status. In recent years, teachers began to assert the importance of their individual rights and freedoms expecting a greater latitude of freedom to pursue and enjoy a private life. While exemplar has a longer history of use, nexus, as embodied in the *Morrison* criteria discussed in Chapter 6, now appears consistently in court decisions nationwide.

A tension emerged between the more subjective standard of exemplar and the more objective standard of nexus. Thus, the tension between who decides who will teach our children arose, not so much over teachers' professional qualifications, but rather over their character.

Parents, who long served as the primary guides and guardians for the children's character, lost some of their parental control with the development of a state system of education and sought to reclaim it as overseers of the private lives of teachers.

The ownership of the role of arbiter and judge of teachers' conduct outside the workday will continue to be contested into the near future. Because teachers work so closely with the children of the community, they hold a special position of trust and responsibility. That relationship is not easily given up. On the other hand, teachers are not likely to give up the greater latitude of action afforded them with nexus. The ownership of the problem will likely remain unresolved well into the future, with both parties' theories of causation acting as a counterbalance to the other. Chapter 8 will explore whether this tension should be resolved in one party's favor or whether it is necessary to maintain a balance between the community and the profession.

> Teachers began to assert that their personal actions off school grounds were their private business, and not their employer's concern. At the same time, administrators continued to claim that teachers serve as role models for their students and must conform to local community mores.
>
> John Trebilcock, "Off Campus School Board Control over Teacher Conduct," *Tulsa Law Journal* 35, no. 2 (1999): 445–65, 448.

NEXT: In the next chapter we explore what it means to be a professional teacher. The discussion of the tension between community and profession benefits from a review of what constitutes a profession and how do educators fit into the understanding of what is a profession and what it means to be a professional. The calculus of community versus profession on the issue of who shall teach our children changes if educators are not members of a profession.

Notes

1 *Adler v. Board of Education of City of New York*. 342 U.S. 485, 493 (1952).
2 David Tyack and Larry Cuban, *Tinkering Toward Utopia: A Century of School Reform* (Cambridge, MA: Harvard University Press, 1995), 42.

3 *Brown v. Board of Education*, 347 U.S. 484, 491(1954).
4 *Plyler v. Doe*, 457 U.S. 202, 221 (1982).
5 Lawrence A. Cremin, *Public Education* (New York: Basic Books, 1976), 74–75.
6 Abraham Lincoln, https://www.brainyquote.com/quotes/abraham_lincoln_133687/. See also, Diogenes, "The foundation of every state is the education of its youth." Ibid.
7 Todd A. DeMitchell and Joseph J. Onosko, "A Parent's Child and the State's Future Citizen: Judicial and Legislative Responses to the Tension Over the Right to Direct an Education," *University of Southern California Interdisciplinary Law Journal* 22, no. 3 (2013): 591–635, 595.
8 Jacqueline A. Meese, "Expectations of the Exemplar: An Exploration of the Burdens in Public School Teachers in the Absence of Tenure," *City University of New York Law Review* 19, no. 1 (2015): 131–164, 133.
9 *Rogliano v. Fayette County Board of Education*, 347 S.E.2d 220, 226 (1986) (Neely, J. dissenting). (See Chapter 8 for a discussion of the case.).
10 Derek W. Black, "The Constitutional Challenge to Teacher Tenure." *California Law Review* 104 (2016): 75–148, 83.
11 See Charlotte Danielson's framework for teaching. The four domains are: (1) Planning and Preparation, (2) Classroom Environment, (3) Instruction, and (4) Professional Responsibilities. Author, "The Framework," The Danielson Group (2017), https://www.danielsongroup.org/framework/; James H. Strong, Thomas J. Ward, and Leslie W. Grant, "What Makes Good Teachers Good? A Cross-Case Analysis of the Connection Between Teacher Effectiveness and Student Achievement," *Journal of Teacher Education* 62 (2011): 339–55, 351 (synthesizing their review of the literature into four dimensions: Instructional Delivery, Student Assessment, Learning Environment, and Personal Qualities). Furthermore, they write, "The common denominator in school improvement and student success is the teacher."
12 Patricia H. Hinchey, *Getting Teacher Assessment Right: What Policymakers Can Learn From Research* (Boulder, CO: National Education Policy Center, Boulder, CO, December 2010), 1, https://nepc.colorado.edu/sites/default/files/PB-TEval-Hinchey_0.pdf. See also, Jennifer K. Rice, *Teacher Quality: Understanding the Effectiveness of Teacher Attributes* (Washington, DC: Economic Policy Institute, August 2003) (writing, "Teacher quality matters. In fact, it is the most important school-related factor influencing student achievement."), 1, https://www.epi.org/publication/books_teacher_quality_execsum_intro/; Demetra Kalogrides, Suzanne Loeb, and Tara Beteille (March 2011). *Power Play? Teacher Characteristics and Class Assignments*. (Washington. D.C.: National Center for Analysis of Longitudinal Data in Education Research, Calder The Urban Institute March 2011), 1, writing, "The effect of teachers on student achievement is particularly well established." http://www.caldercenter.org/upload/CALDERWorkPaper_59.pdf.

13 Eric A. Hanushek, *The Economic Value of Higher Teacher Quality* (Cambridge, MA: National Bureau of Economic Research, December 2010), 3, https://www.nber.org/papers/w16606.pdf.
14 Joseph M. Carroll, *The Copernican Plan Evaluated: The Evolution of a Revolution* (Andover, MA: Regional Library for Educational Improvement of the Northeast and Islands, 1994), 87.
15 Todd A. DeMitchell and Mark A. Paige, *Threading the Evaluation Needle: The Documentation of Teacher Unprofessional Conduct* (Lanham, MD: Rowman & Littlefield, 2020), 1–2.
16 A.R. Brubacher, *Teaching: Profession and Practice* (New York: The Century Company, 1927), 133–4.
17 Floyd G. Delon, *Legal Controls on Teacher Conduct: Teacher Discipline* (Topeka, KS: National Organization on Legal Problems of Education, 1978), 2.
18 Jason R. Fulmer, "Dismissing the 'Immoral' Teacher for Conduct Outside the Workplace—Do Current Laws Protect the Interests of Both School Authorities and Teachers?," *Journal of Law & Education* 31, no. 3 (2002): 271–89, 276.
19 See *Chicago Board of Education v. Payne*, 102 Ill. App. 3d 741, 748 (1981) writing, "We are aware of the special position occupied by a teacher in our society. As a consequence of that elevated stature, a teacher's actions are subject to much greater scrutiny than that given to the activities of the average person."
20 *Ambach v. Norwick*, 441 U.S. 68, 78–9 (1979). See also, *Tingley v. Vaughn*, 17 Ill. App. 347, 351 (1885) ("If suspicion of vice or immorality be once entertained against a teacher, his influence for good is gone. The parents become distrustful, the pupils contemptuous and school discipline essential to success is at an end.").
21 Willard Ellsbree, *The American Teacher* (New York: American Book Co., 1939), 297.
22 *Freeman v. Bourne*, 170 Mass. 289, 294–5 (1898).
23 David B. Tyack and Elisabeth Hansot, *Managers of Virtue: Public School Leadership in America, 1820–1980* (New York: Basic Books, Inc. Publishers, 1982), 174.
24 Howard K. Beale, *Are American Teachers Free? An Analysis of Restraints Upon the Freedom of Teaching in American School* (New York: Charles Scribner's Sons, 1936), 374.
25 Ibid., 388.
26 Carl F. Kaestle, *Pillars of the Republic: Common Schools and American Society, 1780–1860* (New York: Hill and Wang, 1983), 22.
27 *Andrews v. Drew Municipal Separate School District*, 507 F.2d 611, 614 (5th Cir. 1975), *cert. dismissed as improvidently granted*, 425 U.S. 559 (1976).
28 Ibid., 616.

29 Leslie Robert Stellman, "Teacher Terminations: Is the 'Role Model' Concept a Thing of the Past?" Education Law Association Conference (November 2011): 1–11, 3.
30 *Avery v. Homewood City Board of Education*, 674 F.2d 337, 341 (5th Cir. 1982).
31 John H. Chilcott, "Community Restrictions on Teacher Behavior," *The Journal of Educational Sociology* 33, no. 7 (March 1960): 336–8, 338.
32 John Treblicock, "Off Campus School Board Control over Teacher Conduct," *Tulsa Law Journal* 35, no. 2 (1999): 445–65, 447.
33 Ibid., 448.
34 Complaint, *Murmer v. Chesterfield County School Board* No. 3:07CV608, 2007 WL 2914769 (E.D. Va. October 4, 2007).
35 *Fired Art Teacher Wins $65,000 Settlement from Chesterfield County School Board*, ACLU (March 7, 2008), http://www.aclu.org/free-speech/fired-art-teacher-wins-65000-settlement-chesterfield-county-school-board. Following the settlement Stephen Murmer commented, "I hope my case will cause schools to think twice before they fire a teacher for expressing himself outside the classroom. This settlement represents a vindication of me and the First Amendment." Ibid.
36 John E. Rumel, "Beyond Nexus: A Framework for Evaluating K-12 Teacher Off-Duty Conduct and Speech in Adverse Employment and Licensure Proceedings," *University of Cincinnati Law Review* 83 (2015): 685–746, 698, f.n. 78.
37 Suzanne E. Eckes, Todd A. DeMitchell, and Richard Fossey, "Legal Matters for Educators: A Lesson on Social Media," *Principal Leadership* 22, no. 7 (March 2022): 54–5, 55.
38 Joseph R. Gusfield, *The Culture of Public Problems: Drinking, Driving, and the Symbolic Order* (Chicago: The University of Chicago 1981). This discussion is based on the prior work of Todd A. DeMitchell, "Private Lives: Community Control vs. Professional Autonomy," *Education Law Reporter* 78 (1993): 187–97.
39 Ibid., 10.
40 Ibid., 11.
41 Ibid.
42 Ibid.
43 Ibid., 13.
44 Ibid., 14.
45 *Board of Education of Hopkins County v. Wood*, 717 S.W.2d 837, 839 (Ky. 1986).
46 Treblicock, *supra* note 32, 448.
47 M. Chester Nolte, "Establishing the Nexus: A School Board Primer," *Education Law Reporter* 38 (1987): 1–24, 3.

Chapter 4

THE PROFESSIONAL TEACHER

Because the foundation of an educated society relies on the teachers who daily interact with students from early childhood to young adulthood, it is important to understand what it means to be a professional teacher.[1]

Professional educators are connected to their purpose and driven by their moral compass. They have servant hearts and believe deeply in serving others.

Elementary School Assistant Principal (Response to Educators' Descriptors Study of the Profession (2021).[2]

First, what is a profession? A profession is distinguished from an occupation. "Historically, the conceptualization of the professional and of professionalism referred to the level of autonomy and internal regulation exercised by members of an occupation in providing services to society."[3] In Europe, in the eighteenth and nineteenth centuries, occupations were differentiated from professions by the level of required special knowledge, a formal code of conduct, and a mandate to carry out the services that support the legal order and promote the common culture.[4] "Only professionals are *expected* to act in the public interest, to create a calculus that balances self-and-civic interest."[5] The term profession has its etymological roots in Latin for profess (*professio*). The individual makes a public declaration to be an expert in some skill or field of knowledge.

Professional work, by its very nature, is complex and nonroutine. It involves a standard of practice recognized and adhered to by the practitioners operating within the structure of an accepted code of ethics that is adopted in the best interests of the people that a professional serves. Because judgment must be used in applying professional knowledge to meet client's needs, that knowledge cannot be easily reduced to rules or prescriptions. "One size doesn't fit all."[6] Professionals are accorded an exceptional level of deference in society, which allows them a measure of autonomy in their actions. They also are held professionally accountable through licensure and legally through malpractice, except for educators.[7]

State governments are appropriately compelled to protect their citizens. Police and fire services are examples of government actions that protect the citizenry. Another protective activity is the licensing of individuals who provide specific services to the public. Many of these services are provided in the private sector. The practice of law and medicine, for example, are two well-established professions in which a license to practice is required. The state, through its licensing requirements, specifies the conditions that must be met to obtain the license to practice.

Skills and knowledge are often the leading criteria for admission to practice. However, morality is also often a component of the requirements for practicing the right.[8] For example, the Council on Ethical and Judicial Affairs of the American Medical Association requires physicians to act in an ethical manner defined as "moral principles or practices."[9] Admission to the bar in New Hampshire requires applicants to "establish their moral character."[10] Should teachers who work with children also be required to act in an ethical manner and have good moral character, much like physicians and attorneys?[11] The answer is yes.

Professionals hold a special place in our society. William J. Goode, in his study of professions, asserts that there are two general qualities that define professions.[12] The first is a "service orientation." The second pillar of professionalism is the acquisition of a specialized body of knowledge.[13] Simply put, professionals adhere to the standard of accepted practice acknowledged by the profession within the framework of a recognized code of ethics, developed in the best interests of the client, patient, or student. A researcher describes the role of a code of ethics as serving as a guide for determining what actions should be taken and how those actions should be carried out.[14]

Goode's second pillar of professionalism—specialized knowledge— is best categorized as membership in a learned society. Learned societies are traditionally law, medicine, and divinity. These learned professions are "essentially intellectual in character," as described in the influential 1915 Flexner Report on the preparation of physicians.[15] Our preferred definition of the term "professional" is an individual who is a member of a learned society.[16]

Professionals act in the best interests of the person(s) receiving their services. Noted educational policy researcher Linda Darling-Hammond writes, "Professionals are obligated to do whatever is best for the client, not what is easiest, most expedient, or even what the client himself or herself might want."[17] Therefore, the primary goal of a profession is to serve the best interests of the client, not the needs, interests, and desires of the professional.

> Professors Douglas E. Mitchell and Robert K. Ream assert, "education and medicine are unique among the professions in the degree to which they touch our entire citizenry; they are also naturally supportive of common goals." Furthermore, they write, "We take professionalism to mean acceptance of professional responsibility for student and patient outcomes—not just acceptance of responsibility for technical expertise, but commitment to the social norms of the profession, including trustworthiness and responsibility for client well-being."
>
> Douglas E. Mitchell and Robert K. Ream, "A Brief Introduction to the Problem of Professional Responsibility," in *Professional Responsibility: The Fundamental Issue in Education and Health Care Reform*, ed. Douglas E. Mitchell and Robert K. Ream (New York: Springer International, 2015), 1-7, 2.

Building on the concepts of service and a specialized body of knowledge, David Carr identifies five propositions of a profession. His list, which is based on a study of the literature, includes these precepts: (1) professions provide an important public service, (2) these services involve a theoretically as well as practically grounded expertise, (3) professional services have a distinct ethical dimension which calls for expression in a code of practice, (4) they require organization and regulation for purposes of recruitment and discipline, and, (5) professional practitioners require a high degree of individual autonomy for effective practice.[18]

Similarly, Tamar Ruth Horwitz, in her study of professionalism and semi-professionalism in education, states:

1. a profession is based upon a systematic body of knowledge that is both theoretical and practical;

2. the professional mediates between the body of knowledge and the individual;
3. the professional performs an essential service to the community;
4. the professional requires a long period of training;
5. the professional enjoys a high degree of authority;
6. the profession practices a specific code of ethics;
7. the profession involves a high degree of commitment;
8. the profession [requires] intensive "in-service" training.[19]

Professionalism is built around expert knowledge. The work of the professional teacher is complex and not routine or rote. It involves the exercise of discretion in response to a classroom environment filled with young people at varying levels of academic competence, readiness to engage with instruction, and requiring prolonged daily interaction over months.

Teachers' work involves a standard of practice recognized and adhered to by practitioners, applied in varying contexts, even within the same school district. Professionals use their judgment and take actions within the accepted standards of the profession and in the best interests of their students.

Simply put, professionals, including educators, adhere to the standard of accepted practice recognized by their profession within the framework of an established code of ethics, which is offered in the best interests of the client, patient, or student. Their practice is based on a body of specialized knowledge gained through a period of extended study and is grounded in an acceptance of considerable autonomous authority for the practitioner.

The Education Context

Educators lay claim to being members of a profession because the services they provide are a central benefit not only to their students but also to society as a whole. Indeed, all the learned societies are built on a foundation of education. Alice J. Klein writes, "Although definitions of a profession often exclude education, courts have described educators as professionals, and public policy considerations support this proposition."[20] While there is congruence between the professions, there are important points of divergence. For example, "unlike fee-for-service professionals, teachers cannot build a clientele of selected individuals."[21]

As previously discussed, teachers hold a critical position in education. They stand at the crossroads of education, directing students to freeways or byways of educational attainment. The importance of their role in educating the nation's youth is virtually unquestioned. Labor and employment relations professor Robert Bruno, commenting on teacher professionalism, opined on this connection between teachers' importance and their standing as professionals, "This means that a teacher's classroom experiences, and the teacher-student relationship, is what ultimately creates the boundaries for what it means to be a professional."[22]

The Semi-Profession?

Some scholars have questioned whether education is considered a profession on the same level as physicians, dentists, attorneys, and engineers.[23] As Tamar Ruth Horowitz writes, "In certain respects teaching may be defined as a 'profession,' while in other respects it can be more appropriately defined as a 'semi-profession.'"[24] Etizoni's seminal work, *The Semi-Professions and Their Organization: Teachers, Nurses, Social Workers*,[25] which developed the concept of the semi-profession, identified it as consisting of the following characteristics:

1. semi-professions are an integral part of the bureaucratic organization of which it is a part;
2. semi-professionals communicate knowledge rather than applying it;
3. the training required is short and specific;
4. the degree of commitment of the semi-professional is limited; and
5. the practitioners are typically female.[26]

Early studies of the professions focused on the traditional professions: societies of medicine, law, and theology. Consequently, the descriptions reflect the work of the individual professional person with an individual patient, client, or parishioner.

Most of the work performed by practitioners in these three professions is done by individual professionals, often involving interactions of short duration but occasionally of more protracted duration in highly focused situations, such as surgery, administering to a congregant, listening to a confession, and ongoing therapy sessions. Often, there is collaboration with peers on a consulting basis. Their service is delivered with a high degree of autonomy for the practitioner, and deference is shown by the recipient of the service (as exemplified by the familiar refrain of following the doctor's orders, for example). Thus, it makes sense that the descriptors of what constitutes a particular profession inform the foundation of the codes of conduct and ethics for that professional group.

However, the work of teachers does not easily fit the descriptions discussed above. Teachers have prolonged, focused contact with their students, approximately six and a half hours a day, five days a week, 180 days a year. No other professional group has such extended time with their clients or patients. Educators generally interact with groups of students, not individuals, although these groups may vary greatly in size, ranging from physical education classes and music classes to small, advanced placement classes and special education classes.

Whereas most professionals typically practice with one individual at a time (with the exception of small group therapy sessions and sermons to the congregation), giving full attention to that individual, teachers often have a class of fifteen to thirty students in which the knowledge gained and the skills being transmitted must be applied in a group setting with individualized instruction given. In contrast, the teacher still retains full responsibility for the entire class. This is an integral aspect of the educational context; it also adds to the complexity of teaching, delivering instruction, supervising learning activities, and keeping students on task while maintaining a positive classroom climate.[27]

The context of service in the teaching profession is clearly different from that of most traditional professions. For example, a teacher's authority to act and the autonomy to act are manifestly different from those of a legal or medical practitioner. Educational practice is influenced by the inescapable groupness of teaching, which requires adapting to the differing needs and competencies of a classroom of students. While most professionals bring their expertise to bear on one individual at a time, the individual recipient of educational services is almost always part of a larger group.

The Context of Educational Practice

The venue for a professional's practice influences how the professional service is delivered. For example, while the law in a particular jurisdiction remains the same regardless of whether the attorney is a solo practitioner or an associate at a major national law firm, the actual practice of the law is shaped by the context, structure, and procedures of the law. The difference between professions and their practice also varies even though the index used to define a profession is consistent, as discussed above. The context of schools and classrooms also shapes the professional practice of educators. Below are a few of the elements of schooling that impact the professional practice of teachers.

1. Education is a cumulative phenomenon. Current learning is predicated upon prior learning. If a student or a group of students does not have a firm foundation for the curricular goal, teachers must adjust their instruction.
2. Teachers are not only responsible for the effective organization of the curriculum and instructional delivery; they are also responsible for creating and sustaining an environment conducive to student learning. A disciplined classroom is necessary for the focus of instruction and student learning activities. Those who have never been responsible for the behavior of a collection of students, may not be aware of the challenge, the complexity, and stress involved in developing and maintaining a classroom environment that supports learning within a classroom of the willing, the eager, the unconnected, and the defiant. Other professionals are not typically concerned about maintaining control of their patients or clients.
3. Teachers work in a unique learning environment—the school. The school influences the learning conditions in its classrooms through its rules and practices and through the influence of its climate.[28] Classrooms are connected in tangible ways beyond just being connected by common walls and shared hallways. Over half a century ago, in the 1969 landmark student free speech case, *Tinker v. Des Moines Independent School District*, the US Supreme Court noted the "special characteristics of the school environment."[29]
4. Public schools accept all students who reside within their attendance boundary lines. As articulated in a seminal special education case of *Timothy W. v. Rochester School District*,[30] there is a zero rejection of students with disabilities from public education. Special education legal scholars Rud Turnbill and Ann P. Turnbill describe zero rejection as one of the six principles of the National Special Education Law, the Individuals with Disabilities Education Act.[31] They write:

Zero Reject is the principle that no student with a disability can be denied a free, appropriate public education. This is both a civil right under the equal protection doctrine and good social policy, grounded in the individual and social utilitarianism of educating all students.[32] Private schools can establish rules for whom they may admit; thus, their student body is more select than the public schools, which take all children.

The Classroom: The Teacher's Place

The classroom is the teacher's place. It is the environment where their professional practice primarily takes place. It is the refuge that they often seek. It is their place. To understand teachers is to understand their classrooms and the relationships that they forge with their students. This central place helps to identify teachers and their sense of themselves as professionals. Lortie described teachers' view of their classroom in the following manner:

> We found that they want a degree of boundedness around their classrooms; they cathect them, not the organization at large. They want more potentially productive time with students. They depict other adults as intrusive and hindering, and they yearn for more resources as they try to influence their students. Others, they feel, should support them in their work with students—should uphold rather than denigrate their standing.[33]

In other words, teachers seek and reinforce their autonomy over the classroom, not over the school or over the profession. They are centered in their classroom and on their students.

The Educator's Voice on Professionalism

The National Board for Professional Teaching Standards articulates the National Board's five core propositions (2016) of what teachers should know and be able to do. The five core propositions—comparable to medicine's Hippocratic Oath—set for the profession's vision for accomplished teaching:

Proposition 1: Teachers are committed to students and their learning.
Proposition 2: Teachers know the subjects they teach and how to teach those subjects to students.
Proposition 3: Teachers are responsible for managing and monitoring student learning.
Proposition 4: Teachers think systematically about their practices and learn from experience.
Proposition 5: Teachers are members of learning communities.[34]

In the fall of 2021, a qualitative study, the Educators' Descriptors Study of the Profession, was conducted to capture educators' perceptions of their profession.[35] The respondents were asked to list five words "that you believe best describe what is a professional educator." One hundred ninety-six responses were organized into five themes. An emergent inductive qualitative analysis of theme building in which all responses were read and preliminary themes were identified was conducted through an iterative winnowing process. The working themes were distilled into five final themes. The themes are Personal Characteristics, Work Competence, Advanced Education, Relationships, and Ethical Behavior.[36] These themes align with the description of a professional, with some additional elements.

Educators assigned competence to their list of professional attributes and captured the reality of their work, not as solo practitioners but as connected professionals with a symbiotic relationship with other necessary educators and, more importantly, their students. The Personal Characteristics theme had two subthemes, the Individual and Work. Recurring examples of the individual theme include empathy, caring, compassion, respect, and credibility. The respondents did not specifically list role models or exemplars as descriptors. However, the themes of Personal Characteristics, listed above, and the theme of Ethical Behavior may support the professional teacher as a role model. That specific question was not asked.

A decade and a half earlier, Tichenor and Tichenor conducted a focus group study at four elementary schools asking two questions: "What does it mean to be a professional teacher?" and "How do teachers exhibit professionalism?"[37] Their 2004-5 research identified four themes: (1) Character, (2) Commitment to Change and Continuous Improvement, (3) Subject Matter and Pedagogical Knowledge, and (4) Beyond the Classroom. These themes align closely with the findings of the Educators' Descriptors Study of the Profession (2021). Tichenor and Tichenor specifically identified "role model inside and outside the classroom" as part of the theme "Beyond the Classroom." In addition, both studies identify ethics as a personal characteristic.

One of the interesting findings of the 2021 study of teacher professionalism is the perception that educators may hold different views of their practice. While Tichenor and Tichenor identified curricular and pedagogical knowledge, the 2021 study respondents focused on competence, which included knowledge. Specifically, the Work Competence theme was composed of the following descriptors: knowledgeable, experienced, educated, skilled, and qualified/licensed. Coupled with a subtheme example of Work for Personal

Characteristics, hard work emerged as part of the subtheme. The rights associated with practice must first be earned and not granted automatically. This is a very practical approach, possibly influenced by the practicalities of the classroom, reflecting theories in use (demonstrated competence) as opposed to espoused theories (knowledge).

For example, the second part of the educators' descriptor study offered the participants an unstructured opportunity to comment about the professional educator. Responses from twenty-one respondents, some with multiple comments, were analyzed using the same inductive qualitative methods as the five descriptors analysis.

Two respondents raised the interesting question of whether the status of a professional should be conferred upon the completion of extended education and the granting of proper licensure/credentials. These two comments distinguish between the automaticity of being a professional based on a credential and earning the status of a professional based on practice. The two comments follow:

1. "In my mind, you don't automatically become a professional due to being hired. You become a professional based on behavior, achievement, and mindset."
2. "I think what I am getting to is that being a professional is something you demonstrate and earn—not a title given to everyone because they have the same job." (Educators' Descriptors Study)[38]

This assertion that the status of professional must be earned is a deviation from the general literature on professions. The lone exception to the absence of competence in the general professional practice descriptions as a signal of professionalism is the availability of malpractice for a breach of competence resulting in an injury.[39]

We need not resolve the question of where education fits on a continuum of professions. Teachers are subject to discipline, including dismissal, for their unprofessional conduct[40] and other transgressions.[41] The professional responsibilities of teachers extend beyond the classroom and the school; these responsibilities include adherence to a high standard of conduct that extends beyond the schoolhouse gate. Both exemplar and nexus apply to an educator's off-campus behavior as part of the professional responsibilities of educators. As noted in the discussion of a learned society, a code of ethics is an integral guiding influence on the behavior of professionals.

Codes of Ethics

Professional service is individually delivered within the expectations of codes of ethics defining the contours of a professional's obligations. As Bair writes, what distinguishes a profession is "the collective establishment of widely recognized rules of good service ... [it] represents the values of a community of practitioners."[42] Université du Québec à Trois-Rivières professor Bruce Maxwell in his exploration of codes of conduct and ethics in education in five countries (Australia, Canada, England, the Netherlands, and the USA) asserts:

> The positive and constructive roles that a code of professional conduct is meant to play in professional life are clear: inspire public confidence, guide professional conduct, introduce new members to the ethical norms of the profession, and operate as a standard to assess the legitimacy of allegations of professional misconduct.[43]

The values of the community are codified in a code of ethics that forms the foundation for professional practice. A true profession requires its members to abide by a written ethics code promulgated to protect the best interests of the recipient of the services.[44] All professions have a code of ethics that guides the practice of their members.[45] "Professional codes of ethics represent a consensus of the normative values, beliefs, and concerns about appropriate behavior."[46] The code of ethics supports the commitment to serve the public and serves as a balance to professional autonomy. The codes of ethics for professional organizations, including those for teachers, principals (elementary and secondary), and superintendents, are similar in form to those of other professional organizations.[47] Ben-Perez writes that professional teachers' actions must be ethical, comporting with an implicit code of conduct.[48]

The Model Code of Ethics for Educators (2nd Edition: July 2023) Principles

Principle I: Responsibility to the Profession
The professional educator knows that trust in the profession depends upon a level of professional responsibility that may be higher than the minimal standard of policy and law. This

responsibility entails holding oneself and other educators to the same ethical standards.

Principle II: Responsibility for Professional Competence
The professional educator is committed to the highest levels of professional and ethical practice.

Principle III: Responsibility to Students
The professional educator has a primary obligation to promote the health, safety and wellbeing of all students. The professional educator treats students with dignity and respect, and establishes and maintains appropriate verbal, physical, emotional and social boundaries.

Principle IV: Responsibility to the School Community
The professional educator promotes appropriate relationships and effective interactions with members of the school community.

Principle V: Responsible and Ethical Use of Technology
The professional educator considers the impact of consuming, creating, distributing and communicating information through all technologies. The ethical educator is vigilant to ensure appropriate boundaries associated with role, time and place are maintained when using electronic communication.

Author, "MCEE: Model Code of Ethics for Educators," *National Association of State Directors of Teacher Education and Certification* (July 2023), https://cdn.ymaws.com/www.nasdtec.net/resource/resmgr/mcee/mcee_2nd_edition_july_2023.d.pdf.

Educators' codes of ethics are frequently used to define the standard for off-campus behavior, including the use of both exemplar and nexus models. They often provide a legal framework for analysis along with existing state law and court cases in which a particular controversy is analyzed to determine whether an educator can be classified as unprofessional conduct, conduct unbecoming, or immoral conduct.

The right to suspend or revoke an educator's credential or license to teach is not vested in their professional organizations but instead resides in the state boards of education. However, an educator code of ethics, whether developed by a professional organization or by a state, is used to inform the decision as to whether an educator has violated the dismissal or credential revocation standards.

For example, the Nebraska Department of Education's Standards of Conduct and Ethics for holders of public school certificates lists five principles that may form the basis for discipline, including admonishment, reprimand, suspension, and revocation.[49] The five principles follow:

- Principle I: "The educator shall exhibit good moral character, maintain high standards of performance and promote equality of opportunity in fulfillment of the educator's contractual and professional responsibilities."
- Principle II: "The educator shall work to stimulate the spirit of inquiry, the acquisition of knowledge and understanding, and the thoughtful formulation of worthy goals."
- Principle III: "The educator bears particular responsibility for instilling an understanding of and confidence in the rule of law, a respect for individual freedom, and a responsibility to promote respect by the public for the integrity of the profession."
- Principle IV: "The educator shall believe that sound professional relationships with colleagues are built upon personal integrity, dignity, and mutual respect."
- Principle V: "The Educator shall regard the employment agreement as a pledge to be executed both in spirit and in fact. The educator shall believe that sound personnel relationships with governing boards are built upon personal integrity, dignity, and mutual respect."[50]

Due Process and Adverse Employment Action: Dismissal, Credential Suspension, or Revocation.

The touchstone of due process is protection of the individual against arbitrary action of government.[51]

Codes of Ethics provide professional standards for educators who possess state-granted teaching credentials. These standards must be adhered to by educators in the discharge of their professional duties. Failure to meet a professional ethical standard may result in dismissal or nonrenewal of a contract. This decision is made at the local level by the employing school district.

However, the state may also take independent action against an educator in which the educator's credential may be suspended or revoked. To teach (or hold administrative or counseling positions) in a state's public school system, the educator must possess a valid credential. Therefore, the suspension or revocation of an educator's credential is of immense importance. See Chapter 6 for a discussion of a credential revocation case involving a teacher's out-of-school conduct, *Morrison v. State Board of Education*.[52]

A teachers may be fired from a school district while still retaining their teaching credential and the ability to be hired by other public school districts in the state.[53] However, if the teacher's credential is suspended, the teacher is not allowed to teach in the state for the duration of the suspension. If the credential is revoked, the teacher is barred from ever teaching in the state's public schools. Thus, actions by the state to suspend or revoke an educator's credential have extreme negative consequences beyond the loss of current employment; the trajectory of employment in education can be seriously disrupted or terminated. Dismissal from a school district, in the middle of a contract for a nontenured teacher or for tenured teacher, and the suspension or revocation by the state of teaching credential may trigger due process protections for the educator.[54] Due process is discussed below.[55]

Due Process

Due process as a constitutional guarantee is found in the Fifth and Fourteenth Amendments. Due process is central to the relationship between the individual and her/his government. At its core, due process means fundamental fairness—the government must treat an individual fairly before it may infringe on that individual's fundamental rights. Due process requires government to implement fair laws in a fair manner if it infringes upon a person's life, liberty, or property.

The US Supreme Court in *Morrissey v. Brewer* opined, "Once it is determined that due process applies, the question remains what process is due."[56] The process remains flexible, responding to the demands of the particular situation; it is not a "technical concept[] with fixed content."[57] As the Sixth Circuit Court of Appeals stated in a higher education due process case, "The more serious the deprivation, the more demanding the process."[58]

Due process is rooted in common law, dating back to the Magna Carta in 1215. Two elements comprise due process—procedural due process and substantive due process—which are both guaranteed in the Fifth and Fourteenth Amendments of the US Constitution.

Procedural Due Process

Procedural due process guarantees that a person who is deprived by the government of her/his life, liberty, or property is entitled to a fair process. The procedures for possibly taking away a person's life, liberty, or property must meet the requirements of a fair notice and a fair hearing. The Supreme Court underscored the importance of the hearing approximately 110 years ago. In *Grannis v. Ordean*, the Court wrote, "The fundamental requisite of due process of law is the opportunity to be heard."[59]

Discussing due process guarantees, US Supreme Court Justice Frankfurter stated in his concurring opinion, *Joint Anti-Fascist Committee v. McGrath,* "Secrecy is not congenial to truth-seeking, and self-righteousness gives too slender an assurance of rightness. No better instrument has been devised for arriving at truth than to give a person in jeopardy of serious loss notice of the case against him and opportunity to meet it."[60]

The notice must contain specific information about the day, time, and place of the hearing. It must also include, with sufficient specificity, notice of the charges against the person so that he/she can prepare an adequate defense. The hearing must be held before a neutral tribunal with authority in the matter. There must be an orderly proceeding, and the "accused" must have the opportunity to cross-examine witnesses. The hearing, except in the matter of exigency of immediate harm, must be held before the implementation of discipline.

Substantiative Due Process

As law professor and dean Erwin Chemerinsky wrote twenty-five years ago, "There is no concept in American law that is more elusive or more controversial than substantive due process. Substantive due process has been used in this century to protect some of our most precious liberties."[61] A year later, Robert Chesney stated in his law review article, "The doctrine of substantive due process is notorious both for the controversy that perennially surrounds it and the unusual degree of analytical confusion that it generates."[62] These comments are as salient today as they were a quarter century ago.

"Substantive due process allows federal courts to protect certain fundamental rights from government interference under the authority of the due process clauses of the Fifth and Fourteenth Amendments to the Constitution."[63] Substantive due process concerns the substance of the law, rule, or regulation. The law, rule, or regulation that deprives an individual of life, liberty, or property must be reasonable and consistent with the American sense of fairness. It must be clearly and rationally related to a lawful state function. For example, in *Rochin v. California*, the US Supreme Court held that substantive due process is violated when government conduct "offend[s] those canons of decency and fairness."[64]

The Reasonable Person test is used when the issue involves substantive due process. The test asks: "Could a reasonable person understand what to do or not do after reading the law, rule, or regulation?" Substantive due process challenges involve questions of vagueness[65] or overbreadth and about fundamental fairness (conscience-shocking behavior[66]). The US Supreme Court in *FCC v. Fox Television Stations, Inc.* noted that the vagueness doctrine addresses "a fundamental principle in our legal system ... that laws which regulate persons or entities must give fair notice of conduct that is forbidden or required."[67] Vague rules fail to provide adequate notice of what is impermissible and invite uneven, biased, and variable application and the use of "arbitrary power."[68] The Court in *Grayned v. City of Rockford* wrote over fifty years ago that "a vague law impermissibly delegates basic policy matters to policemen, judges, and juries for resolution on an *ad hoc* and subjective basis."[69]

While each state defines the actions/conditions that constitute the basis for an adverse personnel decision, including dismissal and credential revocation, there are some common standards; "good and just cause" is one of those common standards. For example, Ohio Revised Code 3319.16 provides that a teacher may not be terminated except for good and just cause.[70]

The section below will review an egregious example of the violation of the ethics of the profession. The sexual abuse of a student is a profound betrayal of professional ethics and is inappropriate conduct with a student, illegal, and immoral. This section explores the US Supreme Court decision that defines the Title IX requirements regarding the sexual abuse of a student perpetrated by a school employee.

The Sexual Abuse of Students Perpetrated by Educators: A Trust Betrayed[71]

> The sexual abuse of a child is a loathsome act. The act is particularly heinous when it is perpetrated by a person who has power over the child due to a position of trust. In a child's life, parents and teachers

hold recognized and dominant positions of trust ... No harm betrays that trust between educator and student more than the sexual abuse of the student.[72]

Education is one of the great helping professions. It is founded on a trust given by society and parents that the well-being of children will be primary, and the best interests of students shall be served by the actions of those in the teaching profession. As a beginning point for the profession, educators must not harm students and must protect students from foreseeable harm. Harm is not just physical, such as an injury to one's arm, leg, or body. It also includes sexual abuse and its attendant emotional trauma, as well as sexual harassment through allowing a hostile environment that tolerates harassment or abuse. Children must not be treated with indifference by the adults in their lives. This should be an uncontested truth.

There is an "immense trust placed in school employees to keep students safe and to maintain an environment and relationship conducive to learning."[73] If we do not value our students and their well-being at school, nothing else is of sustainable value in our schools. For example, a Tennessee Court of Appeals sustained the dismissal of a teacher after finding that the teacher's inappropriate sexual relationship with a student constituted unprofessional conduct.[74]

United States Secretary of Education Richard Riley stated, "Any sexual harassment of a student—particularly sexual abuse by a teacher—is a basic breach of trust between the school and the student and the family."[75] Educators who sexually abuse their students violate both exemplar and nexus standards.

The most "unprofessional" of acts by an educator, which some could reasonably argue is indifference to the welfare of a student, is sexual abuse. Professional teachers use their power to assist students. This should be an uncontested truth. Predator teachers abuse their power to further their own perverse ends. Professional teachers recognize the inherent boundary limits of their relationship with students. Predatory teachers know no boundaries.

Next, we will discuss *Gebser v. Lago Vista Independent School District*.[76] This US Supreme Court decision held that a school district could violate Title IX when an employee sexually abuses a student.

The Plight of Alida Starr Gebser

In the spring of 1991, Frank Waldrop, a teacher at Lago Vista High School, first met Alida Starr Gebser when she was an eighth grader in one of the district's middle schools during an after-school book discussion at his high school. He made sexually suggestive and unprofessional remarks to students during these sessions, which Alida had received permission to attend.

When Gebser attended high school in the fall as a freshman, she was assigned to Waldrop's classes for both semesters. Waldrop continued to make inappropriate remarks to his students, and he started to target Gebser for many of the more suggestive comments. In the spring of Gebser's freshman year, Waldrop visited Gebser's home, ostensibly to give her a book. He kissed and fondled her while at her house.[77] The two had sexual intercourse soon after on several occasions during the remainder of the school year and, through the summer and into the following school year. They often had intercourse during class time, although never on school property.[78] During the summer, Gebser was Waldrop's only student in an advanced placement class, and the two often had sexual intercourse during the time allotted for the class. It was not until January of 1993 that a police officer discovered Waldrop and the minor Gebser having sexual intercourse that the abusive situation came to light.

Alida did not report the abuse to school officials, testifying that "while she realized Waldrop's conduct was improper, she was uncertain how to react, and she wanted to continue having him as a teacher."[79] Gebser stated that she declined to report the sexual relationship because "if I was to blow the whistle on that, then I wouldn't be able to have this person as a teacher anymore" and that " Waldrop was the person in Lago administration who[m] I trusted."[80] She trusted her teacher, and that trust provided the lever for her abuse. "The trust that a child gives to a teacher is not unlike the trust that the child has for a parent."[81] Because who we place in positions of control over children matters greatly, the sexual abuse of students by educators is an issue of great importance to the community and the profession.

Alida brought suit against the 650-student school district that employed Waldrop and placed him in a position of power over her, alleging a violation of Title IX. The federal district court granted summary judgment for the school district denying relief under Title IX. The Fifth Circuit Court of Appeals rejected Alida's assertion of employer vicarious liability through agency principles[82] and affirmed the lower court's holding. Alida appealed to the US Supreme Court.

The Supreme Court Decides: Actual Notice and Deliberate Indifference

The Supreme Court handed down its ruling on June 22, 1998, after hearing oral arguments on March 25, 1998.[83] The outcome of this case was eagerly awaited in the education community because the Supreme Court had not handed down a definitive ruling on what legal standard applied when a plaintiff student sued a school district for damages under Title IX action alleging sexual abuse perpetrated by an educator.

In a five to four decision, the Court held that "damages may not be recovered for teacher-student sexual harassment in an implied private action under Title IX unless a school district official who, at a minimum, has authority to institute corrective measures on the district's behalf has actual notice of, and is deliberately indifferent to, the teacher's misconduct."[84]

Student Harm Arising from Negligent Supervision and Negligent Hiring

While Title IX is the preferred remedy that student sexual abuse victims seek in federal court, tort liability is also pursued as a cause of action in many such cases. Specifically, students who allege that they were sexually and or physically assaulted by a school employee can sue the school district for negligent supervision. In most states, the action is based on the duty of in loco parentis, which requires educators to abide by the same standard of care expected of parents when supervising their children. Furthermore, under negligence principles, "school have a common law duty to anticipate foreseeable dangers and to take necessary precautions to protect students in their care."[85]

A four-step prima facie test must be met by the plaintiff for the school district to be found liable for negligent supervision by an employee that resulted in harm to the student plaintiff. The test poses four questions that the plaintiff must answer before the defendant school district has to assert a defense. A failure to establish evidence for each test results in a dismissal of the case. The test includes the following.

Duty Owed—Did the educator owe the student a duty to anticipate foreseeable dangers and to take reasonable precautions to protect the student entrusted in their care from such dangers? This standard of care is measured against a reasonable person (educator) standard. Did the educator act as a reasonable and prudent educator would have acted under the same or similar circumstances?

Breach of Duty—Did the educator fail to exercise an appropriate standard of care given the age of the students, the environment, and the type of instructional activity? Did the educator act as a reasonable and prudent educator would act in the same or similar circumstances?

Causation—Actual and Proximate—Did the educator's action or inaction cause the injury?

A. *Cause-in-Fact*—Was there a sequential and continuous connection between the educator's action or inaction and resultant injury, and was that negligence a substantial cause of the harm? "But for" the defendant's action or inaction, the plaintiff would not have suffered an injury.
B. Proximate Cause—Was it foreseeable that the educator's action or inaction would cause the injury?

Actual Injury—Was the injury sufficient to sustain a tort action?[86]

Another basis for bringing a lawsuit against a school district is negligent hiring. An Illinois state court described negligent hiring in the following manner, "Liability for negligent hiring arises only when a particular unfitness of an applicant creates a danger of harm to a third person which the employer knew, or should have known, when he hired and placed this applicant in employment where he could injure others."[87] If the employer fails to use due diligence in the hiring process, a lawsuit for negligent hiring may be successfully brought against the school district. Consequently, employing school districts that do not use care when hiring may face litigation if the employee later causes harm.[88] As the Supreme Court of New York noted in a negligent hiring suit brought by a fifteen-year-old student against his social studies teacher, "A necessary element of a cause of action for negligent hiring is that the employer knew or should have known of an employee's propensity for the conduct that caused the injury."[89]

Furthermore, an Illinois law firm representing schools and colleges reported on the jury award of $2.5 million for the plaintiff in a 2019 negligent hiring case. A former kindergarten teacher was arrested and charged with sexually abusing kindergarten students in 2001–2. Two students brought separate suits against the Cicero school district alleging negligent hiring (asserting a failure to conduct a criminal background check or employment verifications), negligent supervision, and negligent retention. The court found in favor of the school district regarding the supervision and retention claims. However, the jury awarded the plaintiff a multi-million-dollar judgment for negligent hiring. The law firm concluded, "This case serves as a reminder that school districts should thoroughly vet all candidates before allowing them to be with students."[90] This is critically important advice if school districts are to only place qualified and safe employees in their schools and on their buses.

However, not all student lawsuits brought against school districts prevail for the student plaintiff. For example, in a 2023 case, the Supreme Court of New York upheld the dismissal of a case brought by a former high school student against the Hauppauge Union Free School District.[91] The student, John Doe, brought the action alleging that Mark Kimes, a choral teacher, physically and sexually assaulted him while he was attending a party at the teacher's home. John Doe's suit was dismissed for failure to state a cause of action.

In ruling on the student's negligent supervision claim, the court focused on the location of the alleged conduct. The incident occurred at Kimes' home, where the school district had "no custody or control of the plaintiff and no duty to monitor or supervise Kimes' conduct."[92] In addition, the court held that the plaintiff failed to include factual allegations of any improper interaction between him and Kimes on school grounds. Thus, the school district had no notice of the potentiality that Kimes would assault Doe.

Second, the court disposed of the negligent hiring claim in a similar manner. The court stated that John Doe did not show that the school district knew or should have known about Kimes' propensity for this type of assaultive behavior. Furthermore, even if Doe prevailed in demonstrating that Kimes had a propensity for this behavior, he did not demonstrate that there was a nexus between Kimes' employment and the assaults.

While *Gebser* identified a cause of action for an educator's egregious act of abuse of a student through Title IX, common law torts of negligence filed against the employing school district, have a steeper path to climb.[93] Time, commitment, and energy must be invested in the crucial decision of whom to hire to avoid lawsuits and secure professional services that provide a safe and secure environment. Our students deserve no less effort on our part; it is a duty that we owe them.

Ethical Behavior: What and Who Is Valued?

Creating a school culture that protects students is critical. Professional educators must communicate and enforce clear, unambiguous statements about maintaining a professional relationship with students.

Preventing harm and responding to early signs, such as grooming,[94] is a challenge that must be met. The goal must be zero indifference to students and zero tolerance for the sexual abuse of students. It matters not whether the exemplar or nexus standard is used in situations of the sexual abuse of a student that has been proved. The outcome must be the same when students are victimized by teachers who abuse the trust given to them by virtue of their status as educators charged with protecting the children or youth in their care.

Unfortunately, not all schools have placed students four-square in their value system. Too often, a school is more concerned with the school's reputation than the abuse of a student. The "blind eye" approach to reports of suspected sexual abuse by educators is sometimes the first response. These schools fail to ask, "whom do we protect, the student or the school?"

For example, in *Gonzalez v. Ysleta Independent School District*,[95] a school district, instead of reporting a teacher's suspected child abuse, merely moved the teacher to another school. In *Daly v. Derrick*,[96] the faculty of an alternative school negotiated with three female students who were sexually abused by one of their teachers at the school to move the teacher in exchange for the students' silence on the sexual abuse. This practice has often been referred to as the "Turkey Trot," "Passing the Trash,"[97] or the "Dance of the Lemons."

Similarly, in 2010, in the McLean County Unit School District 5, in the face of allegations of sexual abuse by an elementary school teacher, school authorities did not "sound the alarm" by reporting allegations to law enforcement or child-protection officials. Instead, they allowed the teacher to quietly resign and find a new teaching position in the Urbana School district.[98] The minor plaintiff argued that the defendant school district "took deliberate steps" to help the teacher secure a position in the Urbana School District, "all the while concealing [the teacher's] known history of sexual harassment."[99]

The court was asked to decide whether the McLean County School District could be liable for an injury to a student in the school district where the teacher moved. The lower court held that the Mclean County School District did not have the requisite control over the teacher to establish deliberate indifference.

However, the Illinois Court of Appeals found McLean School District's nondisclosure of the teacher's sexual harassment "troubling."[100] The Panel hoped "that school officials would be more proactive in protecting students, even those outside of their own districts, from abusive teachers."[101] The court cautioned that their decision should not be read to suggest "that school districts can quietly shuffle abusive teachers on to the next district with impunity."[102] There should be no impunity, no safe harbor for school districts and their employees who shuffle abusive educators to other school districts, endangering unsuspecting students.

However, as seen by the current moral panic, unfairly characterizing educators without evidence as groomers and pedophiles does not promote a safe environment for all. School law professor Janet R. Decker acknowledged the challenge, writing in her law review article on social networking policies that "administrators and policymakers are confronted with the difficult responsibility of balancing protecting school employees' constitutional rights, safeguarding the image of teachers as role models, and preventing inappropriate employee-student relationships."[103]

A foundation for this balance is the unassailable proposition that the sexual abuse of a student is, *per se*, injurious to the student and harmful to the school environment. Consequently, both tests, exemplar and nexus, are met when the sexual abuse of a student by an educator is established. Justice O'Connor in *Gebser*, noted the "extraordinary harm a student suffers when subjected to abuse by a teacher and that the teacher's reprehensible conduct undermines the basic purpose of the educational system."[104]

NEXT: After discussing the tension between the community and the profession as to who will teach our children—the historical setting for the tension and contour of education as a profession—we now turn to Chapter 5. This chapter continues the exploration of the concept of exemplar and adds a discussion of adverse notoriety and its impact. It also discusses specific court cases that use the mandatory role model status of teachers.

Notes

1 Mercedes S. Tichenor and John M. Tichenor, "Understanding Teachers' Perspectives on Professionalism," *The Professional Educator* XXVII (Fall 2004 & Spring 2005): 89-95, 94.

2 Todd A. DeMitchell, Richard Fossey, and Terri A. DeMitchell, *Raising a Cautionary Flag: Educational Malpractice and the Professional Teacher* (Lanham, MD: Rowman & Littlefield, 2022): 26 (Textbox 2.4). The issue of expectations for the moral conduct of teachers extends not only to the professional association but also to college and university preparation

programs. See Marlynn M. Griffin & Robert L. Lake, "Social Network Postings: View from the School Principals," *Education Policy Analysis Archives* 20(11) (2012): 1-27, 3, http://epaa.asu.edu/ojs/article/view/862. They write that "many colleges of education and state codes of ethics still include an expectation that teachers will exhibit professional dispositions and behavior and will avoid moral turpitude or behavior unbecoming a teacher." (internal citations omitted).

The authors provide examples of student teachers whose social networking site postings were scrutinized. For example, a student teacher removed photos of herself in a bikini after a high school student from her site discovered the pictures. In another case, a student teacher was removed from his field placement site at the request of the host school for a post of a "joke" about child molestation. Ibid., 5. The authors advise, "Teacher education faculty and administrators can better prepare teachers for the professional aspects of their careers when armed with data supporting the need for professional behavior in school and online." Ibid., 17.

3 OECD, *Supporting Teacher Professionalism: Insights from TALIS 2013* (Paris, France: TALIS, OECD, 2016), 28.
4 Ibid.
5 Charles T. Kerchner and Douglas E. Mitchell, *The Changing Idea of a Teachers' Union* (Philadelphia: Falmer Press, 1988), 227 (emphasis in original).
6 James H. Stronge, *Qualities of Effective Teachers* (Washington, D.C.: Association of Supervision and Curriculum Development 64, 2002), 64.
7 See DeMitchell, Fossey, and DeMitchell, *supra* note 2 for a discussion of malpractice in education. The authors conclude,

> And we must continue efforts to define professional practice with more precision and construct clear and valid measures for identifying teachers who fail in their instructional responsibilities. Flying a flag urging caution regarding a change in the public policy that would recognize a tort of educational malpractice is prudent.

Ibid., 193.
8 *See* Marka B. Fleming, Amanda Harmon Cooley, and Gwendolyn McFadden-Wade, *Morals Clauses for Educators in Secondary and Postsecondary Schools: Legal Applications and Constitutional Concerns*, 2009 BYU EDUC. & L.J. 67, 68 (2009). (discussing morals clauses for teachers based partly on the concept that an employee may be terminated "when an employee's conduct is potentially detrimental to the employer's interests.").
9 American Medical Association Code of Ethics, Opinion 1.01 – Terminology (June 1996), http://www.ama-assn.org/ama/pub/physic

ian-resources/medical-ethics/code-medical-ethics/opinion101.shtml (last visited January 20, 2010).
10. Rules of the Supreme Court of the State of New Hampshire, Rule 42. Admission to the Bar: Committee on Character (5)(a). http://www.courts.state.nh.us/rules/scr/scr-42.htm (last visited January 31, 2010).
11. *See also City of San Diego v. Roe*, 543 U.S. 77 (2004) (upholding the dismissal of a police officer for off-duty conduct; he sold videos of himself in his uniform masturbating.).
12. Matthew A. Kraft and Melissa Arnold Lyon, in a 2024 Working Paper (No. 22-679) at the Annenberg Institute at Brown University, assert that occupational prestige is an understudied construct of professionalism in education. "Prestige can be understood to simply mean the respect and social standing that a profession holds in society." They found that perceptions of teacher prestige have fluctuated "considerably" over the last fifty years.
Matthew A. Kraft and Melissa Arnold Lyon. (2024). *The Rise and Fall of the Teaching Profession: Prestige, Interest, Preparation, and Satisfaction over the Last Half Century*. (EdWorkingPaper: 22-679): 1–46, 9, 17. https://doi.org/10.26300/7b1a-vk.
13. William J. Goode, "Encroachment, Charlatanism, and the Emerging Profession: Psychology, Medicine, and Sociology," *American Sociological Review* XXV (1960): 902–65, 903.
14. Satya Sundar Sethy, "Academic Ethics: Teaching Profession and Teaching Professionalism in Higher Education Settings," *Journal of Academic Ethics* 16 (2018): 287–99, 293.
15. Abraham Flexner, *Is Social Work a Profession? Proceedings of the National Conference of Charities and Corrections* (Chicago: Hildmann Printing Co., 1915), 154.
16. For a discussion of the template for a member of a learned society and its application to education, see DeMitchell, Fossey, and DeMitchell, supra note 2, at 35 (Table 2.1), 42–5. The template for a learned society includes four phases—Extensive Knowledge Attainment, Skill Development, Application of Standards of Practice, and Acting in the Best Interests of the Patient/Client/Student—and three influences on the phases—Research-Based Theories, Authority to Act and Autonomy to Act, and a Code of Ethics.
17. Linda Darling-Hammond, "Accountability for Professional Practice," *Teachers College Record* 91 (1989): 59–80, 67. Professor Darling-Hammond, a noted teacher policy expert, states that professionalism is predicated upon these principles:
    1. Knowledge is the basis for permission to practice and for decisions that are made with respect to the unique needs of clients.
    2. The practitioner pledges his[/her] first concern to the welfare of the client.

3. The profession assumes collective responsibility for the definition, transmittal, and enforcement of professional standards of practice and ethics.
Ibid.
18 David Carr, *Professionalism and Ethics in Teaching* (London: Routledge, 2000).
19 Tamar Ruth Horowitz, "Professionalism and Semi-professionalism among Immigrant Teachers from the U.S.S.R. and North America," *Comparative Education* 21 (1985): 297–307, 297.
20 Alice J. Klein, "Educational Malpractice: Can the Judiciary Remedy the Growing Problem of Functional Illiteracy," *Suffolk University Law Review* 13 (1979): 27–62, 41.
21 Dan C. Lortie, *Schoolteacher: A Sociological Study* (Chicago: University of Chicago Press, 1975), 5.
22 Robert Bruno, "When Did the U.S. Stop Seeing Teachers as Professionals?" *Harvard Business Review* (June 20, 2018), https://hbr.org/2018/06/when-did-the-u-s-stop-seeing-teachers-as-professionals.
23 For example, researcher Frederick Hess provocatively stated:

> So—heresy alert—I suspect that the very question we're asking tonight—how to professionalize teaching?—is likely to lead us astray. I'd like to consider the possibility that teaching isn't a profession at all. It's a craft. Like being a plumber, electrician, or air traffic controller. Honorable work. And the people who do this work are pretty good at it. Because they've been *trained* for the job hey're hired to do.

Frederick Hess, "What Exactly is Teacher Professionalism, Anyway?" *Education Next* (October 9, 2018) (emphasis in original), https://www.educationnext.org/what-exactly-is-teacher-professionalism-anyway-reading-pondiscio/.
See also Mary Antony Bair, "Teacher Professionalism: What Educators Can Learn from Social Workers," *Mid-Western Educational Researcher* 26, no. 2 (2014): 28–57, 29–30, writing, "Although the literature is replete with discussions of professionalism and essays bemoaning the de-professionalization of teachers, several scholars have pointed out the scarcity of empirical research on teacher professionalism and the rather surprising gap in our understanding of the institutional contexts for teacher preparation."
24 Tamar Ruth Horowitz, "Professionalism and Semi-Professionalism among Immigrant Teachers from the U.S.S.R. and North America," Comparative Education 21 (1985): 297–307, 297.
25 Amitai Etzioni, ed., *The Semi-Professions and Their Organization. Teachers, Nurses, Social Workers* (New York: Free Press, 1969).
26 Ibid.

27 Matthew A. Kraft, and Melissa Arnold Lyon. "The Rise and Fall of the Teaching Profession: Prestige, Interest, Preparation, and Satisfaction over the Last Half Century" (EdWorkingPaper: 22-679, 2024): 1-46, 3, https://doi.org/10.26300/7b1a-vk. They write, "And unlike most other professions, the public has had ample exposure to what teachers do. Their knowledge is not perceived as exclusive despite the 'irreducible complexity' of teachers' work."
28 School climate refers to the "shared beliefs, values, and attitudes reflecting the quality and character of life in schools." Jacob Olsen, et al., "A Review and Analysis of Selected School Climate Measures," *The Clearing House: A Journal of Educational Strategies, Issues and Ideas* (December 21, 2017): 1-12, 1, https://www.researchgate.net/profile/Jacob-Olsen/publication/321984139_A_Review_and_Analysis_of_Selected_School_Climate_Measures/links/5be06eb2299bf1124fbdfef8/A-Review-and-Analysis-of-Selected-School-Climate-Measures.pdf. "Research shows that a positive school climate directly impacts telling indicators for success such as higher student achievement, lower dropout rates, decreased incidences of violence, and increased teacher retention."
Ibid., 8 (internal citation omitted).
29 393 U.S. 503, 506 (1969). See also *Mahanoy Area School District v. B.L. ex rel. Levy*, 594 U.S. 180, 188 (2021), in which the Supreme Court, in a public school student's off-campus speech, wrote that the "special characteristics" of the public-school context afford schools "special leeway when [they] regulate speech that occurs under [their] supervision."
30 875 F.2d 954 (1st Cir. 1989).
31 *Timothy W.* was tried under the existing Education for All Handicapped Children Act (20 U.S.C. § 1400 et seq.) and codified under current federal special law.
32 Rud Turnbill and Ann P. Turnbill, "Reaching the Idea," *Education Next Forum* 3, no. 1 (July 14, 2006), https://www.educationnext.org/reachingtheideal/.
33 Lortie, *supra* note 20, 201.
34 Author, "Five Propositions," *National Board for Professional Teaching Standards* (2025), https://www.nbpts.org/certification/five-core-propositions/.
35 DeMitchell, Fossey, and DeMitchell, *supra* note 2, 28–34.
36 Ibid., 31.
37 Mercedes S. Tichenor and John M. Tichenor, "Understanding Teachers' Perspectives on Professionalism," *The Professional Educator* XXVII (Fall 2004 and Spring 2005): 89–95, 92-4.
38 DeMitchell, Fossey, and DeMitchell, *supra* note 2, 32.
39 One of the subjects of discussion regarding education as a profession revolves around whether educators are subject to malpractice suits, as are

other professionals. For a discussion of educators and malpractice, see DeMitchell, Fossey, and DeMitchell, *supra* note 2.

40 See Todd A. DeMitchell and Mark A. Paige, *Threading the Evaluation Needle: The Documentation of Teacher Unprofessional Conduct* (Lanham, MD: Rowman & Littlefield, 2020).

41 Conduct unbecoming of a teacher is a standard that is also used in educator discipline cases. An example of applying this standard is found in a Washington case involving both in-school and out-of-school behavior. A teacher was nonrenewed for multiple arrests for alcohol-related offenses. The first offense took place on February 19, 2004, and his fourth arrest occurred on August 4, 2010. On August 29, 2011, he was also arrested for obstructing and resisting arrest. In addition, he was disciplined for harassing a bus driver and inappropriately touching a student (rubbing her stomach), coming to school under the influence of alcohol, in addition to inappropriately touching the school secretary. The school district first placed him in a transition assistance program, issued a written reprimand on May 12, 2009, and initiated the process for nonrenewal and discharge. The hearing officer concluded that Cronin's off-campus conduct and his touching of the student were egregious and materially and substantially affected his teaching performance, efficiency, and effectiveness. The court using nexus upheld the hearing officer's conclusion that Cronin's conduct was "irremediable and materially affected his teaching performance, thus constituting sufficient cause to support his discharge." *Cronin v. Central Valley School District*, 520 P.3d 999, 1033 (Wash. App. Div. 3 2022).

42 Bair, *supra* note 23, 32.

43 Bruce Maxwell, "Codes of Professional Conduct and Ethics Education for Future Teachers," *Philosophical Inquiry in Education* 24, no. 4 (2017): 323–47, 325. Professor Maxwell concludes,

> Society entrusts a relatively wide margin of autonomy to professionals, and recognizes the right for self-regulation, in exchange for a promise that they will work under publicly promulgated and internally enforced standards of ethical conduct.

Ibid., 338.

44 For a comparison of several codes of ethics, including education, see Lynn Hammonds, *Embracing the Model Code of Ethics for Educators Across Multiple Jurisdictions: An Exploratory Multiple Case Study*. Unpublished doctoral dissertation (Ed.D.), University of Hawai'i at Manoa (July 2020); 10–19. The author summarized the similarities of codes of ethics for physicians, attorneys, accountants, and educators:
1. A call for professional competence;
2. Responsibility for the welfare of individuals in their care;

3. The setting of professional boundaries between the professional and those they serve;
4. The requirement for confidentiality to protect personal information; and
5. A responsibility to the greater community that the professional serves. Ibid., 18.

For a discussion of the application of a code of ethics as applied to counselors, see Todd A. DeMitchell, David J. Hebert, and Loan T. Phan, "The University Curriculum and the Constitution: Personal Beliefs and Professional Ethics in Graduate School Counseling Programs," *The Journal of College and University Law* 39, no. 2 (2013): 303–46. The authors conclude, "The professional workspace must be reserved for the ethics of the profession. The college or university must prepare its students to discharge all of the requirements of the profession, not just the ones the student interprets as personally acceptable to his or her beliefs." Ibid., 345.

45 Author, *Professional Ethics*, Center for the Study of Ethics in the Professions (Chicago, IL: Illinois Institute of Technology, 2008), http://ethics.iit.edu/teaching/professional-ethics.

46 Regina Umpstead, Kevin Brady, Elizabeth Lugg, Joann Klinker, and David Thompson, "Educator Ethics: A Comparison of Teacher Professional Responsibility Laws in Four States," *Journal of Law & Education* 42 (2013): 183–225, 186. Furthermore, they write, "Professional codes of ethics in education concern how educators *ought* to conduct themselves within the profession of education." Ibid., 188 (emphasis in original).

47 Patrick D. Pauken and Philip T.K. Daniel, "An Essay: Law, Ethics, and Policy in an Era of Accountability and Responsibility: An Analysis of Codes of Ethics and Conduct," *Education Law Reporter* 223, no. 1 (2007): 1–33, 3. The authors write that professional association codes of ethics "serve not only as guides for individual decision-making but also as unifying documents from one body, offering a sense of confidence to and from the general public and permitting self-regulation at the level where expertise and experience lie." Ibid., 27.

48 Miriam Ben-Perez, "The Impossible Role of Teacher Educators in a Changing World," *Journal of Teacher Education* 52, no. 1 (2001): 48–56, 50.

49
- "Admonishment shall mean a private sanction to an educator that further unprofessional or unethical conduct may result in more serious action, including suspension or revocation of a certificate."
- "Reprimand shall mean a public sanction criticizing or rebuking an educator for unprofessional or unethical conduct."
- "Suspension shall mean a public sanction withdrawing an educator's certificate for a certain period of time. The certificate is automatically reinstated at the expiration of the suspension if it has not expired during the period of suspension."

- "Revocation shall mean a public sanction canceling an educator's certificate for a certain period of time. At the expiration of the revocation period, the former educator may apply for reinstatement."

Nebraska Department of Education, *Standards of Conduct and Ethics for Holders of Public School Certificates* (n.d.). The site was visited on June 15, 2019, and is available at http://nde.ne.gov/CC/standcond.pdf.

50 Ibid.
51 *County of Sacramento v. Lewis*, 523 U.S. 833, 845 (1998) (quoting *Wolff v. McDonnell*, 418 U.S. 539, 558 (1974)).
52 461 P.2d 375 (Cal. 1969).
53 An educator may still face disciplinary action even if the district attorney chooses not to prosecute the educator for criminal conduct. For example, a North Carolina teacher was fired for possessing marijuana in his home even though the criminal charges were dropped. *In re Freeman*, 426 N.E.2d 100 (N.C. Ct. App. 1993).
54 An example of the right to due process for those who possess a professional license from the state, which include educators, is found in New Hampshire's RSA 541-A:30, II. The law provides that:

> An agency shall not revoke, suspend, modify, annul, withdraw, or amend a license unless the agency first gives *notice* to the licensee *of the facts or conduct* upon which the agency intends to base its action, and gives the licensee an opportunity, *through an adjudicative proceeding*, to show compliance with all lawful requirements for the retention of the license. (emphasis added).

See New Hampshire Department of Education regulation, Ed. 501.01(e), which requires that educators facing potential credential discipline be provided a fair hearing with the right to appeal.

55 The discussion on due process rights for educators is based on previous scholarship, including Todd A. DeMitchell and Mark A. Paige, *Threading the Evaluation Needle: The Documentation of Teacher Unprofessional Conduct* (Lanham, MD: Rowman & Littlefield, 2020), 21–25; and for a discussion of due process as applied to public school students, see Todd A. DeMitchell, "Due Process: Fairness in Procedure and Substance in the Public Schools," in *Pedagogies of Punishment: The Ethics of Discipline in Education*, ed. Winston C. Thompson and John Tillson (London: Bloomsbury Academic, 2023), 143–160.
56 408 U.S. 471, 481 (1972).
57 *Cafeteria Workers v. McElroy*, 367 U.S. 886, 895 (1961).
58 *Doe v. University of Cincinnati*, 872 F.3d 393, 400 (6th Cir. 2017).
59 234 U.S. 385, 394 (1914).
60 341 U.S. 123, 171–2 (1951) (Frankfurter, J., concurring).
61 Erwin Chemerinsky, "Substantive Due Process," *Touro Law Review* 15, no. 4 (1999): 1501–34, 1501.

62 Robert Chesney, "Old Wine or New? The Shocks-the-Conscience Standard and the Distinction Between Legislative and Executive Action," *Syracuse Law Review* 50 (2000): 981–1018, 981.
63 Jency Megan Butler, "Shocking the Eight Amendment's Conscience: Applying a Substantive Due Process Test to the Evolving Cruel and Unusual Punishments Clause," *Hastings Constitutional Law Quarterly* 43, no. 4 (2016): 861–84, 873.
64 *Rochin v. California*, 342 U.S. 165, 169 (1972).
65 See, for example, the following cases:
    - *Baggett v. Bullitt*, 377 U.S. 360, 368 (1964) (invalidating on vagueness and overbreadth grounds an oath requiring teachers to forswear an "undefined variety" of behavior considered "subversive" to the government.).
    - "Gang-related activities, such as display of 'colors, symbols, signals, signs, and so on, will not be tolerated on school grounds." The term "gang-related activities" was not defined, and left students unclear about what was allowed and gave school officials too much discretion to decide what constituted a gang symbol (*Stephenson v. Davenport Community School District*, 110 F.3d 1303 (8th Cir. 1997).
    - A rule against "misconduct" (*Soglin v. Kauffman*, 295 F. Supp. 978 (W.D. Wis. 1968, aff'd, 418 F.2d 163 (7th Cir. 1969).
    - A rule forbidding "inappropriate actions" or "unacceptable behavior" (*Galveston Independent School District v. Boothe*, 590 S.W.2d 553 (Tex. Ct. App. 1979).
66 For a discussion of "shocks the conscience" substantive due process as applied to teacher discipline, see Todd A. DeMitchell and Mark A. Paige, "Substantive Due Process. 'Shocks the Conscience Standard' Applied to Educator Discipline," *Education Law Reporter* 424, no. 1 (2024): 15–26. The New York Supreme Court Appellate Division, in a teacher dismissal case, discussed the shocks the conscience standard writing, "the mere fact that a penalty is harsh, and imposes severe consequences on an individual, does not affront our sense of fairness that it shocks the conscience, unless it is obviously disproportionate to the misconduct and in contravention of the public interest and policy reflected by the agency's mission." *Denicolo v. Board of Education of the City of New York*, 98 N.Y.S.3d 578, 579 (App. Div. 1 Dept. 2019) (internal citations omitted).
67 567 U.S. 239, 253 (2012). Furthermore, the Court held, "If arbitrary and discriminatory enforcement is to be prevented, laws must provide explicit standards for those who apply them." *Grayned v. City of Rockford*, 408 U.S. 104, 108 (1972).
68 *Sessions v. Dimaya*, 138 S. Ct. 1204, 1223 (2018) (Gorsuch, J. concurring).
69 408 U.S. 104,108 (1972).
70 See *Chardon Local School District v. Chardon Education Association/ OEA/NEA*, 3 N.E.3d 1224, 1228 (Ohio App. 11 Dist. 2013). In this case, a

teacher was found guilty of vehicular assault, a fourth-degree felony, when she caused a serious motor vehicle accident with significant injuries to the driver of the vehicle she hit by driving on the wrong side of a divided highway.

71 The term "A Trust Betrayed" is borrowed from the title of a three-part Series Special Report published by *Education Week* (December 2, 1998, December 9, 1998, December 16, 1998) that explores when educators cross the line of professionalism and engage in sexual abuse of their students.

72 Todd A. DeMitchell, "The Duty to Protect: Blackstone's Doctrine of *In Loco Parentis*: A Lens for Viewing the Sexual Abuse of Students," *Brigham Young University Education and Law Journal* 2002, no. 1 (2002): 17–52, 17. The author concludes:

> It takes no intuitive leap or well-reasoned analysis to conclude that children should be able to attend school and be free from sexual abuse visited upon them by their teachers, principals, or school bus drivers. Reform efforts that target curriculum, school funding, and teacher preparation, but do not help to make the classroom a more secure place for children make a false promise of improvement

Ibid., 51–2.

73 *Jane Doe A. v. Green*, 298 F. Supp. 2d 1025, 1038 (D. Nev. 2004) (asserting that engaging in sexual relations with students is an "extreme" violation of this trust.).

74 *Crosby v. Holt*, 320 S.W. 3d 805 (Tenn. Ct. App. 2009).

75 Mark Walsh, "Riley Restates Rules Against Harassment," *Education Week* (July 8, 1998), 30.

76 524 U.S. 274 (1998).

77 Ibid., 278.

78 When Waldrop wanted to have sexual intercourse with Gebser at school, they used the code phrase, "Do you want to study psychology." Mark Walsh, "High Court Addresses Harassment," *Education Week* (April 1, 1998), 38.

79 *Gebser*, 524 U.S., 278.

80 Ibid., 299–300 fn. 10 (Stevens, Souter, Ginsburg, & Breyer, JJ., dissenting).

81 DeMitchell, supra note 72, 28.

82 For a discussion of agency principles, see Richard Fossey and Todd A. DeMitchell, "'Let the Master Answer': Holding Schools Vicariously Liable When Employees Sexual Abuse Children," *Journal of Law & Education* 25, no. 4 (Fall 1996): 575–99.

For a recent application of agency principles to the sexual abuse of a student perpetrated by a public school custodian, see Richard Fossey, Todd A. DeMitchell, and Nathan Roberts, "A Louisiana School Is

Vicariously Liable for a School Janitor's Sexual Assault," *Case Closeup* (Education Law Association) 2, no. 6 (June 2022): 9–10.

83 For an expanded discussion of the Gebser case and the deliberate indifference standard, see Richard Fossey and Todd A. DeMitchell, "Title IX's 'Deliberate Indifference' Standard for Determining Liability Under Title IX When Students Are Sexually Abused by School Employees: A Trust Betrayed," Education Law Reporter 299 (2014): 811–42. George Bernard Shaw wrote in The Devil's Disciple, "The worst sin towards our fellow creatures is not to hate them, but to be indifferent to them; that is the essence of inhumanity."
The Devil's Disciple (1901) act 2.

84 *Gebser,* 524 U.S., 277.

85 Martha M. McCarthy and Nelda H. Cambron-McCabe, *Public School Law: Teachers' and Students' Rights* (7th ed.) (Boston: Pearson, 2014), 419.

86 See Todd A. DeMitchell, *Negligence: What Principals Need to Know about Avoiding Liability,* (Lanham, MD: Rowman & Littlefield Education, 2007), 23–46. The obligations that educators owe to their students as part of their duty to the students include (1) providing proper supervision, (2) providing proper instructions, (3) providing properly maintained buildings, grounds, and equipment, and (4) providing warnings regarding known or reasonably foreseeable hazards. Ibid., 27–39.

87 *Fallon v. Indian Trail Sch. Addison Township School District No. 4,* 148 Ill. App. 3d 931, 935 (1986).

88 For a discussion of reasonable hiring practices in education, see Todd A. DeMitchell, "Placing Students in Harm's Way? Exercising Due Diligence: Negligent Hiring and School District Liability," *Labor Law Journal* 72, no. 4 (Winter 2021): 229–39. "The gravamen of negligent hiring claims is whether the plaintiff established facts that 'would plausibly suggest the School Board was on notice of or reasonably could have foreseen, any harmful propensities or unfitness for employment.' This core question of whether the hiring practice and procedures are reasonably calculated to uncover whether the applicant presents a foreseeable risk to students and school personnel." Ibid, 236 (internal citations omitted).

89 *C.M. v. City of New York,* 800 N.Y.S.2d 898, 901 (Sup. 2005).

90 Author, "Cook County Jury Awards $2.5 Million Against Illinois School District for "Negligent Hiring" of Teacher," Hodges, Loizzi, Eisenhammer, Rodrick and Kohn (December 18, 2019), https://hlerk.com/cook-cou nty-jury-awards-2-5-million-against-illinois-school-district-for-neglig ent-hiring-of-teacher/.

91 *Doe v. Hauppauge Union Free School District,* 184 N.Y.S.3d 150, 153 (A.D. 2 Dept. 2023).

92 Ibid.

93 See, for example, a band teacher had an illicit sexual relationship with one of his minor students. Among other complaints, a negligent hiring

claim was brought against the school district. The plaintiffs asserted that the teacher allegedly had sexual relations with two of his students in his former employment, marrying one of the students. The court detailed the hiring process, which included positive recommendations from the former principal and superintendent, possessed a valid teaching credential after passing a criminal background check, completing a questionnaire stating that "he had never been investigated, charged with, or resigned because of any misconduct, including sexual abuse or contact," confirmed that he was not on a list of known sex offenders, and conducted multiple interviews with the principal and assistant superintendent. (*Hansen v. Board. of Trustees of Hamilton Southeastern School Corp*oration, 551, F.3d 599, 610 (7th Cir. 2008)) The Appellate Court held that nothing in the record created an inference that the school district knew or should have known of any negative information regarding the teacher at the time of his employment. "Furthermore, given the school district's hiring process, no evidence indicates that it acted unreasonably in hiring him." Ibid., 612.

94 The Australian National Office for Child Safety, https://www.childsafety.gov.au/about-child-sexual-abuse/grooming#what-is-grooming defines grooming as:

> The term 'grooming' refers to intentional behaviours that manipulate and control a child, as well as their family, kin and carers, other support networks, or organisations in order to perpetrate child sexual abuse.

In the United States, grooming has a similar definition:

> Child grooming refers to an act of deliberately establishing an emotional connection with a child to prepare the child for child abuse. Child grooming is undertaken usually to carry out sexual abuse and other child exploitation like trafficking of children, child prostitution or the production of child pornography. Currently, child grooming occurs through the use of the internet.

It is considered a federal offense pursuant to 18 USCS § 2422. USLegal.com (n.d), https://definitions.uslegal.com/c/child-grooming/.

95 996 F.2d 745 (5th Cir. 1993).
96 230 Cal. App. 3d 1349 (1991).
97 For a 2022 case involving the sexual abuse of students in which a Texas federal district court judge termed part of his analysis on a § 1983 case, "(a) The Pass the Trash Policy Discriminates Against Female Students." The minor female plaintiff students sued the school district and a former male teacher for a due process violation of their rights of personal safety, security, and bodily integrity and violations of their equal protection rights for sexually abusive contact. Before the analysis, in an unusual move, Judge Truncale wrote in pertinent part in bold print:

The Court extends a warning to the reader that parts of this opinion are deeply disturbing. The factual background of this case is challenging to read, and candidly, has been a struggle to write since it involves graphic allegations of systemic child abuse over a forty year period ... The Court relates these facts with great sadness.

Judge Truncale begins his analysis of the first case (2006) writing, "This is not the first time BISD has been ha[u]led into court over allegations of systemic rot."

Doe v. Beaumont Independent School District, 615 F. Supp. 3d 471,481 (E.D. TX. 2022)

98 *Doe-2 v. McLean County Unit District 5 Board of Directors*, 593 F.3d 507, 510 (7th Cir. 2010) (describing the teacher's acts as having students massage him and wrap their legs around him, showing sexually suggestive photographs, and playing the "taste test game" in which "he would blindfold students and then place foods in their mouths using a banana, his hand, or his penis.").
99 Ibid., 516.
100 Ibid.
101 Ibid., 516–17.
102 Ibid., 517. The court further stated that Illinois state law (325 ILCS 5/4-5/4.02) imposes criminal penalties for willful violations of its reporting requirements, "which we trust will give Illinois school officials an extra incentive (if they needed one) to disclose their teachers' known acts of sexual harassment." Ibid.
103 Janet R. Decker, "Facebook Phobia! The Misguided Proliferation of Restrictive Social Networking Policies for School Employees," *Northwestern Journal of Law & Social Policy* 9, no. 2 (2014): 164–205, 166.
104 *Gebser*, 524 U.S., 291.

Chapter 5

TEACHER AS A MANDATORY ROLE MODEL, COMMUNITY CONTROL: EXEMPLAR, ADVERSE NOTORIETY, AND COURT CASES

The US Supreme Court in 1958 stated there is "no requirement in the Federal Constitution that a teacher's classroom conduct be the sole basis for determining his fitness. Fitness for teaching depends on a broad range of factors."[1]

Teachers' private lives are viewed differently from those of other professionals. "[The] calling [of the teacher] is so intimate, its duties so delicate, the things in which a teacher might prove unworthy or would fail are so numerous that they are incapable of enumeration in any legislative enactment. The intimate personal life and habits of a physician or dentist do not necessarily affect his usefulness; he deals with adult persons or children under his protection. But the teacher is entrusted with the custody of children and their high preparation for life.."[2]

The rise of professionalization in teaching, along with the institutionalization of the common school, led to a heightened level of scrutiny of teachers' lives, both inside and outside the school. While teachers are required to be good employees, they are also expected to be good, moral, and upstanding citizens, serving as an example for their students to emulate. Thus, the teacher's life is scrutinized both inside and outside the classroom, as an employee and as a role model for their students. Consequently, "exemplar rests on the belief that students, at least in part, acquire their social attitudes and behaviors by copying those of their teachers."[3]

Therefore, because teachers are considered to be mandatory role models, their conduct in their private lives often affects their standing in the community and their job security. An early Illinois court captured this concept of community control over the lives of teachers, writing, "If suspicion of vice or immorality be once entertained against a teacher, his influence for good is gone. The parents become distrustful, the pupils contemptuous, and school discipline, essential to success, is at an end."[4] In addition to court cases that support the role model standard, the various states enshrine this standard in their laws and regulations. For example, the Ohio licensure code for educators states:

Professional Behavior

Educators shall behave as professionals, realizing that their actions reflect directly on the status and substance of the education profession.

An educator serves as a positive role model to both students and adults and is responsible for preserving the dignity and integrity of the teaching profession and for practicing the profession according to the highest ethical standards.[5]

This chapter discusses the impact of the communities scrutinizing teachers' private lives, from the rise of common schools to the push for civil rights in the 1960s, which moderated the reach and impact of the mandatory role model concept.

Teacher as Exemplar

Teachers, probably more than any other group of public employees, have been required to adhere strictly to the moral code of the community and to project an image of rectitude. The relaxation of many traditional restraints has not permitted public school teachers the same freedoms enjoyed by those in other professions and occupations.[6]

Traditionally, educators have been compelled to adhere more strictly to the community's moral codes than most other professions or occupations. For example, the dissent in a California medical license revocation case captured the difference in social expectations for the two professions: "The gap between a teacher's personal morality and its impact on his ability to function may be very narrow. On the other hand, we do not go to see a doctor because we expect to pattern our lives after his."[7]

Teachers are considered holders of a special position of trust and responsibility because of their relationship with the community's children. Teachers, before the 1960s, led precarious professional lives. They were scrutinized both in the classroom and in their private lives. (See Appendix B). The history of education in the United States is replete with examples of stringent ordinances and school board regulations mandating a higher standard of conduct for teachers than for other community members.

The predominantly rural schools of the early twentieth century were considered an extension of the local community. For example, in a 1942 case, a school board dismissed a teacher for immorality for knowingly making false statements to the Liquor Control Board to procure a liquor license, and the board's dismissal decision was upheld. The teacher's conduct was contrary to ethical conduct and inconsistent with the rules and principles of morality. The court wrote:

> We think it is self-evident that the conduct of a teacher, which is subversive of those standards of moral rectitude, which the law has established both for government and social conduct, is not conducive to the maintenance of the integrity of the public school system.[8]

Parents who smoked, drank, gambled, lied, and committed adultery demanded that a teacher's conduct be above their own. "It was and still is believed that teachers must lead ... exemplary li[ves] so as to properly mold children's virtues."[9] With great sincerity, parents and the community believed that a teacher should serve "the community through an upright exemplary life and whose influence will give their children the characters they themselves aspired to and failed to attain."[10] Even marriage can result in dismissal at various times, often under the assertion that it may be a distraction to the teacher's complete dedication to the community's children.[11]

In the past, the community's control over teachers was pervasive. Not only were the teacher's classroom conduct and skills keenly evaluated, but almost all facets of the teacher's personal conduct were scrutinized. The watch kept over a teacher's private life was taken up by many in some communities. The generalized moral expectations of the community shaped the behavior of educators both in and outside the classroom.[12]

Some communities exercised control over teachers by requiring them to donate both time and money to various civic organizations. Church attendance was mandated in some rural locales. For example, in South Carolina, a teacher was reprimanded for not attending all the town's churches. The teacher taught Sunday school for the Baptist Church, but the town thought that he should show impartiality by attending all the town's churches seriatim. He was, essentially, required to forego his chosen church and conform to all others through his attendance, thus subordinating his religious choice to the community's wishes.[13] However, a 1905 contract in Story County, Iowa, required all teachers to attend church every Sunday and "take an active part, particularly in choir and Sunday school work."[14] The teachers could at least attend the church of their choice but would have to sing.

Before the Second World War, a restriction on a teacher's fundamental right to marry was common in school districts.[15] Communities asserted at various times that married teachers should not be employed.[16] In 1932, a Minnesota court upheld the school board's authority to cancel contracts for female teachers upon their marriage.[17] Beale's 1936 study of teachers' private lives found that in 1903, the New York Board of Education adopted a bylaw forbidding marriage. In 1915, Cleveland implemented a similar rule. A school board in Monroe County, Tennessee, adopted a marriage dismissal rule but added an equality twist. Two school board members proposed enacting a rule to dismiss all married women; two members opposed the policy. The fifth and deciding member, a female member, agreed to vote for the measure if it were amended to apply to all married teachers regardless of gender. Five men and nineteen women were dismissed.[18] Fair is fair; if marriage interferes with a teacher's duties, the board member must have reasoned that no teacher should be allowed to get married.

Emphasizing the reach of the exemplar standard, a Mississippi school district in the mid-1970s passed a policy prohibiting the employment of teachers who were not married but had children.[19] As late as 1985, a teacher was dismissed for going through a divorce.[20]

The tentacles of exemplar control touched almost every facet of a teacher's life. For example, in an 1884 case, the Missouri Court of Appeals upheld the dismissal of a male teacher based on the fact that his wife brought charges of adultery against him, and that had become notorious in the community.[21] Howard K. Beale's 1936 study of teacher freedoms identified several restrictive legislative and employment actions taken as part of the role model requirement. For example, in Tennessee, a pre-1940 act authorized the dismissal of teachers for drinking or refusing to pay their honest debts. In 1929, eleven high school teachers were dismissed for attending a dance at a local country club. In many areas of the country, teachers were not permitted to smoke or consume alcohol, either in private or in public. A teacher caught smoking in public in Omaha, Nebraska, would receive a typewritten notice instructing them to please smoke in private.

Drinking was more restricted than smoking. Teachers in many areas of the country were not allowed to smoke or drink in public or even their private homes. Drunkenness was widespread among colonial teachers, but in 1931, Pennsylvania considered a law requiring all teachers to pledge not to use liquor; in Seattle in 1932, a male teacher was forced to resign because liquor was found in his apartment.[22]

In many locales, a teacher's appearance was circumscribed. In 1928, female teachers in West Virginia were required to fasten their galoshes all the way up. An Arkansas school board prohibited the wearing of transparent hosiery, low-necked dresses, and cosmetics. One country teacher lost her position because the wives of prominent citizens complained about the poor quality of her dresses. The teacher earned forty dollars a month.[23] Teachers led a precarious life, not always knowing what actions might result in discipline.

In 1944, despite the school board finding Edward Schweitzer to be well-qualified, conscientious, and professional, he was fired due to public statements he made affirming that he was a pacifist and would not aid the United States, either as a combatant or noncombatant, during the war. The school board considered his out-of-school conduct and statements to be "inimical to the ideals of citizenship and responsibilities of citizens to their country," thus "rendering him incapable and incompetent to fulfill his duty as a teacher."[24] The court stated that it is the duty of a teacher:

> to labor faithfully and earnestly for the advancement of the pupils in their duties, deportment and morals, and embrace every opportunity to inculcate by precept and example the principles of truth, honesty and patriotism and the practice of every Christian virtue.[25]

Even though Schweitzer was exercising his right to free speech, the court upheld his dismissal for incompetence. The teacher was expected to uphold and adhere to the community standards of thought and action. Beale wrote, "The teacher is still 'only a teacher,' not entitled to vigorous views on things that really matter in the community if his [or her] views differ from those generally accepted."[26]

Examples of Early Cases Under Exemplar

> The proper education of the youth of this country by precept and example is one of the most delicate and important functions of the state, and it is not an arbitrary exercise of power to require that those persons entrusted with such education should themselves possess a good moral character.[27]

In the Dark and Secretive, But "No Immoral Act!" (1931)

L. E. Gover was finishing the first month of his first year of employment as a teacher and football coach at Pritchard High School in Grayson, Kentucky, when written charges were preferred against him, which resulted in his subsequent dismissal. Gover sued the school district in state court to recover the difference between what he earned and what he would have earned had the contract not been terminated. Specifically, he requested $1,025.40 of the total contract amount of $1,600.[28] He argued that his discharge was "without sufficient cause and without any sufficient ground."[29] The lower court supported the dismissal, finding sufficient grounds to do so. Gover appealed.

The applicable statute for Gover's case states that an educator can be dismissed for "immorality, misconduct, incompetency, insubordination, or willful neglect of duty."[30] The court applied the facts of the case, which follows, to the existing legal standard for dismissal.

The undisputed facts of the case were that Jack Jacobs, a young man residing in the town of Grayson, where the school was located, planned to meet three young ladies, one of whom was a pupil at the school after school closed. Upon learning about the clandestine get-together, Gover asked to join them. The five individuals entered the school building one night between eight and nine o'clock and remained there for approximately forty-five minutes to an hour. They did not turn on the lights and kept their meeting a secret for a few days until it was discovered. It had been known from the early morning after the escapade that someone had been in the school building the night before, and which was discovered by the janitor, who found breadcrumbs, cigarette stubs, and other evidence of someone having been in the building after it was closed for the evening.[31]

The testimony from the five participants stated that "no immoral act was perpetrated or attempted during the stay of the party in the school building, nor did they have any such purpose in view."[32] They stated that the lights were kept off to maintain secrecy. The court noted that the testimony was "sufficient to demonstrate a consciousness on the part of [Gover] and his witnesses that their conduct did not measure up to the correct standard, else there would have been no occasion for such cautiousness and secrecy."[33]

The Court of Appeals offered definitions of "misconduct," one of the causes for dismissal, as "conduct amiss; bad behavior." The judges noted that misconduct is broader in scope and more comprehensive than immorality, another reason for dismissal. Behavior that may not constitute immorality could still constitute misconduct. Thus, the court asserted that no immoral conduct occurred, but Gover's actions might still constitute misconduct. Gover, a teacher in the public schools, the Court of Appeals asserted, was so circumstanced as that both patrons and pupils regarded him in the light of an exemplar whose conduct might be followed by his pupils, and the law by necessary intendment demands and requires that he should not engage in any conduct inevitably calculated to invite criticism and of a nature and character justly productive of suspicions of immorality.[34]

Thus, with no evidence of an immoral act being committed by the dismissed teacher and merely suspicions that something inappropriate may have occurred, Gover was terminated. The court asserted that the participants' actions established that misconduct had occurred through keeping the lights off and not disclosing the episode. No effort was made to confirm that the "suspicious" acts actually occurred. The mere existence of a suspicion was enough to lead to the dismissal of a teacher. The court may have realized what may lurk behind the door that was opened—suspicion without evidence of specific wrongdoing—when it concluded with the following explanation:

> "We do not mean by what we have said to prescribe a rule of conduct measuring up to the notions of the self-constituted moralist, nor to require the teacher to abstain from every act that is prescribed by blue law advocates, but we do say that, when he engages in conduct that in the minds of a prudent and cautious person would arouse suspicions of immorality, he is then guilty of such misconduct as is contemplated by the statute."[35]

The court evidently recognized the vagueness of the ruling. Teachers in Kentucky had to guess not only what acts might be immoral but also what "prudent and cautious" citizens might consider actions that constitute suspicious or immoral behavior.

Shaking Dice and Serving Drinks (1939)

Horosko v. School District of Mount Pleasant Township[36] illustrates the reach of exemplar into the private lives of teachers. It is one of the most cited cases of teacher immorality, and its influence was controlling in many instances.

Horosko was a primary school teacher in the small Pennsylvania community of Mount Pleasant. She married the owner of a restaurant located 125 feet from the school where she taught. Beer was served in the restaurant, and patrons enjoyed a pinball machine and a slot machine. Various dice games were also played on the premises. Horosko worked as a waitress after school hours and during the summer months. Students and community members observed her taking an occasional drink of beer, shaking dice with customers, and instructing them on how to play the pinball machine.

Although there was no charge or evidence of disorderly conduct or excessive drinking, the school board dismissed Horosko for immorality. She fought her dismissal all the way to the Supreme Court of Pennsylvania, which upheld her dismissal. The court discussed the exemplary status in which teachers were placed and its relationship to immorality:

> Immorality is not essentially confined to deviation from sex morality; it may be such a course of action as offends the morals of the community and is a bad example to the youth whose ideals a teacher is supposed to foster and to elevate ... It has always been the recognized duty of the teacher to conduct himself in such a way as to command the respect and good will of the community, though one result of the choice of a teacher's vocation may be to deprive him of the same freedom of action enjoyed by persons in other vocations.[37]

Membership in Subversive Organizations: "A Pall of Orthodoxy" (1949)

In 1949, New York enacted the Feinberg Law. The statute made membership in a subversive organization *prima facie* evidence for dismissal of public school employees; mere membership constituted grounds for dismissal. The preamble stated that members of subversive organizations, such as the Communist Party, have been infiltrating the public schools and are teaching and advocating the overthrow of the government by force or violence or by any other unlawful means. "As a result, propaganda can be disseminated among the children by those who teach them and to whom they look for guidance, authority, and leadership."[38] The legislature framed the statute to protect the state's children from propaganda that could be introduced into the classroom by subversive teachers.

In 1952, the US Supreme Court, by a vote of six to three, upheld the constitutionality of the Feinberg Law in *Adler v. Board of Education of the City of New York*.[39] The plaintiffs asserted, to no avail, that the law constituted an abridgment of free speech and assembly. The Court acknowledged that the plaintiffs possessed the right to assemble, speak, and think as they will. They did not have the "right to work for the State in the school system on their own terms."[40] The Court opined:

> They may work for the school system upon the reasonable terms laid down by the proper authorities of New York. If they do not choose to work on such terms, they are at liberty to retain their beliefs and associations and go elsewhere. Has the State thus deprived them of any right to free speech or assembly? We think not.[41]

Furthermore, Justice Minton, writing for the majority, asserted that teachers' work is "sensitive," shaping the "attitude of young minds towards the society in which they live. In this, the state has a vital concern. It must preserve the integrity of the school." Consequently, school officials have the right and the duty to screen educators and employees' associates to determine their fitness and loyalty properly. "One's associates, past and present, as well as one's conduct, may properly be considered in determining fitness and loyalty. From time immemorial, one's reputation has been determined in part by the company he keeps."[42] The Court gave the local boards of education wide discretion in conditioning the terms of employment for teachers and administrators. It also increased the discretion of school boards by allowing the past and present to be considered in determining fitness and loyalty.

Justice Douglas wrote a strongly worded dissent, which foreshadowed many of the changes that would occur in the 1960s and 1970s. He considered the statute a threat to raise "havoc" with academic freedom and a sacrifice of individual civil rights, making teachers second-class citizens by denying them their freedoms of thought and expression. He wrote, "The Constitution guarantees freedom of thought and expression to everyone in our society. All are entitled to it, and none needs it more than the teacher."[43] However, the principle of the Feinberg Law, he asserted, was "repugnant to our society—guilt by association."[44] Justice Douglas cautioned:

> What happens under this law is typical of what happens in a police state. Teachers are under constant surveillance; their pasts are combed for signs of disloyalty; their utterances are watched for clues

to dangerous thoughts. A pall is cast over the classrooms. There can be no real academic freedom in that environment. Where suspicion fills the air and holds scholars in line for fear of their jobs, there can be no exercise of the free intellect. Supineness and dogmatism take the place of inquiry ... A deadening dogma takes the place of free inquiry. Instruction tends to become sterile; pursuit of knowledge is discouraged; discussion leaves off where it should begin.[45]

The language of Justice Douglas's dissent may be an echo from the past that resonates with the current controversy, some seventy years later, over divisive concepts legislation. This has left teachers unsure and afraid of what they can teach and what they cannot teach, under the fear of legal and professional consequences. These divisive concepts and laws have created a high-stakes environment in which teachers "simultaneously must watch their backs and face their students in creative, exciting, and inspiring ways. One cannot face in two directions at the same time."[46]

Justice Hugo Black's Dissent in *Adler v. Board of Education of City of New York*:

Basically, these laws rest on the belief that government should supervise and limit the flow of ideas into the minds of men. The tendency of such governmental policy is to mold people into a common intellectual pattern. Quite a different governmental policy rests on the belief that government should leave the mind and spirit of man absolutely free. Such a governmental policy encourages varied intellectual outlooks in the belief that the best views will prevail. This policy of freedom is, in my judgment, embodied in the First Amendment and made applicable to the states by the Fourteenth Amendment. Because of this policy, public officials cannot be constitutionally vested with powers to select the ideas people can think about, censor the public views they can express, or choose the persons or groups people can associate with. Public officials with such powers are not public servants; they are public masters.

I dissent from the Court's judgment sustaining this law which effectively penalizes school teachers for their thoughts and their associates.

Adler v. Board of Education of City of New York, 342 U.S. 485, 497 (1952) (Black, J., dissenting).

One of the aspects by which the community exercises its influence over the conduct of teachers, including their private conduct, is adverse notoriety. Below, we discuss adverse notoriety and a selected sample of cases in which adverse notoriety plays an important role in court decisions. This section is followed by an exploration of cases on sexual orientation—one of the divisive issues in which some communities asserted that a gay or lesbian teacher's private life is evidence of an immoral lifestyle that is antithetical to the role model status of the profession of teachers.

Adverse Notoriety

When making a decision about the appropriateness of a teacher's lifestyle choice, the courts generally consider *"the notoriety of the conduct and the impact the conduct has on the individual's teaching abilities."*[47]

Adverse notoriety is particularly relevant in this discussion, where a teacher's off-duty conduct receives widespread negative publicity. Such publicity often threatens an educator's employment status. For example, the online Cambridge Dictionary defines "notoriety" as "the state of being famous for doing something bad." The dictionary's cited example is, "The public is unhappy about the notoriety of the Mayor.[48] Furthermore, USLEGAL.com provides the following definition: "Notoriety means the state of being known and spoken of generally for unfavorable acts."[49]

Adverse notoriety, as applied to educator conduct, typically refers to a segment of the community expressing concerns about a teacher's behavior. For example, in *Pettit v. State Board of Education* (discussed in Chapter 6), the California Supreme Court emphasized the significance of the public nature of a teacher's misconduct or the public notoriety of the conduct.[50] The court cited *Morrison* for the proposition that notoriety can be important in establishing harm under the nexus standard. The *Pettit* court wrote, "The [*Morrison*] court suggested that a showing of significant 'harm' could be based upon adverse inferences drawn from the teacher's past conduct as to his probable future teaching ability, as well as upon the likelihood that the publicity surrounding the past conduct 'may in and of itself substantially impair his function as a teacher.'"[51] Conversely, the lack of an adverse community reaction to a teacher's questionable conduct can favor an educator who faces an adverse employment decision.

The adverse notoriety factor discussed above is, followed by an exploration of cases that apply the factor. The chapter will offer a perspective of the tension between exemplar and nexus in determining who will teach our children.

A Sample of Cases Using Adverse Notoriety in Their Analysis

The Mannequin on the Front Lawn (1974)

A Massachusetts case involved a teacher who was dismissed for immorality and conduct unbecoming of a teacher. In March 1972, Wishart's principal wrote in his evaluation that "Mr. Wishart is an excellent teacher. He has a genuine enthusiasm for pupils and teaching, making him a valuable member of the middle School staff."[52] However, starting in the fall of 1971, Wishart began to engage in "unusual conduct"[53] that resulted in his dismissal. He was accused of the following particularized charges of conduct unbecoming of a teacher:

"a. [Y]ou have on various occasions displayed and carried a dress mannequin in the public view on your Spooner Street property, have dressed said mannequin in feminine attire, and have on occasion caressed said mannequin."

"b. [Y]our actions in the public view on your Spooner Street property regarding the dressing and undressing of said dress mannequin in feminine attire have been on various occasions of a suggestive or lewd nature."[54]

The superintendent testified that his recommendation for dismissal was based on his belief that Wishart's Thursday night public conduct on his front lawn had become notorious in the town and had impaired his ability to function as a sixth-grade teacher. Furthermore, the superintendent believed Wishart's conduct indicated possible emotional instability, which was unbefitting a teacher. However, Wishart's psychiatrist testified that Wishart's conduct was unrelated to his performance as a teacher and would not affect classroom conduct.[55]

After his dismissal, Wishart sought relief in the district court, which was denied. The district court rejected the psychiatrist's opinion that Wishart's personality disorder would not affect his classroom performance.

On appeal, the appellate court restated the finding of the trial court:

Even if the Court were to agree (which it is not altogether prepared to do) that plaintiff's problem would in no way reflect on his performance in the classroom, there is still the problem of notoriety and its effect on relationships within the educational process... The Court feels that there was a basis, if somewhat meager, for McDonald's belief that the conduct had, or certainly would in the future, gain a degree of notoriety which would damage plaintiff's effectiveness as a teacher in the school system and his working relationships within the educational process. It cannot be said that the school committee acted arbitrarily or capriciously in sharing in that opinion and following the recommendation to dismiss. Whether or not some of the notoriety was caused by the defendants' investigations and hearings cannot change that result.[56]

Thus, the Court of Appeals affirmed the district court's ruling in favor of the school district.

The *Wishart* case is significant in highlighting the importance of adverse notoriety in evaluating educator out-of-school conduct. Without showing an adverse effect on teaching (nexus), the appellate court allowed a reasonable presumption that Wishart's actions would be considered notorious, thus damaging his teaching effectiveness. A potential for adverse notoriety could infer a negative impact on teaching effectiveness. Another important aspect of this First Circuit case is that investigations and hearings, in and of themselves, do not necessarily disturb a finding of adverse notoriety. At a minimum, reasonable and consistent administrative actions are entitled to some deference to administrative necessity.

This early case is notable in that it finds *Morrison* to be persuasive authority and recognizes that notoriety can be a factor in proving nexus. It also confirmed adverse notoriety as a factor in deciding cases involving a teacher who argues that private, off-duty conduct is immune from discipline or dismissal. While teachers have a right to privacy, *Wishart* emphasizes that they also have a duty to maintain the privacy of their personal lives.

Shoplifting in West Virginia (1981)

In another adverse-notoriety case, the Supreme Court of Appeals of West Virginia found in favor of a guidance counselor. In this case, a school guidance counselor was arrested for felony shoplifting from a department store. She pled *nolo contendere* in a magistrate court and paid a fine of $100 for misdemeanor petty theft. News of the theft was published in the local newspaper. At the school board's dismissal hearing for immorality (shoplifting), Golden explained her conduct, stating that she had been distraught over family issues and inadvertently walked out of the store. She walked about 50 feet from the store when she realized the unpurchased items were in her purse. As she turned to return the items, she was apprehended by the store detective. The board dismissed her for what it characterized as a "serious act of immorality."[57] Golden appealed the decision, and the Circuit Court of Harrison County affirmed the dismissal. She appealed this decision as well.

The appellate court reversed the circuit court and ordered reinstatement with full back pay. The crux of the decision, informed by their discussion of *Morrison*, was to determine "if a 'rational nexus' exists between the conduct complained of and the duties to be performed."[58] The court wrote that a reason for demonstrating nexus was to prevent "dismissal merely upon a showing of some immoral conduct would constitute an unwarranted intrusion upon the teacher's right to privacy."[59] However, the court cautioned that an educator's right to privacy was not absolute and must be balanced against the legitimate interest of the school board. The conduct of a teacher, the court held, ceases to be private in at least two circumstances:

> (1) if the conduct directly affects the performance of the occupational responsibilities of the teacher; or (2) if, without contribution on the part of the school officials, the conduct has become the subject of such notoriety as to significantly and reasonably impair the capability of the particular teacher to discharge the responsibilities of the teaching position.[60]

The court noted a lack of evidence of immorality that would support a finding of unfitness to teach. Indeed, the court concluded that the only evidence submitted was the favorable testimony of her colleagues, both teachers and administrators. No evidence of notoriety had been submitted. This underscores that community involvement does not have to be solely negative to be considered important in weighing the impact of the educator's conduct.

Marijuana Possession (1986)

Anthony Rogliano was a permanent substitute teacher in the Fayette County school system.[61] On February 17, 1982, he was arrested and charged with possession of marijuana, a misdemeanor offense, following a search of his home. The police seized a quantity of seeds and drug paraphernalia. The amount of seized marijuana totaled 0.2 grams.[62] Rogliano was suspended without pay two days after the incident. On March 24, 1982, the school board approved the superintendent's recommendation to extend the suspension "until ... disposition of the charge ... of possession of a controlled substance."[63]

On April 22, 1982, the criminal charges were dismissed based on a defect on the face of the search warrant. The superintendent informed the school board of the dismissed charges and recommended reinstatement, along with back pay. The board, however, was concerned that the charges had been dismissed on a technicality and voted to hold a hearing "for the disposition of [Rogliano'a] suspension and/or dismissal ... on the charge of possession of a controlled substance."[64] At the hearing, the West Virginia Education Association (WVEA) argued that the board had no authority to dismiss Rogliano "because the evidence had not shown a correlation between the alleged misconduct and [his] ability to teach."[65] Nevertheless, the board voted to dismiss him.

Rogliano brought a lawsuit in the Fayette County Circuit Court seeking reinstatement, back pay, and attorney fees. He raised the same issue as the WVEA. The court found that Rogliano had possessed and used marijuana. However, the court also found no evidence showing that his misconduct had impaired his ability to teach. The court remanded the case to the Board of Education for further proceedings on that issue.[66] Rogliano was reinstated on April 20, 1982, without assignment, and no back pay was awarded.

The board conducted a hearing on June 13, 1982. Rogliano presented evidence from his last teacher evaluation, conducted just before his arrest, which rated his classroom performance as average, above average, and excellent in various categories. In addition, he offered several witnesses who testified "that they were satisfied with the manner in which the appellant had taught their children in the past and that they did not believe his arrest, the publicity attendant to it or his alleged possession of marijuana had adversely affected his ability to teach or his reputation in the schools or in the community."[67]

Rogliano also denied the substance of the charges against him, offering testimony from Michael Lloyd that it was Lloyd's marijuana that was seized and not Rogliano's.

After requesting an extension of time to gather information on the effect of Rogliano's conduct, the administration presented the testimony that drug use by teachers violated the moral standards of the community and that the publicity surrounding his conduct besmirched him as a role model and an exemplar for his students.

On July 23, 1983, the board issued its findings: (1) that the teacher had a general reputation in the community as a drug user, heightened by the publicity resulting from his arrest for possession; (2) that the use of marijuana indicated "a defect of character inconsistent with the community's standards of morality"; and (3) that the notoriety surrounding his arrest rendered him less effective as a role model in the community. The board then unanimously voted to dismiss him.[68]

Rogliano again filed a petition with the court asserting that the school board erred in not granting him back pay. The court denied the petition and affirmed the board's ruling. Rogliano appealed.

The Supreme Court of Appeals held that there was no direct evidence of Rogliano's alleged misconduct. The court stated that the vast majority of evidence was favorable to Rogliano. However, the circuit court concluded that the evidence showed that "the appellant had become the subject of such notoriety in the community as to impair, indirectly, his ability to function as a teacher."[69]

The appellate court stated that there was little evidence of notoriety before Rogliano's reinstatement in April 1983. The school administrators who testified in the case "did not recall much discussion of the case or any complaints about [Rogliano] at that time."[70] Furthermore, no evidence was offered in the board's hearing on May 18, 1982, regarding the effect of the behavior on his ability to teach or that demonstrated "widespread adverse public reaction to his remaining in the schools."[71]

As stated above, the school district's failure to consider the lack of adverse notoriety led the circuit court to reinstate Rogliano. The board took almost a year to reinstate him. By then, there was some adverse community reaction against him. In addition, the administration required more time and further proceedings to marshal its witnesses, which also provided additional publicity. The Supreme Court of Appeals concluded that the Board's failure to comply with the mandate of *Golden* (direct evidence of a negative effect or significant adverse notoriety) "unnecessarily protracted the proceedings against the appellant, thereby contributing to whatever notoriety he may have attained in the community as a result of his arrest."[72]

The court clarified that the fact that a disciplinary proceeding against a teacher gives rise to adverse publicity is not sufficient in and of itself to preclude dismissing a teacher in appropriate circumstances. "We merely hold that in these circumstances and upon the particular facts of this case, we believe the adverse publicity was attributable, at least in part, to the Board."[73]

The court went on to note that Rogliano was an above-average teacher who was well-liked by his students. In addition, the misconduct occurred in private and did not directly involve school personnel or students. Furthermore, Rogliano "was only charged with a misdemeanor for possession of a small amount of marijuana, [and thus] the evidence was insufficient to warrant the termination of his employment."[74] The case was reversed and remanded.

Chief Justice Neely filed a dissent in which Justice Brotherton joined him. Using an exemplar argument, the dissent argued that the majority construed the duties of a teacher too narrowly. The dissent wrote:

> If the state may require parents to relinquish their children to the influence of public school teachers on a daily basis, then surely it is reasonable for parents to demand that public school teachers adhere to standards of conduct consonant with the moral standards of the community, especially when such conduct is required by law.[75]

Justice Neely went on to assert that the majority's decision subjected the children of the community to be involuntarily subjected to the influence "of an authority figure and role model who advocates, at least by example, the use of illegal drugs."[76]

After discussing the illegality and danger of marijuana, Justice Neely made a questionable adverse nexus connection. "The parents of Fayette County have, through their elected representatives on the board of education, determined that they do not wish to maintain appellant in a position of authority and influence with respect to their children."[77] Because the elected school board dismissed Rogliano, adverse notoriety had been established.

In this situation, following the dissent's logic, it did not matter whether there was any evidence showing that Rogliano's conduct adversely affected his teaching or whether the marijuana incident gave rise to significant notoriety. Under the dissent's line of reasoning, lack of evidence did not matter because the Board's decision was the decision of the community that elected them and was imputed to the community, thereby establishing adverse notoriety *per se*.

The Bachelor/Bachelorette Party, the Male Mannequin, and the Internet Pictures (2010)

Middle school teacher Anna Land attended a bachelor/bachelorette party during the summer of 2005. The party was invitation only and no minors were in attendance. At some time during the party, Land engaged in a simulation of fellatio with a male mannequin. An unknown person uploaded pictures of her behavior without Land's permission. Rumors of the pictures surfaced at her school, and some students gained access to the pictures.

At Land's request, the pictures were removed from the website. In the meantime, however, she was suspended. On the recommendation of the superintendent, the school board dismissed Land for "engaging in lewd behavior contrary to the moral values of the educational and school community, which undermined her moral authority and professional responsibilities as a role model for students."[78]

The Administrative Law Judge (ALJ) issued a preliminary decision, finding that the charges had been proven and that they constituted reasonable and just cause for her dismissal. Land appealed to the Michigan State Tenure Commission. The commission reversed the ALJ's decision. The commission found that the incident occurred two years before she was dismissed and was not illegal. Additionally, Land's conduct took place off school grounds, did not involve a school activity, and was not part of her duties as a teacher. Moreover, Land did not discuss the incident at school or advocate the type of conduct in which she was photographed.

Accordingly, the commission determined that petitioner did not engage in professional misconduct and that, absent such a showing, any negative publicity arising from petitioner's conduct did not provide reasonable and just cause for petitioner's discharge.[79]

The school district appealed, challenging the commission's decision as arbitrary, capricious, and contrary to law. The Michigan State Tenure Commission, in an unpublished opinion, disagreed with the school board's decision to dismiss.

The Court of Appeals referenced *Morrison v. State Board of Education*[80] as persuasive authority along with *Beebee v. Haslett Public Schools*,[81] which quoted *Morrison*. The *Beebee* court stated: Activities outside the classroom have warranted discharge where they brought such notoriety to the teacher that his teaching ability was impaired. Special care must be taken to show this link between out-of-school acts and in- school behavior.[82]

The Appellate Court affirmed the Commission's decision, summarizing its decision as follows:

> Examination of the entire record reveals that the photographs engendered widespread gossip and some students and parents

lost respect for petitioner. Further, there was expert testimony that the conduct depicted in the photographs would tend to cause students to lose respect for their teacher, and could adversely affect learning. However, some parents testified that while the internet posting of the photographs was unfortunate, they had not lost respect for petitioner as a teacher or a person. Moreover, there was overwhelming evidence that petitioner was an excellent teacher who went above and beyond her responsibilities to assist her students to learn and enjoy the material, and to assist students and parents with other issues that might arise. Mindful of the applicable standard of review, we conclude that the commission did not act arbitrarily or capriciously in deciding that, where there is no professional misconduct, the notoriety of a tenured teacher's off-duty, off-premises, lawful conduct, not involving students or school activities, by itself, will not constitute reasonable and just cause for discipline.[83]

It is important to note the court considered adverse notoriety as a factor in disciplinary proceedings but not a dispositive factor. The lawfulness of the conduct, the location of the conduct, whether the conduct was associated with the teacher's professional duties and responsibilities of the educator, and whether the conduct involved students must also be part of the calculus.

A School Guidance Counselor Facebook Post (2020)

On February 15, 2017, Patricia Crawford served as a high school counselor in good standing at Rubidoux High School (RHS) in the Jurupa Unified School District in California. Her standing would not last beyond the rest of the school year.[84] While this case involved faculty speech transmitted on the school's Facebook page about a recent school event, it is instructive for a discussion on adverse notoriety. A posted message on a school's social media site may be viewed as a personal communication even though it is conveyed through school resources. Thus, it is helpful to include it in our discussion.

On February 16, 2017, one-quarter of RHS's students, of which 90 percent are Hispanic, boycotted school to attend the nationwide "A Day Without Immigration" boycott.[85] Several faculty members, including Crawford, participated in a discussion of the event over email and on the public (RHS) Facebook page. On the morning of the protest, a teacher emailed the staff about the high rate of absences in her classes. Crawford responded, "The PROFESSIONAL staff members and SERIOUS students are here today, boycott be darned."[86] The posts went viral in the community and beyond with "many, many negative replies."[87]

Another teacher, Geoffrey Greer, also posted a negative opinion about the student boycott. Greer expressed the view that the boycott temporarily reduced overcrowding in his classroom and said, "That's what you get when you jump on some sort of bandwagon cause as an excuse to be lazy and/or get drunk. Best school day ever."

The following day, Greer's classroom and the classroom of another teacher were vandalized with "F" words, including "F**K YOUR OPINION," and 350 students staged a walkout in response to Greer's comments and other Facebook comments that were critical of the boycott. Four days later, at the public comment portion of the District's regularly scheduled board meeting, several people criticized some of the Facebook postings that had expressed negative views of the walkout. Eleven people specifically referred to Crawford, and no one voiced support for her.

In the aftermath of these Facebook postings, Crawford, Greer, and other faculty members who commented on Greer's post were put on administrative leave. Two months later, Crawford was placed on paid leave and informed of the district's intent to dismiss her.

Subsequently, the school board dismissed Crawford for engaging in immoral conduct and for evident unfitness to teach, and the Commission on Professional Competence (CPC) and a California superior court upheld that decision. Crawford then appealed to the California Fourth Circuit Court of Appeal. The issue before the appellate court was whether there was substantial evidence to support the trial court's conclusion that the weight of evidence supported the CPC's findings of fact. The court rejected Crawford's argument that the *Morrison* criteria was not applicable. Instead, it found that applying the *Morrison* criteria provided an objective measure of immoral conduct, indicating that an employee is unfit to teach.[88]

As a prelude to the court's application of *Morrison*, it dismissed Crawford's contention that terminating her based on the public's response to her posts would allow her to be fired for virtually any statement she made.[89] Possibly harkening back to exemplar, the appellate court asserted that the *Morrison* court underscored that the public's opinion of a teacher's conduct "bears on the employee's ability to teach."[90]

The *Crawford* court stated that adverse notoriety formed in response to Crawford's public posts could be appropriately considered in a termination decision. "After all, the impact of publicity resulting from the employee's conduct is an appropriate consideration under Morrison, because the public's response may affect a permanent employee's ability to perform their job."[91]

The court emphasized that Crawford was not dismissed because her Facebook comments were controversial. Rather, "the District dismissed Crawford because of the adverse effect her comments had on her professional reputation, her ability to counsel students effectively, and her relationship with RHS generally." As the CPC found, Crawford's comments had a negative impact on students, the school, the district, and the community.[92]

Adverse Notoriety: A Factor Under Both the Exemplar and Nexus Standards

Adverse notoriety is crucial in determining when a teacher's off-duty conduct impairs that individual's effectiveness in the classroom. Under the exemplar standard, a teacher's off-duty conduct can diminish the teacher's status as a role model. Under the nexus standard, a teacher's behavior outside the school day may attract so much negative publicity that the teacher loses the respect of parents, students, and the community and becomes an ineffective pedagogue.

Adverse notoriety is a critical metric because it recognizes that parents have a voice in determining who should teach their children or, in dismissal cases, who should be retained to teach them. It acknowledges the inherent connection between parents and schools.

Parents and the community have a legitimate concern about the qualifications and actions of the individuals the school district places in positions of power and trust over their children. Listening to their concerns is not only reasonable but also necessary. Teachers often stand in place of parents while a child is at school. In addition, a parent's right to criticize a teacher is clearly acknowledged in that parents have qualified immunity from a defamation lawsuit to lodge complaints about teachers to the proper educational authorities.[93] The public's views about a teacher's fitness to teach cannot be disregarded.[94]

However, parental and community concerns must not automatically result in adverse employment decisions. School boards and administrators making high-stakes employment decisions must balance competing legal and professional responsibilities. They must adequately buffer teachers from unwarranted parental intrusion into their private lives and not heedlessly cave under pressure.

Examining adverse notoriety through a bifocal lens that views a teacher's private conduct from both an exemplar and nexus perspective is helpful.[95] A review of the cases discussed above shows that an adverse notoriety analysis typically asks two questions. The first asks whether the conduct is consistent with that of a role model. The second asks whether the questioned conduct negatively impacted the educator's ability to discharge their professional duties effectively.

While the two concepts appear to use different lenses, caselaw reveals that adverse notoriety is a factor in evaluating a teacher's off-duty conduct under both the exemplar and nexus standards. A bifocal optic clarifies that the lens of exemplar focuses on a teacher's out-of-school behavior and its impact on that teacher's role-model status. In contrast, the nexus lens examines whether a teacher's questionable conduct has a negative impact on the teacher's classroom effectiveness.

Next, we examine several key cases involving sexual orientation. This aspect of an individual's private life spawns much public debate and is one of the fronts in the so-called culture wars. Public school teachers have not been spared in this controversy. If anything, because of their special role with children, the focus on their private lives has sharpened and been brought into high magnification. We next discuss a teacher's sexual orientation and its application to their role model status.

Sexual Orientation

The history of the climate for gay and lesbian teachers reveals how contentious being gay and being a teacher has been and still is.[96]

In the 1960s and 1970s, there appeared to be an uptick in court cases in which gay and lesbian teachers turned to the courts to redress adverse employment decisions that were made as a result of their sexual orientation. These cases track the transition from the development of nexus. For example, the federal district court in the Washington District of Columbia wrote, "Homosexual conduct may not be protected under the right of privacy, and homosexuals may not qualify as a suspect class. Nonetheless, the government may not discriminate against homosexuals for the sake of discrimination, or for no reason at all."[97] Below, several cases in which gay and lesbian teachers sued their school are discussed.

James Gaylord as Role Model: "A Publicly Known Homosexual"
On November 21, 1972, James Gaylord, a Phi Beta Kappa graduate from the University of Washington, received a letter from his employer, the Board of Directors of the Tacoma School District No. 10, which stated in part as follows:

> The specific probable cause for your discharge is that you have admitted occupying a public status that is incompatible with the conduct required of teachers in this district. Specifically, that you have admitted being a publicly known homosexual.[98]

Gaylord had taught for twelve years in the school district with no problems. He had consistently received "favorable evaluations of his teaching."[99] The precipitating event that moved Gaylord from a "favorable" teacher to an immoral teacher was the revelation that Gaylord was gay.[100] He was dismissed for his status of being gay, not for any specific act. Specifically, he was dismissed for immorality on the basis that he was gay.

Gaylord sought relief from the state courts. He lost and appealed. The appeal resulted in a remand, but the ultimate result was the same. His appeal reached the Washington Supreme Court, which settled the matter of his dismissal.

The court considered immorality to be a volitional choice. The court offered an odd explanation of choice, stating, "One who has a disease, for example, cannot be held morally responsible for his condition. Homosexuality is not a disease."[101] The court noted that Gaylord was "comfortable" with his sexuality and did not seek psychiatric help to change his orientation.[102] Therefore, the court asserted, "He has made a voluntary choice for which he must be held morally responsible."[103] Gaylord "chose" to be gay or to remain gay and that choice was a choice to be immoral, or so the Supreme Court reasoned.

Next, the State's high court turned to whether public knowledge that Gaylord was a teacher who happened to be gay would sufficiently impair his performance. The court found that the knowledge of his sexual orientation would result in impairment. The State Supreme Court cited one of the trial court's findings of fact:

> A teacher's efficiency is determined by his relationship with students, their parents, fellow teachers and school administrators. In all of these areas the continued employment of [Gaylord] after he became known as a homosexual would result, had he not been discharged, in confusion, suspicion, fear, expressed parental concern and pressure

upon the administration from students, parents and fellow teachers, all of which would impair [Gaylord's] efficiency as a teacher and injure the school.[104]

The court reasoned that Gaylord's sexual orientation was immoral and could cause harm once his sexual orientation became public knowledge. According to the Washington Supreme Court, gay and lesbian teachers could not be role models because of their sexual orientation. Being a gay or a lesbian, the Washington Supreme Court reasoned, was *per se* immoral.

However, the dissent pointed out that "homosexuality per se does not preclude competence."[105] And, in a nod to *Morrison v. State Board of Education*, discussed in Chapter 6, the dissenting judge stated, "mere speculation coupled with status is not enough."[106] In other words, just being gay should not automatically lead to an irrebuttable conclusion of immorality, the dissent asserted. While the dissent signaled the use of nexus, the majority stayed in the subjective exemplar lane for judging the teacher's out-of-school life. This case appears to be the last appellate case in which the role model concept was applied with no showing of harm to students or criminal conviction. Instead, it was based on a conclusion that being gay is *per se* immoral.

Exemplar has receded as arbiter of the sexual orientation of an educator as a statement of immorality and/or in the ability of the educator to serve as the community as a role model. Legal strides have been made to end, or at least curtail state sanctioned discrimination based on an individual's sexual orientation. The Supreme Court in 1984, acknowledged that an individual may have a personal bias and hold discriminatory views, however, the State cannot. Chief Justice Burger, writing for a unanimous Court, stated that the "Constitution cannot control such prejudices but neither can it tolerate them. Private biases may be outside the reach of the law, but the law cannot, directly or indirectly give them effect."[107]

The issue of whether gays or lesbians can serve as role models because of their sexual orientation has largely been a controversy over their private lives contested in the courts. However, the issue of sexual orientation has also arisen in other countries such as the United Kingdom. Their controversy largely played out in parliament. On March 24, 1988, the Local Government Act was passed. It included sections on housing and dog licenses. However, it also added Section 2A, which came to be known as Section 28. The title of the section was "Prohibition on promoting homosexuality by teaching or by publishing material."[108] Section 28 (1)(a) of the section stated, "A local authority shall not—intentionally promote homosexuality or publish material with the intention of promoting homosexuality."

A negative response over the law's passage followed, to which the government sought to clarify the legislation quickly, noting that there was fear of irrational interpretations. Their circular stated:

> It will not prevent the objective discussion of homosexuality in the classroom, nor the counselling of pupils concerned about their sexuality. Local Government Act: Circular. Catalogue reference:113/4[109]

However, the impact of Section 28 was felt, spawning a campaign group "Outrage!" The group argued that a lack of awareness "perpetuates the isolation, fear, and guilt experienced by so many young lesbians and gays."[110] Gay and lesbian teachers were also affected by the Section. "The late 20th century was meant to be better, but teachers still felt unable to be themselves at work and unable to offer support on sexuality to their students."[111]

However, just as public attitudes toward gay and lesbian neighbors and citizens were changing in the United States, they were also changing in the United Kingdom. The Scottish Parliament, in one of its newly formed Acts,[112] passed the Ethical Standards in Public Life etc. (Scotland) Act 2000.[113] By 2002, the cabinet office was feeling the pressure of restrictive LGBTQ+ legislation, especially from the negativity and fear associated with the Section. On November 18, 2003, Section 28 was eliminated. It would no longer cast "a shadow over lesbian, gay and bisexual lives in England, Wales and Scotland."[114]

Pregnant Teachers

Teachers have historically been considered mandatory community role models, even when they are off duty. "In the early 1970s, public school systems across the country excluded pregnant women and new mothers from the workplace."[115] The author continued, "The pregnancy dismissal policies embodied traditional ideals about sexuality, pregnancy, and gender roles. First, the dismissal policies suggested that pregnancy, as a visual representation of female sexuality, represented an inappropriate presence in the classroom."[116]

Senator Elizabeth Warren in 2019 while campaigning shared her experience of being a pregnant teacher on "X" (formerly known as Twitter). She wrote on the social media site on October 8, 2019:

> When I was 22 and finishing my first year of teaching, I had an experience millions of women will recognize. By June I was visibly pregnant—and the principal told me the job I'd already been promised for the next year would go to someone else. Oct. 8, 2019 9:08 AM
>
> This was 1971, years before Congress outlawed pregnancy discrimination[117]—but we know it still happens in subtle and not-so-subtle ways. We can fight back by telling our stories. I tell mine on the campaign trail, and I hope to hear yours.

She received 765 replies and 15.5 million likes.[118]

In 1974, three years after the passage of the pregnancy antidiscrimination legislation a federal court held that a school district had violated a pregnant teacher's constitutional right of privacy.[119] The teacher was single and a few months pregnant as revealed by her physician who had not received a right to disclose from the teacher. Her fiancé was the father of her child. "The Board made no finding that Drake's claimed immorality had affected her competency or fitness as a teacher, and no such nexus was developed in the evidence."[120]

However, Judge Varner dissented. He wrote:

> I cannot agree that Miss Drake, at the time of her hearing, a public school teacher whose morals were street talk in Florala [her community], had any remaining right of privacy.
>
> If she had such a right, I think it was subrogated to a strong and compelling State interest in the morality of the State's public school system itself.[121]

His position is grounded in exemplar while the majority found that Drake has a right to privacy and that no nexus existed to support a dismissal. Judge Varner argued:

> Her claim that her sexual conduct was private paled when she admitted that it was publicly discussed in [the community]. Rumor of immorality of a public schoolteacher in a small town

travels fast and has a larger impact on the educational process than in a city.[122]

Judge Varner's argument made two important assumptions. First, talk among members of the community is enough to establish a showing of harm. Second, Judge Varner implicitly assumed that exemplar is contextually and geographically defined. Would a violation of the status of role model be determined differently in different locales even though state laws apply and are defined equally throughout a state and a teacher's teaching credential is valid throughout a state?

Conclusion

The breadth of control that the community had over the private lives of its teachers throughout the nineteenth and early twentieth centuries was extensive. The community decided who should teach its children not just through the teacher selection process but also through the retention process. Reflecting on these prohibitions placed on teachers' private conduct, Elsbree wrote:

> Emphasis has been placed upon the peculiar nature of the vocation of teaching—the fashioning of human lives—and upon the importance of exemplary conduct on the part of teachers, both within and without the classroom. At no time in our history have lawyers, doctors, and other professional workers been expected to maintain a comparable level of righteousness with that required of school teachers.[123]

Exemplar holds that a teacher is a mandatory role model because of the special role that teachers play in our society.[124] For example, a dean of students on Staten Island was responsible for enforcing rules prohibiting drug use among students. The dean was arrested in Brooklyn with one bag of marijuana on his person and ten bags of cocaine in his car. He pled guilty to attempted criminal possession of a controlled substance. The felony charges were dismissed against him in exchange for participating in a drug program, but the school board dismissed him. The hearing officer held that the dean should be able to be reinstated in the school district upon the successful completion of the treatment program. The school district brought suit.

On appeal, a New York appeals court considered the hearing officer's determination "to be returned to his former or similar position in the District ... to be irrational and to defy common sense. Such a conclusion would allow him to be placed back into a position where he would administer a program to discourage drug use among students."[125] In other words, how could the dean enforce a regulation he himself broke? The dean did not model that which he was required to enforce.

While the weight of exemplar has abated somewhat, many communities still judge school educators by the exemplar standard in this century. For example, a Texas Classroom Teachers Association publication titled "Professional boundaries with students" states at the top of its web page:

> Teachers are perceived as role models in the community, and the laws and regulations that mandate appropriate standards of conduct reflect that expectation. Failure to comply with these standards can lead to adverse employment action, certification sanctions and possible prosecution for criminal violations.[126]

It is clear that public school teachers are role models at all times—not just when they stand in a classroom in front of their students, but at home, on the weekend, or on vacation. (See, for example, the discussion on the Perils of Technology in Chapter 7). For example, in 2011, a teacher was dismissed for posting a picture on Facebook in which she was holding a drink while on vacation in Europe. Jonathan Turley, a law professor at George Washington University, wrote critically in a *Los Angeles Times* op-ed piece about this incident, observing that we expect a lot from teachers who put in long hours in overcrowded classrooms while making lower salaries than comparable professionals. "For this sacrifice, we now demand that they live their lives according to a morality standard set to satisfy the lowest common denominator of parental sensibilities."[127]

NEXT: Our next chapter continues the discussion of the tension over who decides who shall teach our children. Exemplar was discussed above. Its counterpoint, nexus, is discussed next. The seminal case of *Morrison v. State Board of Education* forms the foundation for the discussion. Times were changing in the 1960s. Teachers were caught in the push for greater rights.

Notes

1 *Beilan v. Board of Education*, 357 U.S. 399, 406 (1958).
2 *Goldsmith v. Board of Education*, 225 P. 783, 787, 66 Cal. App. 157, 168 (Cal. Ct. App. 1924).
3 Clifford P. Hooker, "Terminating Teachers and Revoking Their Licensure for Conduct Beyond the Schoolhouse Gate," *Education Law Reporter* 96 (1994): 1–22, 2.
4 *Tingley v. Vaughn*, 17 Ill. App. 347, 351 (1985).
5 Ohio Department of Education, Licensure Code of Professional Conduct for Ohio Educators (September 17, 2019): 4, https://dam.assets.ohio.gov/image/upload/sboe.ohio.gov/Professional-Conduct/Licensure-Code-of-Professional-Conduct.pdf. For an application of this Code section to a credential revocation of "Conduct unbecoming to the profession" see, *Prude v. Ohio State Board of Education*, 214 N.E.3d 1164, 1178–9 (Ohio App. 8 Dist. 2023).
6 Samuel N. Francis and Charles E. Stacey, "Law and the Sensual Teacher," *Phi Delta Kappan* 59, no. 2 (October 1977): 98–102, 98.
7 *McLaughlin v. Board of Medical Examiners*, 35 Cal. App. 3d 1010, 1021 (Cal. Ct. App. 1973) (Kraus, P.J. dissenting).
8 *In Batrus Appeal*, 148 Pa. Superior Ct. 587, 594 (1942).
9 Todd A. DeMitchell and Richard Fossey,*The Limits of Law-Based School Reform: Vain Hopes and False Promises* (Lancaster, PA: Technomic Publishing Company, 1997), 53.
10 Howard K. Beale, *Are American Teachers Free? An Analysis of Restraints Upon the Freedom of Teaching in American Schools* 407 (New York: Charles Scribner's & Sons 1936), 407.
11 Former School Board Member, "What About the Married Teacher?" *The American School Board Journal* 71, no. 6 (December 1925): 42,
12 David B. Tyack and Elizabeth Hansot, *Managers of Virtue: Public School Leadership in America, 1820–1980* (New York: Basic Books, 1986), 174.
13 Beale, *supra* note 10, 394
14 Kyle Greenwalt, "Even when they aren't fired for being pregnant or gay, teachers face strict moral demands," *The Conversation* (October 22, 2017), https://theconversation.com/even-when-they-arent-fired-for-being-pregnant-or-gay-teachers-face-strict-moral-demands-125353.
15 Regarding teachers and pregnancy, education journalist Madeline Will writes, "Experts say it was extremely common for pregnant teachers to be forced out of the classroom through the 1970s. In fact, up until the World War II era, it was common for teachers to be asked to leave or be fired when they got married." Madeline Will, "Pregnant. Here's What You Should Know," *Education Week* (October 10, 2019), https://www.edweek.org/teaching-learning/yes-teachers-once-could-be-fired-for-being-pregnant-heres-what-you-should-know/2019/10.

16 Former School Board Member, "What About the Married Teacher? *The American School Board Journal* 71, no. 6 (December 1925): 42.
17 *Backie v. Cromwell Consolidated School District No. 133*, 186 Minn. 38, 39–44 (1932).
18 Beale, *supra* note 10, 384–5.
19 *Andrews v. Drew Municipal. Separate School District*, 507 F.2d 611 (5th Cir. 1975). Even though the federal appellate court invalidated the policy, it is striking that such a policy was adopted so late in the twentieth century.
20 *Littlejohn v. Rose*, 786 F.2d 765 (6th Cir. 1985).
21 *McLellan v. Board. of Presidents, etc. of Public Schools. of St. Louis*, 15 Mo. App. 362, 366 (1884). The court opined that the dismissal was necessary because the teacher taught students age fourteen to twenty and that the dismissal "would be the common sense of all fathers and mothers having a parental regard for the morals of their children."
22 Beale, *supra* note 10.
23 Ibid., 391.
24 *State Ex Rel. Schweitzer v. Turner*, 19 So. 2d 832, 833 (Fla. 1944).
25 Ibid.
26 Howard K. Beale, *A History of Freedom of Teaching in American Schools* (New York: Charles Scribner's & Sons, 1941), 244.
27 *People ex rel. Odel v. Flaningam*, 179 N.E. 823, 826 (ILL. 1932).
28 *Gover v. Stovall*, 237 Ky. 172, 173 (Ky. Ct. App. 1931). This discussion will not include the second issue before the court as to whether Gover was entitled to a written contract under state law. Instead, we focused on Gover's dismissal for off-duty conduct.
29 Ibid.
30 Ibid., 176.
31 Ibid.
32 Ibid., 177.
33 Ibid.
34 Ibid.
35 Ibid., 178.
36 6 A.2d 866 (1939).
37 Ibid., 868.
38 *Adler v. Board of Education of City of New York*, 342 U.S. 485, 489 (1952).
39 342 U.S. 485 (1952).
40 Ibid., 492.
41 Ibid.
42 Ibid., 493.
43 Ibid., 508 (Douglas, J., dissenting). He further wrote, "The public school is, in most respects, the cradle of our democracy." Ibid.
44 Ibid.
45 Ibid., 510.

46 Jacob A. Bennett and Todd A. DeMitchell, "Federal District Court Finds Plausible Claims Against 'Divisive Concepts' Law: Local 8027, AFT-CIO-N.H., AFL-Cio v. Edelblut," *Education Law Reporter* 414, no. 1 (2023): 1–17, 7. In a summary judgment finding, the federal district court found that the disputed provisions of New Hampshire's divisive concepts law are unconstitutionally vague. "Teachers could face severe consequences if they taught or advocated banned concepts. . . . The legislation did not provide sufficient specificity to allow the reasonable educator to know what instruction must be avoided." The First Circuit of Appeals in a New England teacher speech case wrote thirty years ago with the same salience today, "If teachers must fear retaliation for every utterance, they will fear teaching." And students will lose. *Ward v. Hickey*, 996 F.2d 448, 453 (1st Cir. 1993).
47 David Schimmel, Suzanne Eckes, and Matthew Militello, *Principals Teaching the Law: 10 Legal Lessons Your Teachers Must Know* (Thousand Oaks, CA: Corwin, 2010), 124. (emphasis in original).
48 Author, "Notoriety," *Cambridge Dictionary* (n.d.), https://dictionary.cambridge.org/us/dictionary/english/notoriety#.
49 Author, Notoriety "Law and Legal Definition", *USLEGAL.COM*, (n.d.), https://definitions.uslegal.com/n/notoriety/#:~:text=Notoriety%20means%20the%20state%20of,said%20to%20have%20achieved%20notoriety.
50 10 Cal.3d 29, 35, note 5 (1973).
51 Ibid., 34.
52 *Wishart v. McDonald*, 500 F.2d 1110, 1111 (1st Cir. 1974).
53 Wishart's psychiatrist testified that Wishart's behavior was symptomatic of a personality disorder characterized by the displacement of sexual interest into a dress. Ibid. 1112.
54 Ibid., 1113.
55 Ibid.
56 Ibid.
57 *Golden v. Board of Education*, 169 W.Va. 63, 63–5 (W. Va.1981).
58 Ibid., 67.
59 Ibid., 69.
60 Ibid.
61 *Rogliano v. Fayette County Board of Education*, 347 S.E.2d 220 (1986).
62 Ibid., 222.
63 Ibid.
64 Ibid.
65 Ibid.
66 Ibid.
67 Ibid., 223.
68 Ibid.
69 Ibid. 224.
70 Ibid., 225.

71 Ibid.
72 Ibid.
73 Ibid.
74 Ibid.
75 Ibid., 226 (Neely, J., dissenting).
76 Ibid.
77 Ibid.
78 *Land v. L'Anse Creuse Public School Board of Education*, No. 288612 (Mich. Ct. App. 2010), *2, https://cases.justia.com/michigan/court-of-appeals-unpublished/20100527_C288612_50_288612.OPN.PDF?ts=1396125917.
79 Ibid.
80 461 P2d 375 (1969).
81 66 Mich App 718, *rev'd*,406 Mich 224 (1979).
82 Ibid.
83 *Land v. L'Anse Creuse Public School Board of Education*, *8.
84 *Crawford v. Commission on Professional Competence*, 267 Cal. Rptr. 3d 520 (Cal. Ct. App. 2020). For a discussion of this case, see Todd A. DeMitchell, Suzanne Eckes, and Richard Fossey, "Adverse Notoriety, the Student Protest, & the Viral Facebook Posts: Immoral Conduct and Evident Unfitness to Serve. *Crawford v. Commission on Professional Competence*," *Education Law Reporter* 391 (2021): 426–35, 426.
85 The boycott protested President Donald J. Trump's immigration policies. It was intended to show the economic impact of immigrants. *See* Bill Chappell, 'A Day Without Immigrants' Promises A National Strike Thursday, NPR (Feb. 16, 2017), https://www.npr.org/sections/the-two-way/2017/02/16/515555428/a-day-without-immigrants-promises-a-national-strike-thursday.
86 *Crawford v. Commission on Professional Competence*, 267 Cal. Rptr. 3d at 524 (emphasis in original). See DeMitchell, et al. supra note 85, for an abbreviated discussion of the posts.
87 Ibid., 525.
88 Ibid., at 529.
89 Ibid.
90 Ibid. at 530. See, e.g., *Pettit v. State Bd. of Educ.* (1973) 10 Cal. 3d 29, 35, n. 5, 513 P.2d 889, 109 Cal. Rptr. 665 (writing, "Various cases have emphasized the significance of the public nature of a teacher's misconduct, or the notoriety and publicity accorded it."
91 Ibid.
92 Ibid. (internal punctuation omitted).
93 *Desselle v. Guillory*, 407 So.2d 79 (La. Ct. App. 1981).
94 Todd A. DeMitchell, "Counterpoint – Immorality, Teacher Private Conduct, and Adverse Notoriety: A Needed Recalculation of Nexus?," *Journal of Law & Education* 40, no. 2 (April 2011): 327–39, 337–8.

95 DeMitchell, Eckes, and Fossey, *supra* note 85 discuss and apply the bifocal lens as part of their analysis of the *Crawford* decision.
96 Janna M. Jackson, *Unmasking Identities: An Exploration of the Lives of Gay and Lesbian Teachers* (Lanham, MD: Rowman & Littlefield, 2007), 8. See also, *High Tech Gays v. Defense Industrial. Security Clearance Office*, 895 F.2d 563, 573 (9th Cir. 1990) (recognizing that "homosexuals have suffered a history of discrimination").
97 *Swift v. United States*, 649, F. Supp. 596, 602 (D.D.C. 1986).
98 *Gaylord v. Tacoma School District No. 10*, 535 P.2d 804, 807 (Wash. 1975) (Ringold, J. concurring in part and dissenting in part).
99 *Gaylord v. Tacoma School District No. 10*, 559 P.2d 1340, 1346 (Wash. 1977).
100 The vice principal of Gaylord's school received a communication in which the former student stated, "he thought Gaylord was a homosexual." The vice principal confronted Gaylord who admitted that he was gay. Ibid., 1342.
101 Ibid., 1345.
102 Ibid., 1346.
103 Ibid. To support its contention that homosexuality is immoral, the court stated, "Homosexuality is widely condemned as immoral and was so condemned as immoral during Biblical times." Ibid., 1345. The court went so far as to state that Gaylord's sexual orientation would "hurt his parents." Ibid., 1342.
104 Ibid., 1346.
105 Ibid., 1349 (Dolliver, J. dissenting).
106 Ibid., 1350.
107 *Palmore v. Sodoti*, 466 U.S. 429, 433 (1984).
108 See Vicky Iglikowski-Broad, "The Origins of Section 28," *The National Archives* (n.d.), https://beta.nationalarchives.gov.uk/explore-the-collection/stories/origins-section-28/.
109 Vicky Iglikowski-Broad, "Section 28: impact, fightback and repeal," *The National Archives* (n.d.), https://beta.nationalarchives.gov.uk/explore-the-collection/stories/section-28-impact-fightback-repeal/.
110 Ibid.
111 Ibid.
112 UK Parliament, "The 20th anniversary of the repeal of Section 28 of the Local Government Act of 1988," *House of Commons Library* (n.d.), https://commonslibrary.parliament.uk/research-briefings/cdp-2023-0213/.
113 Ethical Standards in Public Life etc. (Scotland Act 2000, Section 34(94.)) This section repeals section 2A of the Local Government Act 1986, which was inserted in that Act by section 28 of the Local Government Act 1988, https://www.legislation.gov.uk/asp/2000/7/notes/division/2/2/6/1.

114 Vicky Iglikowski-Broad, "Section 28: impact, fightback and repeal," *The National Archives* (n.d.), https://beta.nationalarchives.gov.uk/explore-the-collection/stories/section-28-impact-fightback-repeal/.
115 Deborah Dinner, "Recovering the *LaFleur* Doctrine," *Yale Journal of Law and Feminism* 22, no. 2 (2010): 343–406, 352.
116 Ibid., 353.
117 See, U.S. Equal Employment Opportunity Commission, "Pregnancy Discrimination and Pregnancy-Related Disability Discrimination," (n.d.), https://www.eeoc.gov/pregnancy-discrimination; U.S. Department of Education, Office for Civil Rights, "Know Your Rights: Pregnant or Parenting? Title IX Protects You from Discrimination at School," OCR-00070 (n.d.), https://www.ed.gov/media/document/dcl-know-your-rights-2013-title-ix-21502.pdf.
118 Kyle Greenwalt, "Even when they aren't fired for being pregnant or gay, teachers face strict moral demands," *The Conversation* (October 22, 2019), https://theconversation.com/even-when-they-arent-fired-for-being-pregnant-or-gay-teachers-face-strict-moral-demands-125353.
119 *Drake v. Covington County Board of Education*, 371 F.Supp. 974, 979 (M.D. Ala. 1974).
120 Ibid.
121 Ibid., 981.
122 Ibid.
123 Willard S. Ellsbree, *The American Teacher* (New York: American Book Company, 1939), 535.
124 See *Chicago Board of Education v. Payne*, 430 N.E.2d 310, 315 (Ill. App. Ct. 1981) ("Teachers occupy a special position in our society. As a consequence of that elevated stature, a teacher's actions are subject to much greater scrutiny than that given to the activities of an average person.").
125 *City School District. of City of New York v. Campbell*, 798 N.Y.S.D. 54, 56 (N.Y. App. Div. 2005).
126 Texas Classroom Teachers Association, "Professional boundaries with students," (2024), https://www.tcta.org/legal-services/legal-issues-a-to-z/professional-boundaries-with-students.
127 Jonathan Turley, "Teachers Under the Morality Microscope," *Los Angeles Times* (April 2, 2012), http://articles.latimes.com/2012/apr/02/opinion/la-oe-turley-teachers-under-scrutiny-20120402. He concluded, "[Teachers] live under the transparent conditions of celebrities without any of the benefits, with parental paparazzi eager to catch them in an unguarded moment. They deserve better." Ibid.

Chapter 6

MORRISON AND THE RISE OF PROFESSIONAL AUTONOMY: FINDING A NEXUS

Today's morals may be tomorrow's ancient and absurd customs. ... And conversely, conduct socially acceptable today may be anathema tomorrow.[1]

Although teachers are generally held to a higher standard of conduct than the general population, they are afforded some protections regarding their out-of-school conduct. As aptly noted by the federal Eastern District Court of Virgina the privacy interests of the educator must be balanced with the needs of the public school district.[2] Specifically, citizens' rights to privacy are an implied right under the concept of personal liberty embodied in the Fourteenth Amendment, and this constitutional right to privacy has been invoked by citizens, including teachers, when governmental authorities try to punish private behavior. In addition, courts have recognized equal protection, due process,[3] freedom of speech, and other legal claims when school boards have disciplined or dismissed teachers for their off-duty conduct.

The acceleration of individual rights in the 1960s and 1970s caught teachers in a whirlwind. The college free speech movement, the baby boomer generation, and serious scholars and policymakers have called many long-held beliefs about the relationship between government and the individual before the bar of reason and found some practices lacking.[4] There was a swing toward greater freedom of action and speech. Individual rights were now being balanced against the interests of the community. "A local school board's power to control the personal lives of its teachers has unquestionably diminished during the second half of the twentieth century."[5] School law researcher M. Chester Nolte wrote in 1972 that "what was once thought well settled law relating to the relationship of the teacher to his employer, the board of education, has been opened for further consideration in light of the civil rights movement."[6]

For example, the US Supreme Court's 1960 decision in *Shelton v. Tucker* signaled the beginning of a shift in the courts' view of teachers' rights. The Court overturned an Arkansas law requiring public school teachers and college professors to file an affidavit listing any organization they had belonged to or supported through regular contributions in the last five years. Failure to file the affidavit was grounds for dismissal (voiding their contract), and the employing school district could retrieve any compensation paid. B. T. Shelton, a twenty-five-year veteran of the Little Rock School District, declined to file the document and was dismissed at the end of the year. He brought a lawsuit challenging the constitutionality of the law. At the trial, it was discovered that he was not a member of the Communist Party, but he was a member of the National Association for the Advancement of Colored People (NAACP).

The Arkansas Supreme Court upheld the mandatory disclosure law. However, in a five–four decision, the US Supreme Court held that the Act was unconstitutional. The majority broke new ground by applying a least restrictive standard, writing: "Even though the governmental purpose be legitimate and substantial, that purpose cannot be pursued by means that broadly stifle fundamental personal liberties when the end can be more narrowly achieved."[7] Justice Stewart described the breadth of the legislation as "completely unlimited"[8] in the following manner:

The statute requires a teacher to reveal the church to which he belongs, or to which he has given financial support. It requires him to disclose his political party, and every political organization to which he may have contributed over a five-year period. It requires him to list, without number, every conceivable kind of associational tie—social, professional, political, avocational, or religious. Many such relationships could have no possible bearing upon the teacher's occupational competence or fitness.[9]

The last sentence on teacher behavior and fitness to teach appears to presage the emergence of the concept of nexus.

Since *Shelton* was decided, there has been a swing toward greater freedom of action and speech for classroom teachers. Writing at this time, Earl Hoffman noted several reasons for the change in educator rights. He listed these contributing factors:

1. General relaxation of social restraints on all people.
2. Improved educational standards of teachers and administrators.

3. Organizational efforts of the teaching profession and the usurpation of responsibilities.
4. Decisions in various court cases which have confirmed many common law rights for teachers.[10]

Morrison and Nexus

The limit of a private right is reached where public injury begins.[11]

As discussed in Chapter 5, the acceleration of individual rights in the 1960s and 1970s significantly impacted the right of teachers to be free from close oversight of their private lives as a mandatory role model. There was a swing toward greater freedom of action and speech. Individual rights were now being balanced against the interests of the community. An example of the weakening of *Horosko* and its role model responsibility, discussed in Chapter 5 and cited in the following case, was decided in Ohio in 1967.

Jarvella, a teacher, wrote two letters in July and December to an eighteen-year-old former student, Ben Nichols, who had recently graduated from high school in June of the same year. The letters were addressed to the student, Ben Nichols, and mailed via regular first-class mail. The letters contained language that "many adults would find vulgar and offensive and which some 18-year-old males would find unsurprising and fairly routine."[12] Nichols's mother found both letters and turned them over to the Willoughby Police Department on December 22, 1966, which turned them over to the school district.

Jarvella was briefly suspended while the district investigated the situation, but was reinstated. Subsequently, the local newspapers wrote several articles about the letters. On February 7, 1967, the county prosecuting attorney was quoted as saying that the letters were hard-core obscenity and that "it seemed obvious that a person who would write letters of this kind is not fit to be a school teacher [sic]."[13] Six days later, the board notified Jarvella in writing of its intent to dismiss him. On March 8, after the board had heard evidence in private, it voted to terminate his contract for immorality. Jarvella appealed to the Court of Common Pleas.

The court concluded that Jarvella was a teacher of "exceptional merit," as verified by the testimony of fellow teachers and administrative superiors as well as a review of all of his written evaluations from 1963. The court wrote:

> He was dedicated to his work, enthusiastic and successful. He had a personal commitment to his students beyond the norm, devoting much free time to extra-curricular school activities. More than this, he had a sensitivity and concern for the students' personal problems, which they recognized, for he enjoyed their confidence and respect and had an excellent rapport with them.[14]

The court held that there was no evidence, nor even an inference of evidence, that the knowledge of the letters adversely affected the welfare of the school community. The court spoke, in an often-quoted passage, to the balance of a teacher's private life and protection of the education process, writing:

> The private conduct of a man, who is also a teacher, is a proper concern to those who employ him only to the extent it mars him as a teacher, who is also a man. Where his professional achievement is unaffected, where the school community is placed in no jeopardy, his private acts are his own business and may not be the basis of discipline.[15]

Jarvella signaled the ebb of *Horosko's* influence, which had imposed community moral standards upon teachers as a condition of employment. It marked the beginning of the concept that a nexus, a connection, must exist between an educator's behavior and harm to teaching performance or to the educational program interfering with student learning.

The Morrison Case

> In other words, very little weight was placed on the teachers' side of the scale [in the judicial balancing of the community and teacher privacy]. However, the judicially-spawned "Rights Revolution" of the late-1960s and early 1970s signaled increases in the property, liberty, privacy, speech and associational rights of individuals in the public employment setting and elsewhere, as well as a concomitant reduction in the power of the government to deprive public employees and other individuals of those same rights.[16]

Approximately two years after *Jarvella*, the California Supreme Court decided the watershed case of *Morrison v. State Board of Education*.[17] This case best illustrates the move away from the ability of school boards to police the private lives of teachers. Another legal concept regarding the impact of teachers' private lives on their teaching responsibilities—nexus—serves as a counterbalance to the exemplar. Under the nexus theory, a teacher's questionable personal conduct only results in employment sanctions if the conduct affects the teacher's ability to teach or harms the learning environment. Nexus seeks to balance competing legitimate interests—a teacher's private life and the school district's "strong interest in protecting the school community."[18] While *Morrison* is a California Supreme Court decision, the case has been cited as persuasive authority in many jurisdictions.[19]

Marc S. Morrison was a successful teacher in the Lowell Joint School District for several years before 1964. A review of his record revealed no complaints or criticism of his performance as a teacher. In 1963, he developed a close friendship with Mr. and Mrs. Schneringer; Mr. Schneringer taught in the same school district as Morrison. When the Schneringers experienced marital and financial difficulties, Morrison provided counsel and advice to Mr. Schneringer, who frequently visited Morrison's apartment. During one week in April of 1963, the two men engaged in a limited, noncriminal physical relationship in Morrison's apartment. Morrison described these activities as being homosexual in nature.[20] Morrison was never accused or convicted of any criminal activity, nor was there any evidence of continued homosexual activity by Morrison after the incidents. After Schneringer separated from his wife, Morrison suggested several women whom Schneringer might date.

One year after the April incidents, Schneringer reported his homosexual conduct with Morrison to the superintendent of the district. Morrison resigned from his teaching position in May of 1964. Nineteen months after the report was submitted, the California State Board of Education conducted a hearing regarding the possible revocation of Morrison's life teaching credential. No evidence was presented at the hearing that Morrison had ever committed any act of misconduct while teaching. Nevertheless, the Board of Education revoked Morrison's credential some three years after the Schneringer incidents, concluding that Morrison's behavior constituted immorality and unprofessional conduct.

Morrison sought a writ of mandamus from the Superior Court of Los Angeles to compel the Board to set aside its decision and restore his credential. The court denied the writ. The trial court held that Morrison had "committed the homosexual acts involving moral turpitude and that such acts constituted immoral and unprofessional conduct."[21]

Morrison appealed and lost. However, the Supreme Court of California heard his case.

The California State Supreme Court's decision was and remains seminal not just for the private conduct of gay and lesbian teachers but for any private conduct of educators that may form the basis for adverse employment action. To help frame the issue of private human conduct, the court stated: "Today's morals may be tomorrow's ancient and absurd customs. And conversely, conduct socially acceptable today may be anathema tomorrow."[22]

To help determine what constitutes immoral and unprofessional conduct as envisioned by the Education Code, the California Supreme Court cited a 1965 study from the *Report of the Subcommittee on Personnel Problems of the Assembly Interim Committee on Education*. The report found that in "the opinion of many people, laziness, gluttony, vanity, selfishness, avarice, and cowardice constitute immoral conduct" and "unprofessional conduct might include imbibing alcoholic beverages, use of tobacco, signing petitions, revealing contents of school documents to legislative committees, appealing directly to one's legislative representative, and opposing majority opinions."[23]

This list of immoral and unprofessional conduct may have reinforced the court's wariness about using ancient and absurd customs to define morality. The court cautioned, "It is dangerous to allow the terms 'immoral' and 'unprofessional' to be broadly interpreted ... Therefore, unless these terms are carefully and narrowly interpreted, they could be applied to most teachers in the state."[24] Furthermore, the court observed, extramarital heterosexual sex against a background of years of satisfactory teaching performance "would not constitute immoral conduct sufficient to justify revocation of a [teaching credential] without any showing of adverse effect on fitness to teach."[25] In pursuit of the relationship between a teacher's out-of-school activities and dismissal for immorality or unprofessional conduct, the court held:

> Terms such as "immoral or unprofessional conduct" or "moral turpitude" stretch over so wide a range that they embrace an unlimited area of conduct. In using them, the Legislature surely did not mean to endow the employing agency with the power to dismiss any employee whose personal, private conduct incurred its disapproval. A teacher's behavior should disqualify him only when it is clearly related to his effectiveness in his job. When his job as a teacher is not affected, his private behavior is his own business and should not form a basis for discipline. [26]

The court was concerned about the statute's reach as affording "too great a potential for arbitrary and discriminatory application and administration."[27]

The court offered several considerations for determining the impact of a teacher's out-of-school conduct on the school setting. These include the following:

1. Would the conduct adversely affect the students or fellow teachers;
2. the proximity or remoteness in time of conduct;
3. the age of the students that the teacher works with;
4. the extenuating or aggravating circumstances surrounding the conduct;
5. the praiseworthiness or blameworthiness of the motives resulting in the conduct;
6. the likelihood of recurrence; and
7. the extent to which disciplinary action may inflict a chilling effect on the rights of teachers.[28]

The court concluded:

> Thus, an individual can be removed from the teaching profession only upon a showing that his retention in the profession poses a significant danger of harm to either students, school employees, or others who might be affected by his actions as a teacher.[29]

A new theory of causation emerged from the *Morrison* decision—nexus, a connecting link between the questioned conduct and the educator's ability to perform the assigned duties.[30] This theory asserts that school authorities must demonstrate that the teacher's behavior has adversely affected the school or reduced the teacher's effectiveness in the classroom.

The teaching profession now had a theory it could assert as it struggled to balance the weight of community control against a teacher's right to a private life. However, while the court held that a nexus must exist between a teacher's questioned conduct and harm to the school's educational mission, "the court did not rule out the community's subjective values as a significant factor in making that determination."[31] Consequently, the community's sensibilities can be taken into account in the form of adverse notoriety when school authorities assess whether a teacher's off-duty conduct provides grounds for dismissal. Adverse notoriety will be discussed in Chapter 8.

Next, we discuss several cases that followed *Morrison* to gain insight into the application of *Morrison*.

Early Selected Court Cases Following the Morrison Decision

It is well settled under the concept of *stare decisis* that courts within a jurisdiction follow the precedent established by higher courts. Thus, it is expected that the California state courts would follow the precedent established by the California Supreme Court's *Morrison* decision. However, the *Morrison* rationale soon spread to other states and federal jurisdictions, where it was cited not as precedent but as persuasive authority. The discussion will first focus on the early application of nexus in California and then look beyond the California borders.

Pettit v. State Board of Education was the first decision by the California Supreme Court to apply the *Morrison* nexus standard. *Pettit* is instructive in part because California's highest court placed some limits on *Morrison*.

The Swingers Party, Privacy, and Notoriety: Pettit v. State Board of Education

Four years after *Morrison*, the California Supreme Court heard a case in which a public school teacher's teaching credential was revoked for sexual conduct that occurred in her private life.[32] The court upheld the credential revocation as supported by evidence of her unfitness to teach.

In 1966, Elizabeth Pettit, a special education teacher, and her husband appeared on two occasions on a television program to discuss "nonconventional sexual lifestyles," including adultery and wife swapping. While the couple wore masks and the husband wore a fake beard, one of Pettit's fellow teachers recognized them and discussed their televised statements with the superintendent and other teachers. There was no statement in the court's decision indicating that a follow-up school district investigation of the television appearance had occurred.

In November 1967, Pettit and her husband applied for membership in "The Swingers," a private club in Los Angeles primarily promoting "diverse sexual activities between members at club parties."[33] At this time, the club was under investigation by the Los Angeles Police Department. As part of the investigation, an undercover police sergeant applied for membership in the club. On December 2, 1967, the sergeant attended a club party at a private residence. While at the party, he observed couples engaging in sexual intercourse. Over a one-hour period, the sergeant observed Pettit engage in oral sex with three different men at the party. All participants were undressed. These acts took place in front of other club members. Approximately sixteen to twenty people were present at the club party.[34]

Pettit was subsequently arrested and charged with violating Penal Code Section 288a (oral copulation). However, in a plea bargain, she pleaded guilty to Penal Code Section 650 ½ (outraging public decency). She received a fine and was placed on probation. The probation was terminated once Petit paid the fine, and the criminal proceedings were dismissed. Pettit was awarded a contract for the 1968–9 school year.

However, more than a year later, the California State Board of Education commenced a disciplinary proceeding to revoke Pettit's teaching credential. The grounds for the revocation included the allegation that her conduct involved moral turpitude and demonstrated her unfitness to teach. Ms. Pettit did not testify, but her husband testified concerning their participation in the club's sexual activities as well as their television appearances. In addition, two superintendents and one assistant superintendent testified that Pettit's conduct rendered her unfit to teach. Their testimony primarily centered on exemplar rather than the newly articulated *Morrison* standard of finding a nexus between the contested conduct and harm to the teacher's effectiveness.

The school administrators' expert testimony, in pertinent part, supported Elizabeth Pettit's teaching credential revocation. Their selected statements are part of the California Supreme Court decision. While the Court's Morrison decision was published four years earlier, the cited parts of the witnesses' testimonies are more consistent with the exemplar standard than their nexus standard.

William B. Calton, superintendent of the Cypress School District which employed Ms. Pettit.

- "[A] person who committed the sexual acts performed by plaintiff would be unfit to teach in an elementary school . . . [A] teacher has the responsibility to practice as well as teach moral values; one who failed to practice morality would have difficulty teaching it."

> Sylvester A. Moffett, superintendent of the Huntington Beach City Schools,
> - "[E]very teacher should possess high morals, and that it would be difficult to teach morality without practicing it."
>
> Archie J. Haskins, assistant superintendent of the Magnolia School District.
> - "[A] teacher must set a good moral example for her pupils, for she spends much time with them and has a strong influence over them."
>
> *Pettit v. State Board of Education*, 10 Cal. 3d 29, 32 (Cal. 1973).

The hearing officer, while stating that it was unlikely that she would repeat the "sexual misconduct, she has engaged in immoral and unprofessional conduct, in acts involving moral turpitude, and in acts evidencing her unfitness for service."[35] The hearing officer concluded that cause exists for the revocation of Pettit's life credential. The board adopted the findings and conclusions *in toto*. On appeal, the superior court upheld the board's revocation decision.

The California Supreme Court reviewed its *Morrison* decision as part of the Pettit appeal. The court stated that the facts in *Pettit* distinguished it from *Morrison*.[36] First, Morrison's behavior was noncriminal in nature. However, Pettit's behavior was criminal and a violation of public decency. According to the California Supreme Court, the second distinguishing factor was that Morrison's conduct occurred entirely in private and involved only two partners.

In contrast, Pettit's actions involved three partners and were witnessed by several strangers. It also took place in a club party's "semi-public" atmosphere. The court wrote:

> Plaintiff's performance certainly reflected a total lack of concern for privacy, decorum, or preservation of her dignity and reputation. Even without expert testimony, the board was entitled to conclude that plaintiff's flagrant display indicated a serious defect of moral character, normal prudence and good common sense. A further indication that plaintiff lacked that minimum degree of discretion and regard for propriety expected of a public school teacher is

disclosed by her television appearances, giving notoriety to her unorthodox views regarding sexual morals.[37]

The semipublic nature of the conduct encompasses the concept of adverse notoriety, in which the public not only has knowledge of the questionable behavior but also recognizes that the response to the conduct of a public school educator is contrary to the high expectations held for such public employees.

Third, the Supreme Court majority noted that, unlike *Morrison*, where school authorities provided no evidence of unfitness to teach, three expert witnesses testified that Pettit was unfit to teach. The school administrators stated that Pettit could not "set a proper example for her pupils or teach moral principles to them" as required by state law.[38]

Furthermore, the court noted the notoriety of the conduct as supporting the adverse employment decision of credential revocation. The majority wrote, "A further indication that plaintiff [Pettit] lacked that minimum degree of discretion and regard for propriety expected of a public school teacher is disclosed by her television appearances, giving notoriety to her unorthodox views regarding sexual morals."[39] The majority concluded that her conduct "reflected a total lack of concern for privacy, decorum or preservation of her dignity and reputation, displaying a serious defect of moral character, normal prudence and good common sense."[40]

Morrison was not overturned as California precedent for the standard for unfitness to teach. However, three factors were added to the *Morrison* nexus analysis: Is the behavior criminal? Did it occur in a private or semi-public setting? and Does expert witness testimony support a finding of unfitness to teach based on the questioned conduct?

The Dissent

Justice Tobriner began his lengthy dissent with a recap of the implications of revoking Pettit's teaching credential. He noted that Pettit's competence had never been questioned throughout her career. "One can ask for no better proof of fitness to teach than this record of consistent, capable performance," Judge Tobriner argued.[41] The revocation of Pettit's credential not only applied to dismissal from her current job. She was also barred from employment in any public school district in the state of California. In addition to Pettit's loss of earnings and "psychological damage," Justice Tobriner remarked, the school district lost a "skilled and dedicated teacher."[42]

After laying out the consequences of upholding the credential revocation, the dissent questioned whether the school board had relied on credible evidence of unfitness to teach. Instead, the Judge asserted, "the board has acted on the basis of questionable conjecture."[43] Specifically, the dissent wrote, "Yet this important issue of plaintiff's right teach should not turn on the personal distaste of judges; the test, as this court has announced in this case, is the rational one of the effect of the conduct, if any, on the teacher's fitness to teach."[44] Judge Tobriner concluded:

> In conclusion, I submit that the majority opinion is blind to the reality of sexual behavior. Its view that teachers in their private lives should exemplify Victorian principles of sexual morality, and in the classroom should subliminally indoctrinate the pupils in such principles, is hopelessly unrealistic and atavistic. The children of California are entitled to competent and dedicated teachers; when, as in this case, such a teacher is forced to abandon her lifetime profession, the children are the losers.[45]

Adultery: Erb v. Iowa State Board of Public Instruction

The central issue in this case[46] was whether a teacher could have his teaching certificate revoked upon an allegation of moral unfitness because of his adulterous relations with another teacher. Richard Erb taught art, coached wrestling, assisted with football, and acted as senior class sponsor at Nashua Valley Community School. He taught there for eleven years. He had two sons and was married.

Margaret Johnson taught home economics in the same school. She planned to quit teaching and open a boutique in a nearby town. Erb helped her with the store design. Their affair began in the early spring of 1970.

Mr. Johnson became suspicious about his wife's frequent late-night absences. One night, Mr. Johnson hid in the trunk of his wife's car. She drove the car to school that night, worked for a while, and later drove to a secluded area where she met Erb. Mr. Johnson, while still hiding in the trunk, heard his wife and Erb having sexual intercourse in the back seat of her car. Mr. Johnson did not confront his wife about the affair.

Instead, Mr. Johnson consulted a lawyer and learned that his pending divorce proceedings would be better served if he had witnesses to the affair. After several attempts to catch them together, he organized a "raiding party." Johnson and colleagues "located the couple one night in June, parked in a remote area. Johnson and the others surrounded the car and took photographs of Margaret and Erb, who were partially disrobed in the back seat."[47]

Later, Mr. Johnson complained to the school authorities, hoping to remove Erb from the school, stating that he was not seeking the revocation of Erb's credential. Upon hearing of the complaint, Erb offered to resign, but the local school board would not accept his resignation. However, in a hearing before the state Board of Education into the matter, Erb's certificate was revoked by a vote of five to four. Erb sought relief from the courts.

The trial court held that Erb's adulterous conduct was a sufficient cause upon which to base the revocation of his teaching certificate. On appeal, the Iowa Supreme Court, relying heavily on *Morrison* as persuasive authority, reversed the lower court's decision. First, the court found extensive evidence of the regulation of teacher conduct. They first cited the California case, *Board of Education v. Swan*,[48] in which the court held that a public school teacher is subject to reasonable administrative supervision and restriction to maintain proper discipline and that the teacher's conduct will neither disrupt nor impair the educational process. "A teacher occupies a sensitive position. Since students are taught by example as well as lecture, the teacher's out-of-school conduct may affect his classroom fitness."[49] The comment about the teacher as an exemplar was followed by the often-quoted statement from *Jarvella* on the "private conduct of a man who is also a teacher."[50]

The Iowa Supreme Court, citing the *Morrison* criteria, held that the adulterous conduct must adversely affect the teacher's performance before revocation can be upheld. Citing *Morrison*, the court stated, "Surely incidents of extramarital heterosexual conduct against a background of years of satisfactory teaching would not constitute 'immoral conduct' sufficient to justify revocation of a life diploma without any showing of an adverse effect on fitness to teach."[51]

The Iowa Supreme Court concluded that there was no evidence of such an adverse effect; a nexus was not established between the teacher's personal conduct and a corresponding detriment to the school or the teacher's ability to teach. The Iowa Supreme Court concluded with a nod to *Morrison*:

> The evidence showed Erb to be a teacher of exceptional merit. He is dedicated, hardworking, and effective. There was no evidence to show his affair with Margaret Johnson had or is likely to have an adverse effect upon his relationship with the school administration, fellow teachers, the student body or the community.[52]

With an apparent reference to *Morrison*, the court held that to sustain a revocation of a teaching credential, there must be a showing that the teacher's retention in the profession will adversely affect the school community.

In an interesting comment that may seek to place exemplar in brackets, the court wrote:

> We emphasize the board's power to revoke teaching certificates is neither punitive nor intended to permit exercise of personal moral judgment by members of the board. Punishment is left to the criminal law, and the personal moral views of board members cannot be relevant.[53]

Overnight Male Guests: Fisher v. Snyder

Nexus is further illustrated in *Fisher v. Snyder*, a 1973 decision.[54] Prior to this case, actions on the part of a teacher that raised the mere specter of wrongdoing would implicate the status of exemplar.

Fisher, a middle-aged divorced high school teacher in a rural Nebraska community, was discharged because she had overnight male guests stay in her one-bedroom apartment. Most of the guests were young men and friends of Mrs. Fisher's son, who taught school in a neighboring community. The hotel accommodations were limited in the town, and upon advice from the school board's secretary, Mrs. Fisher extended the hospitality of her residence to her son's friends. There was no attempt to conceal the presence of her visitors.

In the Spring of 1972, Mrs. Fisher was notified that her contract would not be renewed at the end of the school year. After exhausting her quest for an administrative remedy, she was dismissed for unbecoming conduct outside the classroom.[55] The school board took the position that "the inferences from her social behavior are that there was a strong potential of sexual misconduct. The board does not actually accuse Mrs. Fisher of immoral conduct but of social misbehavior that is not conducive to the maintenance of the integrity of the public school system."[56]

Mrs. Fisher turned to the federal court system. She brought an action against the board members under 42 U.S.C. 1983, alleging that her dismissal was unconstitutional. The district court held that her dismissal was impermissible because it was arbitrary and capricious. The court ordered her reinstated. The school board appealed.

The Court of Appeals affirmed the lower court's ruling that the dismissal was arbitrary and capricious. It based its decision on the argument that "each of the stated reasons ... is trivial, or is unrelated to the educational process or to working relationships within the educational institution, or is wholly unsupported by a basis in fact."[57] The appellate court held that a school board cannot infer wrongdoing based on unsupported conclusions. It must prove wrongdoing before a teacher can be dismissed. The stated reasons for dismissal can be successfully challenged as arbitrary and capricious if it can be proved by the plaintiff teacher that each stated reason for the dismissal is trivial or is "unrelated to the educational process or to working relationships within the educational institution or is wholly unsupported by a basis in fact."[58] Clearly, the court articulated a requirement that the nexus standard must be applied based on objective evidence and not mere suspicions or speculation.

The *Fisher* decision contrasts with *Gover v. Stovall*, previously discussed in Chapter 4, which relied on exemplar as justification for dismissal based on the mere inference of potential wrongdoing.[59] L. E. Gover, a high school teacher and coach, was in his school between eight and nine o'clock at night with another man and three young ladies, one of whom was a pupil at the school. The group left the lights off and kept their meeting a secret for several days. Although no evidence was introduced of actual wrongdoing, the court upheld Gover's dismissal based on facts that inferred misbehavior.

A 1996 opinion by a Michigan appellate court illustrates how the concept of a nexus has been applied in subsequent cases to substantiate a dismissal charge. In *Satterfield v. Board of Education of Grand Rapids Public Schools*,[60] the court accepted testimony that a teacher's conviction for embezzlement[61] created a nexus between his nonteaching behavior and his professional duties that impacted his teaching. The testimony asserted that retaining Satterfield would "affect the school's reputation, would affect referrals, and would make it more difficult to work in a team."[62] The court affirmed Satterfield's dismissal. Thus, finding a nexus was not a bar to dismissing an educator whose behavior directly harmed the school, the students, or the teacher's ability to be effective.

Exemplar, Reduced, but Not Replaced

While nexus has protected teachers from many of the unreasonable aspects of exemplar, it has not relieved teachers from the burden of becoming mandatory role models.[63]

Nexus is not a license for the teacher to engage in any off-duty conduct whatsoever. For example, in the *Jarvella* case discussed above, an Ohio court protected the plaintiff's letters to his former student. Still, it acknowledged that some restraints placed on teachers' private conduct are permissible to safeguard the school community's welfare and the "protection of students from corruption." In the court's view, "this is a proper exercise of the power of a state to abridge personal liberty and to protect larger interests."[64]

The courts may sometimes infer harm where there has been no direct showing of harm to students, the school, or the teaching performance. This is especially true when the conduct involves students. For example, the Supreme Court of Kentucky, in the *Board of Education of Hopkins County v. Wood*,[65] upheld the termination of two teachers who were discharged for smoking marijuana with two female students in the privacy of their off-campus apartment during the summer. The court stated that "immoral or unbecoming conduct sufficient to merit discharge of a tenured teacher, when it occurs in a context other than professional competency in the classroom, must have some nexus to the teacher's occupation."[66] Although the court applied the *Morrison* criteria, the dismissals were upheld despite the absence of direct evidence of harm. The court seemed willing to infer harm, similar to the 1931 decision in *Gover v. Stovall*, involving a teacher who met with young women in a school at night.[67] (See Chapter 5 for a discussion of *Gover*.) The *Wood* court wrote:

> A teacher is held to a standard of personal conduct which does not permit the commission of immoral or criminal acts because of the harmful impression made on students. The schoolteacher has traditionally been regarded as a moral example for students.[68]

Even though the Supreme Court of Kentucky offered nexus as the rule to be followed in resolving this issue of out-of-school behavior, the court clearly grounded its finding in exemplar. The court discussed nexus and the need for a showing of harm but was willing to infer harm for conduct that involved drugs and students.

In another post-*Morrison* drug case, a nontenured junior high school teacher was indicted for intent to distribute cocaine. The teacher was suspended without pay. He sought payment of his salary and benefits. The Superior Court awarded the teacher the amount of his unpaid salary withheld, asserting that the "alleged criminal conduct was unconnected to his school-related duties, activities, or contacts."⁶⁹ The court used a nexus argument to find for the plaintiff teacher.

However, the Appeals Court of Massachusetts reversed the lower court using exemplar. The Appellate Court wrote:

> This special role of teachers on impressionable and not fully tutored minds distinguishes them from other public officials and, we think, also informs the term "misconduct in office" as applied to teachers. For this reason, and because of the specific statutory duty of drug education imposed on schools ... we view an indictment of a teacher for a drug felony to be sufficient grounds for suspension.⁷⁰

In another out-of-school behavior case, a ninth-grade English teacher with an exemplary teaching record was dismissed for immorality when she was convicted of intentionally shooting her estranged husband's girlfriend. The teacher argued that there was "insufficient evidence to show a nexus between her conduct and performance of duties."⁷¹ The Missouri Court of Appeals applied a version of the *Morrison* criteria to demonstrate that only a "likelihood that the teacher's conduct will have an adverse effect on students or other teachers need be demonstrated." This likelihood was shown by the Board's findings that the teacher's students were at an impressionable age and would receive a mixed message about violence if she continued to teach.⁷² In addition, the court held:

> The use of violence by a teacher to solve personal problems was likely to have an adverse effect on her students by confusing the violence-free message promoted by the school and the community. In addition, [the] teacher's violent behavior would adversely affect other faculty and parents because her conduct was a breach of both policy and law, impacting her role as a role model and authority figure.⁷³

As with the *Wood* case, the Missouri court was prepared to find harm for certain types of private conduct even when it had not been established that actual harm occurred.

Hoffman and the Adult Bookstore

James Hoffman, a high school art teacher and department chair, had an excellent reputation that spanned thirty years. However, his record did not remain spotless. On October 30, 1998, Hoffman was arrested at the House of Books, an adult bookstore, for public indecency, a fourth-degree misdemeanor. The conduct occurred in a non-private setting and did not involve any students. He pleaded no contest, and he was fined $250.[74]

This incident received significant media attention at the high school when a reporter attempted to interview Hoffman. Additionally, the administration team instructed Hoffman to cease soliciting letters of support from his students immediately. He agreed and stated that it would not happen again. There were no protests calling for his ouster.

The Shaker Heights Board of Education considered the matter and decided, due to Mr. Hoffman's spotless employment record, not to impose any disciplinary action. However, the State Board of Education passed a resolution at its July 12–13, 1999 meeting stating its intent to limit Hoffman's teaching credential. In response, Hoffman requested a hearing. At the hearing, four witnesses testified that Hoffman's conviction did not diminish his effectiveness as a teacher or undermine his authority or reputation. No adverse witnesses gave testimony.

The hearing officer recommended a one-year suspension, concluding that Hoffman's conduct in voluntarily engaging in sexual conduct in a non-private setting constituted conduct that was unbecoming to the position of teacher. The State Board of Education, after receiving the hearing officer's recommendation, revoked Hoffman's teaching certificate for a minimum of two years for violating the law on public decency. The Court of Common Pleas affirmed the decision of the State Board of Education. Hoffman appealed, asserting that the court "abused its discretion when it determined the State Board's decision was supported by reliable, probative and substantial evidence."[75]

On the first assignment of error, the appellate court concluded, without providing any analysis, that Hoffman's behavior impacted his role as a teacher. "While this incident did not occur on school grounds, during school hours, or involve students, it received media attention and impacted his professional life."[76]

Next, Hoffman argued that the revocation of his teaching certificate was not done in accordance with state law. Essentially, he claimed that the applicable state law for revocation of a license required a showing that he had committed "an immoral act," demonstrated "incompetence," or had negligently engaged in conduct that was "unbecoming to the applicant's or person's position."[77] His argument was based on two previous cases, which required a showing of a "nexus between the teacher's conduct and the teacher's duties."[78]

The Court of Appeals noted that the trial court failed to apply the nexus requirement. "However, based on the facts, Mr. Hoffman established the nexus between his conduct and his teaching duties when he solicited students to write letters on his behalf. Thus, we cannot conclude the trial court abused its discretion."[79]

Thus, the Court of Appeals determined that the lower court had not properly applied the nexus test. However, the appellate court did not properly apply the nexus standard when it upheld the suspension of Hoffman's teaching certificate without demonstrating harm resulting from the connection between Hoffman's off-duty conduct and his professional life. On the contrary, the evidence before the court showed no adverse notoriety within the community. Moreover, the school board supported Hoffman, and all testimony before the hearing officer supported him as well.

The causal connection between Hoffman's controversial behavior and its negative impact on his teaching appears to be missing. However, as discussed earlier, when an educator's off-duty, controversial action involves students, the courts appear motivated to establish a nexus.

See, for example, the "steamy photos" of a high school guidance counselor in "seductive undies" that led to her dismissal for conduct unbecoming of a teacher. After twelve years of service in New York City schools, Tiffany Webb was fired for the photo shoots when she was eighteen to twenty years old. She disclosed her previous career as a lingerie and bikini model when she was hired. The photos kept appearing on the internet without her permission, with virtually all of them being photoshopped.

Her prior work was investigated three times, and she was cleared to return to her guidance counseling responsibilities each time. However, when a student reportedly showed the principal pictures of the "scantily clad" guidance counselor, she was investigated one more time, and a three-member chancellor's committee ruled two–one that the photos were accessible to "impressionable adolescents" and that the counselor's "behavior had a potentially adverse influence on her ability to counsel students and be regarded as a role model." However, the dissenting member reasonably argued that "her professional work as a guidance counselor has been outstanding, and she should not be punished for something that happened years ago."[80] There was no showing of adverse effect on her professional role, only the stated possibility of it occurring. Most likely, the change from the earlier investigations was the student's report. No nexus was established between her past conduct and her counseling responsibilities. Instead, the court's decision was based on the exemplar standard.

Craigslist and Teacher Morality and Fitness to Teach: Applying Morrison

The geography between school and outside of school is being redefined. One commentator observed, "Twenty-first-century technology has transformed human relations."[81]

In a 2011 decision, the California Court of Appeal examined whether a teacher's private, non-school-related electronic social media actions had any connection with the teacher's fitness to teach. This case inquires whether an advertisement posted on Craigslist, accompanied by pictures, can serve as the basis for dismissing a teacher with a previously unblemished fitness record.[82]

The Facts

Frank Lampedusa, a tenured teacher, taught middle school literacy (grades six through eight) for five years before being promoted to dean of students. His principal characterized Lampedusa as doing a "good job" and acting professionally.[83] On June 22, 2008, a school district police dispatcher received an anonymous tip from a parent that Lampedusa had a listing on Craigslist section for "men seeking men" titled "Horned up all weekend and need release."[84] The section had disclaimers regarding the age to enter (eighteen years old) and a notice that the site contained adult content. To enter the site, viewers had to click the disclaimer. The ad did not contain Lampedusa's name or occupation. The ad included four pictures of Lampedusa: two images were of his face and upper torso, the third was of his anus, and the fourth was of his genitalia.[85] The ad was very graphic, using descriptive, vulgar language.

The tip about the ad was relayed to the Area Three Superintendent, Rich Cansdale, who met with Lampedusa at his school. Cansdale suggested that Lampedusa remove the listing. Lampedusa agreed and immediately left the school to remove the listing and all known links to it. The ad had been up for two days before it was discovered. Lampedusa had posted five or six previous ads on Craigslist soliciting sex.

On July 17, 2008, Lampedusa was placed on paid administrative leave, which he served without incident. On November 10, 2008, he was served with a notice of suspension and dismissal charges for evident unfitness for service and immoral conduct, as outlined in the California Education Code.[86]

The Legal History

Lampedusa requested a hearing before the three-member panel of the Commission on Professional Competence to contest the dismissal charges. He asserted that he never intended for students to view the Website and did not use school time, equipment, or resources to develop or post the listing. Furthermore, he stated that it was the responsibility of parents and students not to access Craigslist ads, saying, "I would assume parents are taking their responsibilities to monitor children and what they're doing on the Internet."[87]

He also testified before the hearing panel that while he understood that "educators at his school would be uncomfortable with what he did," he did not believe that he acted in an immoral manner.[88] He stated that he would continue to place ads soliciting sex but that he would be more cautious about the choice of pictures and would censor the material more effectively.

The principal told the panel that "she had lost confidence in Lampedusa and questioned his ability to serve as a role model for students as either the dean of students or as a teacher."[89] She had viewed the ad before her testimony.

The Commission found Lampedusa's conduct of placing the ad as "vulgar and inappropriate and demonstrating a serious lapse of judgment." However, despite strongly condemning Lampedusa's behavior, the Commission concluded that the school district had failed to establish a nexus between the placing of the ad and his employment. In other words, the school district had not shown that his conduct harmed the school or affected his teaching ability. Specifically, the Commission noted:

> Had any student, parent, or teacher viewed respondent's ad, it surely would have washed over into his professional life and interfered with his ability to serve as a role model at school. However, that never happened in this case.[90]

Moreover, the panel stated that there was no adverse notoriety associated with his act of placing the ad. Thus, there was no showing that Lampedusa's conduct harmed the school or diminished his ability to fulfill his professional duties effectively.

The district filed a writ of mandate challenging the Commission's decision, arguing that it lacked sufficient evidence to support the dismissal of the charges. The trial court adopted the Commission's findings and conclusions. It held that the weight of evidence supported the Commission's decision. The court denied the writ of mandate, holding that "Lampedusa's conduct did not affect students or teachers, and by all accounts he was a competent teacher and Dean of Students."[91]

Court of Appeal

The California Court of Appeal used the *Morrison v. State Board of Education* criteria for analyzing evident unfitness to teach. This analysis requires a nexus between the questioned conduct and employment. The trial court used the same test but arrived at a different result. The appellate court concluded that there was no substantial evidence to support the Commission's decision; instead, the evidence showed Lampedusa's evident unfitness to serve as a teacher, which constituted adequate grounds for termination. The following is the Court of Appeal's *Morrison* analysis of the facts, which is instructive whenever school officials face issues of an educator's out-of-school behavior.[92]

1. *Adverse Effect on Students or Teachers*: Contrary to the Commission's finding, the Court of Appeal noted that a parent (the anonymous tip) and an educator (the principal) had viewed the ad, and both evinced concern about it. Thus, Lampedusa's conduct "washed over into his professional life."[93] His ability to serve as a role model was compromised by the "pornographic nature of the ad," and the impairment of his relationship with his principal established an adverse effect. Furthermore, the court held that educators are regarded as exemplars with responsibilities and limitations on their actions.
2. *Proximity or remoteness in time of the conduct*: The ad was placed in June, and the District brought charges in November of the same year. "Thus, the District promptly served Lampedusa with the charges, and the conduct was not remote in time."[94]
3. *Type of teaching certificate held by the teacher*: Lampedusa held secondary teaching credentials in social studies, a supplement in English, and an administrative services credential. "Lampedusa's public posting of his pornographic ad is inconsistent with teaching middle school students and serving as an administrator."[95]
4. *The extenuating or aggravating circumstances surrounding the conduct*: The Commission found no aggravating circumstances, noting that Lampedusa promptly removed the ad. The Court of Appeal disagreed. It found that Lampedusa had posted "graphic,

pornographic photos, and obscene written material" on a site open to the public.[96] The court noted that he had done this before and would likely do it again; he attempted to shift responsibility to parents and students and did not believe that he had done anything immoral.
5. *Praiseworthiness or blameworthiness of the motive*: While the court found that Lampedusa's desire to seek a date was not blameworthy, "it was extremely blameworthy in the pornographic, obscene manner that he did so."[97]
6. *Likelihood of recurrence of the conduct*: Lampedusa posted ads previously. He said that he would do so again, and he failed to accept responsibility for his actions, giving the District "little comfort that the conduct would not recur."[98]
7. *Chilling effect on constitutional rights of teachers*: The court concluded there was no chilling effect on the constitutional rights of others. It cited the United States Supreme Court case *City of San Diego v. Roe*.[99] In this case, a police officer sold sexually explicit videos of himself on eBay during his off-duty hours. Like Lampedusa, the officer did not identify himself, his city, or his employment as a police officer. The Supreme Court found that his conduct was detrimental to his employer, the police department of San Diego, and that his constitutional rights were not violated. "Thus, it is established that disciplining Lampedusa for publicly posting his ad does not infringe on his constitutional rights or the rights of other teachers."[100]

The Court of Appeal found a nexus between Lampedusa's conduct and his teaching fitness. In the appellate court's view, the public posting of pictures of his anus and genitals, accompanied by sexually explicit text, "demonstrated a serious lapse in good judgment," and argued for a finding that "given his position as a teacher and role model, demonstrates evident unfitness to teach."[101]

The court quickly dispatched the issue of whether the acts met the criteria for immorality. The court concluded that the "pornographic photos and obscene text constitute immoral conduct in that it evidences 'indecency' and 'moral indifference.'"[102] Lampedusa's conduct was immoral.

The superior court was directed to issue a writ of mandate instructing the Commission to set aside its decision and find that Lampedusa's conduct constituted grounds for dismissal for evident unfitness to teach and immorality.

Discussion: Finding a Nexus

The Court of Appeal found Lampedusa's ad, and, probably just as importantly, his response to concerns about the ad, to be unacceptable behavior for a teacher charged with being a role model for students. The finding under *Morrison* did not require a showing of adverse notoriety or a significant negative response to placing the ad. Sexually charged behavior that is intentionally placed before the public carries a burden for the educator. A toned-down, less sexually explicit ad for a date might not have garnered the negative attention that Lampedusa's explicit ad did. Also, Lampedusa's defense would have been better served had he shown an appreciation of the status of mandatory role model even when acting in the privacy of one's home.

As discussed above, these post-*Morrison* courts imputed harm for some types of out-of-school behavior. Conduct that is clearly immoral or the commission of a felony is seen as acts that occasion an inference by the courts of harm to students and the teaching profession. For example, in *Kenai Peninsula Borough Board of Education v. Brown* (1984), the Alaskan court upheld the discharge of a teacher who had been convicted of diverting electricity. The court held that "the finding that a crime involving moral turpitude has been committed raises at least a presumption that there is a nexus between the teacher's act and fitness to teach."[103]

Similarly, in a case involving burglary, the Supreme Court of Kansas wrote, "Teachers are role models for their students ... There is at least a presumption that the felonious conduct has sufficient relationship or nexus to Hainline's fitness to teach to warrant action by the Board herein."[104] Therefore, in some situations, nexus is not established through fact-finding, but rather inferred by the court.

Nexus is tempered by exemplar; however, some out-of-school conduct rises to the level of imputing harm with its establishment in fact. Apparently, the court finds some behavior objectionable, tacitly applying nexus but employing exemplar. While nexus has protected teachers from many unreasonable aspects of exemplar, teachers are not relieved of the burden of serving as mandatory role models for the students.

Conclusion

We are reminded of the admonition that educators have a right to a private life, but they also have a corresponding duty to keep it private. As stated before, Susan Moore Johnson correctly wrote, "Who teaches matters."[105] And what educators do away from school also matters to the community. The Fourth Circuit Court of Appeal's 1992 holding reflects Professor Johnson's statement, underscoring the critical importance of who is placed in front of the community's children in a position of authority and influence. The court wrote:

> Public education is recognized as one of the most important public services offered by state government, and the maintenance of a professional and dedicated teaching staff to provide that service continuously ranks among the State's highest concerns.[106]

While the current, most used legal test is nexus, it is clear that courts continue to rely on the exemplar standard when determining whether a teacher's private, off-duty conduct can form the basis for discipline or dismissal. Exemplar has not been abandoned; it continues to shape the public conversation and influence judicial decision-making. Given the growing influence of social media in publicizing private behavior, a teacher's private life will continue to be scrutinized under both the exemplar and nexus standards.

NEXT: In this chapter, we discussed the evolution of the concept of nexus and its response to exemplar. The California Supreme Court's seminal *Morrison* decision and its influence nationwide were discussed. In Chapter 7, we move to a contemporary application of nexus to specific issues such as LGBTQ+ teachers, drug and alcohol use, and the pervasive impact of technology, including social media and communication platforms.

Notes

1 *Morrison v. State Board of Education*, 461 P.2d 375, 383 (Cal. 1969).
2 *Ponton v. Newport News School Board*, 632 F. Supp. 1056, 1062 (E. D. Va. 1986).
3 "The tenured public employee is entitled to oral or written notice of the charges against him, an explanation of the employer's evidence, and an opportunity to present his side of the story." *Cleveland Board of Education v. Loudermill*, 470 U.S. 532, 546 (1985).
4 Todd A. DeMitchell, Suzanne Eckes, and Richard Fossey, "Sexual Orientation and the Public School Teacher," *Boston University Public Interest Law Journal* 19, no. 1 (2009): 65–105, 74. Law professor Stuart Biegel wrote that this time of cultural transition has opened an expanded view of individual rights, including the rights of LGBTQ persons, "Indeed,

a principled reading of current legal doctrine reveals that, in our pluralistic society, all persons have a right to be open regarding fundamental aspects of identity, personhood, and group affiliations." Stuart Biegel, *The Right to be Out: Sexual Orientation and Gender Identity in America's Public Schools* (Minneapolis, MN: University of Minnesota Press, 2010), xiii.

5 Donald M. Sacken, "The Limits to a Teacher's Privacy Rights: Ponton v. Newport News School Board," *Education Law Reporter* 42 (1987): 19.

6 M. Chester Nolte, "Teachers and Other Employees," in *The Yearbook of School Law 1972*, ed. Leroy J. Peterson (Topeka, KS: National Organization on Legal Problems of Education, 1972), 158. See also Fleming's 1978 analysis of teacher dismissals and public morality in which he found that teacher's traditional status of exemplar "has increasingly become the subject of considerable controversy and scrutiny." Courts were providing a "sympathetic forum" for changing social mores, including private sexual conduct. Thomas Fleming, "Teacher Dismissal for Cause: Public and Private Morality," *Journal of Law and Education* 7, no. 3 (July 1978): 423–30, 423–4.

7 Ibid., 488.

8 Ibid., 487.

9 Ibid., 488

10 Earl Hoffman, "Are Teachers Citizens of Their Communities?" *School Management* 16 (1972): 8–12, 10.

11 *Jarvella v. Willoughby-Eastlake City School District Board of Education*, 12 Ohio Misc. 288, 291 (1967).

12 *Ibid.*, 289.

13 Ibid.

14 Ibid., 290.

15 Ibid., 291.

16 John E. Rumel, "Beyond Nexus: A Framework for Evaluating K-12 Teacher Off-Duty Conduct and Speech in Adverse Employment and Licensure Proceedings," *University of Cincinnati Law Review* 83 (2015): 685–746, 693–4.

17 461 P.2d 375 (Cal. 1969).

18 Jason R. Fulmer, "Dismissing the "Immoral" Teacher for Conduct Outside the Workplace—Do Current Laws Protect the Interests of Both School Authorities and Teachers?" 31 *Journal of Law & Education* 271, 282 (2002).

19 See West Virginia Code § 18A-3-6, which reads in pertinent part "... there must be a rational nexus between the conduct of the teacher and the performance of his or her job." This code section was applied to a teacher who was convicted, under a plea agreement, to one count of a misdemeanor offense for domestic battery for beating his son with a belt. *Powell v. Paine*, 655 S.E.2d 204 (W. Va. 2007).

20 *Morrison v. State Board of Education*, 461 P.2d., 377–8.

21 Ibid., 396. Since the acts were not criminal, it can be inferred from the court's statement that the homosexual acts were *per se* immoral and unprofessional, thus creating an irrebuttable conclusion.
22 Ibid., 383–84.
23 Ibid.
24 Ibid., 383.
25 Ibid.,
26 Ibid., 382.
27 Ibid., 383, n. 15.
28 Ibid., 386.
29 Ibid., 395.
30 The court found that the "board failed to show that [Morrison's] conduct in any manner affected his performance as a teacher. There was not the slightest suggestion that [Morrison] ever attempted, sought, or even considered any form of physical or otherwise improper relationship with any student.... There is no reason to believe that the ... incident affected [his] apparently satisfactory relationship with his coworkers." Ibid., 392.
31 Leslie Robert Stellman, "Teacher Terminations: Is the 'Role Model' Concept a Thing of the Past?," Education Law Association (November 2011): 1–11, 5.
32 Pettit v. State Board of Education, 10 Cal.3d 29 (Cal. 1973).
33 Ibid., 30.
34 Ibid., 31.
35 Ibid., 33.
36 Ibid. 34 citing that *Morrison* did not involve oral copulation, which was defined in the Education Code as a sex crime (see *Morrison*, 1 Cal 3d at 218, fn 4).
37 Ibid., 35.
38 Ibid., 36. The court referred to California Education Code § 13556.5 which states the duty of teachers "to endeavor to impress upon the minds of the pupils the principles of morality . . . and to instruct them in manners and morals."
39 Ibid., 35.
40 Ibid., 33.
41 Ibid., 37 (Tobrinner, J., dissenting).
42 Ibid.
43 Ibid. Justice Tobriner wrote,

> In proceedings for the disbarment of attorneys or for the revocation of real estate licenses, the courts have held that "guilt must be established to a reasonable certainty . . . and cannot be based on surmise or conjecture, suspicion or theoretical conclusions, or uncorroborated hearsay."

Ibid., citing *Small* v. *Smith*, 16 Cal. App. 3d 450, 457 (1971).

44 Ibid., 41.
45 Ibid., 44.
46 *Erb v. State Board of Education*, 216 N.W.2d 339 (1974).
47 Ibid., 341. Mr. Johnson told Erb to tell his wife about the affair, which he did. Erb and Margaret ended their affair. Ibid. "Erb made no effort to justify it; instead, he sought to show he regretted it, it did not reflect his true character, and it would not be repeated." Ibid., 344.
48 *Board of Education of the City of Los Angeles v. Swan*, 41 Cal.2d 546 (1953).
49 Ibid., 552.
50 Erb, 216 N.W.2d at 341, citing to *Jarvella*, 12 Ohio Misc., 291.
51 Ibid., 343., citing *Morrison*.
52 Ibid., 344.
53 Ibid., 343.
54 Fisher v. Snyder, 467 F.2d (8th Cir. 1973).
55 The charge and justification of the school board reads,
   (a) Frances A. Fish [sic] is a single woman.
   (b) That on several occasions during the current school year, men not related to Francis A. Fisher, stayed in her apartment in Tryon, McPherson County, Nebraska, on several occasions ranging from one night to a period of at least one week, this constitutes conduct unbecoming a teacher.
   Ibid., 376.
56 Ibid., 377.
57 Ibid.
58 Ibid., 378.
59 *Gover v. Stovall*, 237 Ky. 172 (Ky. Ct. App. 1931).
60 556 N.W.2d 888 (Mich. Ct. App. 1996).
61 Satterfield embezzled from a company where he worked part-time. Ibid., 889.
62 Ibid., 890.
63 Todd A. DeMitchell, "Teacher Conduct Outside the Schoolhouse Gate: Exemplar or Nexus?," *International Journal of Educational Reform* 6, no. 1 (1997): 91–6, 95.
64 *Jarvella*, 12 Ohio Misc., 290.
65 *Board of Education of Hopkins County v. Wood*, 717 S.W.2d 837 (Ky. 1986).
66 Ibid., 840.
67 *Gover v. Stovall*, 237 Ky. 172 (Ky. Ct. App. 1931).
68 *Board of Education of Hopkins County v. Wood*, 717 S.W.2d., 839.
69 *Dupree v. School Committee of Boston*, 15 Mass. App.535, 536 (1983).
70 Ibid., 539.
71 *In Re Thomas*, 926 S.W.2d 163, 165, 166 (Mo. App. E.D. 1996).
72 Ibid.
73 Ibid.

74 *Hoffman v. State Board of Education*, 145 Ohio App. 3d 392, 393 (Ohio Ct. App. 2001).
75 Ibid.
76 Ibid., 395.
77 Ohio Rev. Code § 3319.31(B)(1).
78 *Hoffman v. State Board of Education*, 145 Ohio App. 3d, at 396.
79 Ibid.
80 Susan Edelman, "Manhattan HS guidance counselor stripped of job over steamy-photo past," *New York Post* (October 7, 2012), https://nypost.com/2012/10/07/manhattan-hs-guidance-counselor-stripped-of-job-over-steamy-photo-past/.
81 Terri Day, "The New Digital Dating Behavior – Sexting: Teens' Explicit Love Letters: Criminal Justice or Civil Liability," *Hastings Communication & Entertainment Law Journal* 33, no. 1 (2010): 69–110, 69.
82 *San Diego Unified School District v. Commission on Professional Competence*, 124 Cal.Rptr.3d 320 (Cal.App. 4 Dist. 2011).
83 Ibid., 323.
84 Ibid.
85 Ibid.
86 Ibid., 323–4.
87 Ibid., 324.
88 Ibid.
89 Ibid.
90 Ibid.
91 Ibid., 325.
92 Ibid., 327.
93 Ibid.
94 Ibid.
95 Ibid.
96 Ibid., 328.
97 Ibid.
98 Ibid.
99 543 U.S. 77 (2004).
100 *San Diego Unified School District v. Commission on Professional Competence*, 124 Cal.Rptr.3d 320, 329 (Cal.App. 4 Dist. 2011).
101 Ibid.
102 Ibid.
103 *Kenai Peninsula Borough Board of Education v. Brown*, 691 P.2d 1034, 1041 (Alaska 1984).
104 *Hainline v. Bond*, 824 P.2d 959, 964 (Kan. 1992).
105 Susan Moore Johnson, *Teachers at Work: Achieving Success in Our Schools* (New York: Basic Books, 1990), xiii.
106 *Stroman v. Colleton County School District*, 981 F.2d 152, 158 (4th Cir. 1992). Stroman was dismissed for sending a letter to fellow faculty

members to take "sham" sick leave during student exams to pressure the school district during negotiations. The court upheld his dismissal stating,

> He suborned a misrepresentation about sick leave and encouraged a deliberate violation of regulation and employment terms, for which the provided sanction is dismissal. He also took aim at established standards of professionalism by urging teachers to abandon their duties during exam week when supervision would be particularly needed.

Ibid.

Chapter 7

ONGOING TENSIONS ABOUT TEACHERS' OUT-OF-SCHOOL CONDUCT

As times have changed, a teacher's private life outside the workplace has been scrutinized for breaches of exemplar that reflect contemporary tensions. Some of these contemporary issues relating to teachers' out-of-school conduct include such activities as smoking marijuana in states that have enacted recreational marijuana laws, "conduct from earlier years, posting videos or pictures on the internet that may be considered by some to be inappropriate, and past criminal activities that may or may not impact their job responsibilities."[1]

Around 200 years ago, the concept that teachers were exemplars emerged with the advent of the common school movement and its scrutiny of teachers' private, out-of-school activities. This was especially true for females who were leaving their homes to enter the workforce as teachers—one of the few occupations open to women. As public education became more bureaucratized and controlled by educational professionals, the tension between the community and the profession coalesced around who should be permitted to teach our children. DeMitchell and Onosko write of this tension:

> Maintaining an appropriate balance between the parental right to control their child's education and the community's obligation to create future citizens has been a persistent conundrum. Parents seek to mold their children in ways consistent with their ideals, social understandings, and aspirations, while communities and the state seek to form the ideal citizen through discourse and the democratic process. It is not surprising that these visions often collide.[2]

Parents and community members hold teachers to high standards for their private conduct. In the early twentieth century, parents sought to exert control over the private lives of teachers as well as their in-class activity and the content of their teaching.[3] Professor Kristin Shotwell asserted in 2010, "Now teachers are facing renewed intrusions into their private lives from parents and community members seeking to monitor their private, off-duty conduct through the use of social networking websites, online public records, and drug testing requirements."[4] The scrutiny over the private lives of teachers appears not to have abated.

Below, we explore several recent out-of-school activities that reflect the tension over who shall teach our children. What behaviors of educators best serve as indicators of their fitness to teach? The tension between the community and the profession over control of who shall be hired and retained to teach the community's children persists.

LGBTQ+ Teachers, Exemplar and Nexus

Board members and administrators must protect teachers from discrimination just as they must protect students from discrimination. If powerful figures in the life of a student cannot be protected, is it a stretch for students to question whether those same board members and school administrators can protect them?

If schools are not safe for the most vulnerable, are they safe for anyone? ... Laws, professional ethics, and community standards should and must make sexual orientation irrelevant in deciding who will teach our children.[5]

The contours of exemplar can be oppressive, smothering teachers' private lives and reducing them to mere appendages of the community. This has been especially true for LGBTQ+ teachers.[6] For example, in *McConnell v. Anderson*, a 1971 opinion, the Eighth Circuit Court of Appeals upheld the school board's refusal to hire a homosexual school librarian whose application for a marriage certificate to another male was widely reported in the news media. The court asserted that to force the employer to hire the plaintiff would "foist tacit approval of this socially repugnant concept upon his employer."[7]

While the ability to convey knowledge, teach skills, challenge, and inspire students should determine an individual's fitness to teach, lamentably, these measures have not always been the yardstick that is used. Unfortunately, the Nation's gay, lesbian, bisexual, and transgender teachers are often judged by different standards than the standards that apply to other teachers. For example, Justice Brennan's dissent from the Supreme Court's 1985 denial of certiorari in *Rowland v. Mad River School District* captures the challenge that LGBTQ+ teachers have faced. In this case, a bisexual guidance counselor was dismissed, and her equal protection claim failed. Justice Brennan asserted in his dissent that "homosexuals have been the historical object of 'pernicious and sustained hostility.'"[8]

The acceptance and participation of gay, lesbian, and particularly transgender individuals[9] in today's contentious political environment have been and remain divisive issues. Some argue that, at best, gays and lesbians should remain closeted, while others maintain that they should openly take their place in society alongside all other members of the community.[10] There may be few places in society where this dispute has generated more passion than in the public schools.

Even when a teacher's dismissal violated constitutional principles, a court might not order reinstatement. For example, an Oregon federal district court in *Burton v. Cascade School District Union High School, No. 5*,[11] decided whether a teacher's sexual orientation provided grounds for dismissal two years before the *Gaylord* case (discussed in Chapter 5). In *Burton*, Peggy Burton was dismissed for her sexual orientation. At the beginning of her second year of teaching, the principal of her high school confronted Burton with information from the mother of a student that Ms. Burton was a lesbian. She admitted to the principal and again to the school board at a special meeting that she "was a practicing homosexual." She was first suspended and then dismissed for immorality based solely on her sexual orientation. She brought a lawsuit in federal court against the school board, challenging the constitutionality of the dismissal statute. She sought declaratory relief, damages, and reinstatement to her teaching position.

The district court reviewed Burton's complaint that asserted that the statute was unconstitutionally vague and overbroad. The court held:

> A statute so broad makes those charged with its enforcement the arbiters of morality for the entire community. In doing so, it subjects the livelihood of every teacher in the state to the irrationality and irregularity of such judgments.[12]

The district court judge found that the statute upon which the dismissal was based was unconstitutionally vague. However, the court limited its relief to damages equal to one-half of Burton's salary for 1971–2 and one-half of her wages for the following school year. In addition, she was awarded $750 for attorney fees and costs and an order directing the school district to expunge all references to her dismissal from its records. The court did not order reinstatement.

Burton appealed the non-reinstatement order, and the school board appealed the money damages. The Ninth Circuit Court of Appeals majority affirmed the district court's judgment. The appellate court noted that Burton was a nontenured teacher and thus had no expectation of continued employment. Consequently, the total one-year reimbursement was sufficient and in accordance with her one-year contract. However, the court also accepted the school board's assertion that her reinstatement was not required because the community resentment directed at public school teachers who were homosexual was "legitimate."

Judge Lumbard's dissent argued that it was "inappropriate" to consider community resentment in determining whether to reinstate a teacher who had been unconstitutionally removed from her employment. The dissent supported a one-year reinstatement for Burton.[13]

Weaver v. Nebo School District

Wendy Weaver earned an unblemished record as a teacher. In addition to her teaching duties, she served as the girls' volleyball coach at Spanish Fork High School in Nebo, Utah. After a hiatus from coaching, Weaver informed the principal that she was ready to return to coaching. As in the past, Weaver organized two summer volleyball camps. She telephoned prospective volleyball team members to inform them of the schedule. During one of her calls, a senior team member asked her if she was gay. Weaver responded truthfully that she was gay. The team member informed Weaver that she would not play on the volleyball team in the fall. That single question and Weaver's truthful response led to the loss of Weaver's coaching position, a letter directing what Weaver could say to students, and Weaver filing a federal lawsuit against her school district.[14]

Weaver alleged that the letter, which restricted her speech, violated her constitutional right to freedom of expression and that she was denied equal protection under the law. Both parties filed for summary judgment. This discussion will only focus on the equal protection portion of the proceedings.[15]

The first task in an equal protection analysis is selecting the appropriate test. Weaver asserted that she had been denied her right to equal protection when the school district removed her from her coaching position solely based on her sexual orientation. The court started by noting that the Supreme Court had not recognized a "person's sexual orientation as a status that deserves heightened protection."[16] Consequently, the court in *Weaver* applied the lowest standard of scrutiny, known as rational basis.[17]

The rational basis analysis began with the US Supreme Court's articulated proposition that an "irrational prejudice" cannot provide the rational basis to support state action against an equal protection challenge.[18] Acknowledging that prejudices existed in the case, District Court Judge Jenkins noted that "although the Constitution cannot control prejudices, neither this court nor any other court should, directly or indirectly, legitimize them."[19] Consequently, the court found that the defendants' assertion that the rational basis for their decision to remove her as a volleyball coach was based on a negative reaction from the community "failed to advance any justification" for not assigning her to the position.[20] Accordingly, Weaver prevailed on her motion for summary judgment.

Regarding her second equal protection claim—that she was restricted from discussing her sexual orientation—Weaver was also successful. The court quickly dispatched this claim by writing, "simple as it may sound, as a matter of fairness and evenhandedness, homosexuals should not be sanctioned or restricted for speech that heterosexuals are not likewise sanctioned or restricted for."[21] In other words, heterosexual teachers had not been restricted from discussing their sexual orientation; thus, a lesbian teacher could not be restricted from discussing her sexual orientation.

While Weaver won her case on a motion for summary judgment, the issue of her sexual orientation was not without further controversy. Soon after Weaver initiated her lawsuit, parents, students, and community members submitted formal complaints to the school board. A group called the Citizens of Nebo School District for Moral and Legal Values sought redress of their grievances by submitting a petition signed by 3,000 residents of the school district.[22] When their requests were unmet, they sought relief in the state courts. The defendants essentially wanted a court to do what neither the school district nor the State Board of Education would do—fire Weaver. They alleged that Weaver had violated state law concerning the conduct of teachers, and they sought to have the law, as they interpreted it, enforced by the court. They further argued that they had the right to bring a private right of action "to enforce statutory and regulatory requirements for public school employees."[23] The plaintiffs lost at the trial court level and did not prevail on appeal. The Citizens of the Nebo School District lost their case, and Weaver was granted her costs on appeal.[24]

Unfortunately, the nation's gay, lesbian, bisexual, and transgender (LGBTQ+) teachers are often judged by different standards than the standards that apply to other teachers. In staffing decisions, the consistent use of quality teaching practices, the ability to inspire students, and the tenacity to believe in students and to help them achieve more than they thought possible too often take a back seat to the examination of the teacher's private sex life.

How has the concept of exemplar affected the lives of LGBTQ+ teachers? Just over fifteen years ago, Professor Janna M. Jackson, in her qualitative study of gay and lesbian teachers, wrote, with salience today, that "the history of the climate for gay and lesbian teachers reveals how contentious being gay and being a teacher has been and still is."[25]

Hillary Clinton, in her concession speech after running to be the Democratic Party's nominee for president in 2016, stated that "there are no acceptable limits and there are no acceptable prejudices in the 21st century."[26] Nevertheless, prejudice against LGBTQ+ teachers is still common in the twenty-first century in spite of expanded legal protections for LGBTQ+ community.

Marijuana Use

In 1971, a California appellate court upheld the dismissal of Garnet Brennan, a teacher who signed an affidavit telling of her "long and beneficial use of marijuana." The school district's board of trustees began dismissal proceedings against her for immoral conduct. While the court agreed that the questioned conduct must indicate unfitness to teach to justify dismissal under the nexus standard, citing *Morrison* and other decisions, it rejected Brennan's argument that such a nexus was not established.[27] The court noted that the affidavit received extensive publicity in the press, on radio, and on television—both locally and nationally. Thus, her actions resulted in adverse notoriety. Furthermore, the court reasoned that it could have been anticipated that children and their parents would learn of it. Acknowledging that no evidence had been submitted regarding the affidavit's impact on students, the court ruled that competent evidence of such harmful effects was required. The court found this evidence in the testimony of the district superintendent, who said that students were likely to follow Brennan's example. The court observed that *Morrison* does not indicate that the student body must be examined to determine the effect of a teacher's conduct on students.

However, perceptions of marijuana use are changing. States are legalizing and decriminalizing marijuana use in addition to allowing the use of marijuana for medical purposes.[28] This has ramifications for educators. In states where marijuana has been either decriminalized or legalized, would a school district still be able to discipline an educator for use under existing morality regulations? An interesting case arose in Texas in 2017.

The Texas Education Agency, Educator Leadership and Quality Division, brought charges, asking the State Board for Educator Certification to take disciplinary action against Maryam Roland. The division staff recommended that her educator certification (science, grades 8–12) be suspended for two years for violations of the Code of Ethics. Specifically, the staff of the Division claimed that Ms. Roland "lacks good moral character and is unworthy to instruct or supervise the youth of this state."[29]

The case began when a former bookkeeping clerk implicated Ms. Roland in a series of emails about a teacher at Roland's school who allegedly used and distributed cocaine, including possessing cocaine on the school campus. Several employees at the school were identified, but no details were provided regarding their actions.[30] Roland was not mentioned in this email. However, it was reported that the former clerk implicated Roland in a phone call to district personnel. During the investigative interview, Roland stated that she had smoked marijuana but not for the last half-month and that she was in rehab. She never specifically admitted that she used marijuana in Texas.

Roland resigned but submitted samples of her breath, hair, and urine for testing. The breath test indicated no trace of alcohol. The urine test did not indicate that she had consumed marijuana or other drugs. However, the test of her hair showed that she had consumed marijuana in the past, but no other drugs. During the hearing before an Administrative Law Judge (ALJ), she testified that she ate an edible product that contained marijuana during the 2014–15 Christmas break a couple of months before the February investigation, which she believed was legal in Colorado, where she was vacationing. Colorado legalized marijuana in November 2012.

"At the hearing, [Ms. Roland] denied ever selling, buying, possessing, consuming, or being under the influence of any illicit drug or alcohol while on District property, during work hours, or a school-related activity."[31] No evidence was presented to contradict her testimony. The investigator stated during the hearing that he had no reason to think that Ms. Roland was under the influence of alcohol or a drug at the time of the interview or at any other time while she was at school or a school-related activity. He also confirmed that she had not previously been disciplined or investigated by the district for misconduct.[32]

The ALJ recommended that no action be taken against Ms. Roland's teaching certificate. The ALJ's pertinent findings of fact supporting his conclusion, included the following:

1. The evidence did not establish reasonable suspicion that a search of hair would uncover evidence of work-related misconduct for alcohol or controlled substances.
2. There was no evidence that she was under the influence of marijuana or any other controlled substance while at school or a school-related activity.
3. The evidence also did not demonstrate that Ms. Roland had ever consumed or possessed marijuana in Texas. However, she did consume an edible product of marijuana while on vacation in Colorado (where it is legal).[33]

Ms. Roland did not violate any laws while in Texas. Her lawful behavior in another state could not be used as evidence in disciplinary proceedings in the state of employment or in proceedings to revoke or suspend her teaching credential. The ALJ's analysis was consistent with the nexus standard in that it sought evidence of activity within her employment. Notably, the concept exemplar was not part of the analysis except when discussing the inability to instruct or supervise.[34] There was no discussion of community standards or exemplar.

However, the reach of exemplar is still felt in many of the Nation's schools. For example, a dean of students on Staten Island was responsible for enforcing rules prohibiting drug use among students. The dean was arrested in Brooklyn with one bag of marijuana on his person and ten bags of cocaine in his car. He pleaded guilty to attempted criminal possession of a controlled substance. The felony charges were dismissed against him in exchange for participating in a drug program, but the school board dismissed him. The hearing officer held that the dean should be reinstated in the school district upon completing the treatment program. The school district brought suit.

On appeal, a New York appeals court considered the hearing officer's determination "to be returned to his former or similar position in the district ... to be irrational and to defy common sense. Such a conclusion would allow him to be placed back into a position where he would administer a program to discourage drug use among students."[35] In other words, how could the dean enforce a regulation that he himself had broken? The dean did not model what he was required to enforce.

Alcohol-Related Offenses

Even though educators are adults and can legally buy and imbibe alcoholic beverages, the weight of exemplar impacts this legal right. Early contracts and rules for teachers restricted their use of alcohol. A pre-*Morrison* case captures the public concern with a teacher's alcohol use.

In *Scott v. Board of Education of Alton*, decided in 1959, a school board dismissed a teacher who had been arrested four times for public intoxication.[36] The adverse employment decision was made despite undisputed evidence that Scott was an excellent teacher, had a good reputation, and her students did not exhibit a lack of discipline or respect for her in the classroom.[37] In upholding Scott's dismissal, the appellate court emphasized that Scott's arrests had "received publicity." The court held that a teacher is "a leader of pupils of tender age, resulting in admiration and emulation and that the Board might properly fear the effect of social conduct in public, not in keeping with the dignity and leadership they desired from teachers."[38] In particular, multiple convictions for driving while impaired burden the expectations of the community for their teachers.

A 1971 post-*Morrison* case involved the denial of a teaching credential to Joseph Watson, Jr., based on six convictions involving alcohol use. The California Court of Appeals eschewed the use of nexus and found no evidence that Watson's teaching was negatively affected. Nonetheless, the court held that his conduct was a poor example for students. The court stated that Watson's multiple convictions for alcohol-related offenses "amply demonstrates his unfitness to teach in the public schools." After all, the court pointed out, "one of the main concerns of parents and school administrators is the effect of the use of and overindulgence in alcohol on their youngsters."[39]

Furthermore, the Court of Appeals was concerned with the public nature of Watson's conduct, as well as the repetition of criminal conduct of driving while intoxicated extending over a ten-year period. "There is here involved no private, isolated, noncriminal act which occurred years before, but a series of convictions for criminal offenses, all involving the use of alcohol, constituting a continuing course of conduct, public in nature."[40] And, of greatest concern to the court was that the criminal convictions were contrary to instilling respect for the law. The court stated, "As between a teacher and his student, 'an important part of the education … is the instilling of a proper respect for authority and obedience to necessary discipline.' Lessons are learned from example as well as from precept."[41] The California Court of Appeals asserted that exemplar, not nexus, is the standard for analyzing Watson's convictions.

In a similar case, a public school teacher who taught in an alternative education program operated by a drug and alcohol residential treatment facility was dismissed for immorality after her third driving under the influence conviction and driving without a license.[42] The court wrote that her convictions for three drunk driving convictions and driving without a license "is, *per se*, conduct that is a bad example to students whose ideals as a teacher is supposed to foster. This affects her credibility and impacts her ability to teach."[43]

The Principal's DUI Convictions

Joseph P. Moffitt served as the principal of two elementary schools in Pennsylvania. In June 2010, he was arrested for driving under the influence (DUI). Four years later, in April of 2014, he was once again arrested for DUI. He pleaded guilty in October 2015 and had his driver's license suspended for twelve months. He received ninety days of house arrest, fines, and probation for five years.[44] Moffitt was suspended without pay on March 14, 2016. The evidentiary hearings included the following findings:

1. The Acting Superintendent testified that the two DUI offenses "caused irreparable damage to Moffitt's reputation and ability to lead the schools; that his behavior was contrary to the School District's attempts to discourage students from drinking and driving; and that allowing him to return to his position would send mixed messages to School District student."
2. A teacher in the school district and resident in the school district stated that the "two DUI offenses constituted immorality and

expressed her thoughts concerning the bad example his conduct has set for students."
3. The former Educational Services Program Director for the school district and the acting principal for Moffitt's two elementary schools and resident asserted that "Moffitt's actions constituted immorality because they set a bad example for School District students and he could not serve as an effective role model."
4. A parent testified that Moffitt's actions "constituted immorality because they set a bad example for students regarding responsibility, character, and integrity."
5. Another parent stated that his actions were "unacceptable and rendered him unable to be a good role model—and that his actions went beyond impacting the children and their future choices and impacted the morale of the school."[45]

The school board dismissed Moffitt, and the state hearing officer, supported by the Secretary of Education, denied Moffitt's administrative appeal. The Secretary wrote that he found credible evidence supporting dismissal and that the school district had established grounds for termination by a preponderance of the evidence.

On appeal, a court found that the Secretary and the school board met the burden of proving that the "(1) conduct occurred, (2) the conduct offends the morals of the community, and the conduct is a bad example to the youth whose ideals the educator is supposed to foster and elevate."[46] Moffitt's DUIs constituted immorality. He appealed the decision.

The Commonwealth Court of Pennsylvania reviewed whether there was sufficient evidence to support the finding that the principal's dismissal for two DUI convictions in an approximately four-year period offended the community's morals. Senior Judge Collins considered the second DUI as constituting immorality as a "difficult one." Previously, the court, in an earlier case involving a teacher who had three drunken driving offenses, had opined that the third conviction was "not a single act of misjudgment, but rather a pattern of conduct that is not only damaging to [the teacher], but also puts the public in serious danger."[47] Although the Secretary of Education did not find that Moffitt's two convictions amounted to *per se* justification for dismissal, the multiple convictions for DUI appeared to constitute *per se* justification under the previous case. The court did not explicitly address whether two convictions constitute a pattern of immoral conduct. The court concluded:

> Given the weight of evidence presented by parents and teachers in the community that Moffitt's conduct involving drinking and driving set a bad example for students and was offensive to the morals of their community, the Secretary's decision to dismiss Moffitt for immorality under the School Code must be affirmed.[48]

California and a Teacher's DUIs

A last case for discussion, which occurred in California and was decided in 2010, combined the concept of adverse notoriety of exemplar and its impact on the application of the *Morrison* nexus test. Shirley Marie Broney, an elementary school teacher, described by her principal as "a very dedicated and talented teacher who works well with children,"[49] received three driving-under-the-influence citations between 1987 and 2002. However, upon cross-examination, the principal agreed that teachers act as role models, and that "it was important how a teacher acted outside of school, and that a teacher who drank and drove, and who was arrested and convicted of DUI, engaged in unprofessional conduct."[50]

Broney's teaching credential was suspended for sixty days by the California Commission on Teacher Credentialing. Pertinent to our discussion, the Commission's authority to regulate the profession "cannot be used arbitrarily to penalize conduct having no demonstrable bearing upon fitness of practice."[51]

The Commission's action barred Broney from teaching in the public schools of California, including her employing school district; and she subsequently brought a lawsuit challenging the suspension of her credential. The Superior Court of Sacramento County denied the petition to set aside the suspension. The court held that the three convictions rendered Broney unfit to teach *per se*. She appealed the court's decision.

The appellate court held that the lower court's *per se* rule was in error. It held that a conviction of a crime not listed as an automatic credential revocation or dismissal in the Education Code is not, *per se*, unfit to serve. Instead, the educator is entitled to a fitness hearing. This statement is counter to a traditional exemplar argument that would most likely uphold a *per se* dismissal based on a criminal conviction.[52] The court applied an abbreviated version of the *Morrison* analysis.

The court observed that Broney's ankle bracelet, a visual reminder of her DUI convictions, may have diminished students' respect for her in the classroom. This case used the language of nexus and found harm to students. The court wrote. "We agree with the trial court that plaintiff's wearing an ankle bracelet to school for a month may have adversely affected others. It would have adversely impacted plaintiff's ability to earn the respect of her students."[53] The number of arrests supported the use of *Morrison*'s likelihood of the "recurrence" nexus criterion. And, under the factor type of teaching credential, the court cited the lower court's analysis, holding: "Given the impressionable nature of children at that age," the court wrote, "which is not disputed here, [plaintiff's] multiple alcohol-related convictions are of serious concern."[54]

The Court of Appeals, while rejecting the lower court's *per se* ruling regarding Broney's criminal conviction, applied a fitness-to-teach test under *Morrison* and upheld the lower court's finding that Broney was unfit to teach.

The Last Chance Agreement

John Bender, an assistant principal, was scheduled to host an award ceremony on June 15, 2015, but was admittedly under the influence of alcohol. He disregarded his principal's instructions and attempted to drive home. He was arrested for driving while intoxicated. The arrest was widely reported in the media and sparked social media comments from parents and students. The board chose not to initiate termination proceedings against Bender asserting that because he was a highly regarded educator it was a mitigating factor for adopting a lesser penalty short of immediate dismissal. Instead, the board offered him a "last chance agreement." Under the terms of the agreement, Bender agreed to undergo counseling and to comply with specific reporting requirements. In addition, he agreed to waive his hearing rights if the school board terminated him for testing positive for alcohol on school grounds or if he was convicted of an alcohol-related offense.

On September 11, 2015, it was reported that Bender appeared to be intoxicated, but there was no verified blood alcohol test taken. However, in less than a month, on October 2, 2015, he was arrested for driving under the influence of alcohol. The school board opted to initiate a dismissal proceeding. The hearing officer supported the termination. However, on appeal, the court set aside the hearing officer's decision, asserting that the termination was "shockingly disproportionate to petitioner's misconduct inasmuch as that misconduct did not occur on school grounds."[55]

On appeal, a New York appellate court reversed the lower court's decision and upheld the "last chance agreement." Furthermore, it asserted that Bender had "squandered the opportunity of the agreement by committing another serious alcohol-related driving offense."⁵⁶ The court concluded:

> Given the seriousness of [Bender's] offenses and his position as a role model for young adults, we cannot conclude that the Hearing Officer's penalty of termination was shocking to the conscience.⁵⁷ In vacating the penalty, the [lower] court inappropriately substituted its judgment for that of the Hearing Officer.⁵⁸

Sexual Behavior: Past and Present

A teacher's private life before taking a teaching position and while teaching have both led to employment problems. In many cases, the teacher was disciplined for lawful work that pushed the boundaries of "socially acceptable" behavior. For example, Jonathan Turley, in his 2012 *Los Angeles Times* Op-Ed, discussed examples of such situations, including an Oxnard, California middle school teacher who was placed on administrative leave when it was revealed that she had been a porn actress before becoming a teacher.

Across the country, a male substitute teacher, Shawn Loftis, was fired for conduct that reflected negatively on him and the school community. The Florida Department of Education barred Loftus from obtaining a teaching certificate for five years. However, the ban was reversed by the Florida Practices Commission, which ruled that he could obtain a teaching credential. Nevertheless, "local officials were quick to assure citizens that they would not have to hire Loftis even if he were certified."⁵⁹

Most cases involving teachers outside employment are brought under the exemplary standard, but some are based on nexus. Lawful action is not necessarily a shield for immoral conduct or conduct unbecoming of a teacher. This section will discuss a few of these situations.

Hot for Teachers

Linda Janack taught reading in a Michigan elementary school for several years. She earned a sterling reputation as an educator. However, in the summer of 2018, her students' parents discovered her second job. In cooperation with her husband, Janack performed on an internet X-rated porn site, Hot for Teachers.

Parents complained about the site. When the news broke, the school board had not yet decided whether Janack would return to work in the fall. The teacher and school officials were still in discussions about the situation.

A mother whose child had Janack as a teacher stated, "My kids, when they talked about her, really liked ... her. But that's not OK, and I can't believe [that] if the district knows about it, they're still allowing it." While Janack's activities were not illegal, it "wasn't any solace for the mother."[60]

Bob's Videos

Forty-nine-year-old Robert Walenski, affectionately called "Bubba" by his students, taught English at Dennis-Yarmouth Regional High School for twenty-eight years. He also spent school vacations and breaks producing and starring in adult films in California. His school district placed him on administrative leave. Then, it dismissed him for "conduct unbecoming of a teacher" when a parent came across one of his movies and informed the school superintendent. The Massachusetts Department of Education stated that it would move to revoke his teaching credential.

The superintendent purchased the film "Mood Pieces" and watched it. The superintendent asked, "How could he teach love sonnets when he is engaged in these activities?"[61] However, students protested his dismissal, and the town was divided over whether he should be returned to the classroom.[62] One student stated that "filmmaking is legal. It's not like he's drunk or something." However, the superintendent said, "My concern is that all our teachers be appropriate role models."[63]

Walenski's dismissal was predicated on the allegation that he had approached a female student about appearing in one of his "Bob's Videos," a charge that Walenski denied. The solicitation of a student for pornographic acts, however, framed this issue differently than the constitutionally protected activity of producing and starring in pornographic films. In the *Janack* case, there were no allegations of involvement with students or minors. The *Walenski* case, if it were proven that he invited his student to participate in pornographic filmmaking, would come to the courts with a heavy presumption in favor of a school district's authority to discipline or dismiss the accused teacher. Questionable actions with students cross the court's (and everyone else's) line of acceptability and would constitute immorality or unprofessional conduct.

A Prior Porn Star

Whereas Janack and Walenski were involved in X-rated adult content contemporaneously with their teaching, prior work in the adult entertainment industry is also perilous for educators. Sex-related behaviors coupled with role model expectations for teachers may tend to dampen the effect of the *Morrison* criteria of proximity or remoteness in time.

For example, Stacie Halas, a California school teacher, was dismissed after school officials learned that she had been a porn star before becoming a teacher.[64] In a decision issued by the Commission on Professional Competence, the Commission found that some of the earlier pornographic items were still available on the internet and that these materials would impede Halas' ability to be effective in the classroom or respected by colleagues. In one of the sex videos, Halas talked about being a teacher. Although the videos were not created while the school district employed her, students located several of these videos and began calling her by her stage name. The district superintendent remarked that the Halas' choice to "engage in pornography was incompatible with her responsibilities as a role model for students and would present an insurmountable, recurring disruption to our schools should she be allowed to remain as a teacher."[65]

The Perils of Technology

> Nationwide reports of scandals and abuses involving social media have contributed to increasing concern and public interest in the allegations of unprofessional conduct by teachers, including inappropriate relationships between teachers and students.[66]

Social media has introduced a new arena for scrutinizing teachers' private lives. "Now, teachers are facing renewed intrusions into their private lives from parents and community members seeking to monitor their private, off-duty conduct through social networking websites, online public records, and drug testing requirements."[67] The technology-driven social media world offers teachers creative opportunities, but challenges them to establish professional and appropriate boundaries for their behavior. For example, a first-grade teacher lost her appeal for dismissal for posting comments about her class on her Facebook page. She posted the following: "I'm not a teacher—I'm a warden for future criminals!" and "They had a scared straight program in school—why couldn't [I] bring [first] graders."[68]

The internet has made teachers' private lives more accessible and, in many ways, more vulnerable. "Teachers are not immune to the changes wrought by the technology-created social media."[69] The impact of educators' postings on social networking sites affects their employment prospects and their ability to secure a teaching position. A study of social networking sites on principals' perceptions of applicants' postings found that a job applicant's postings could impact principals' hiring decisions.[70]

For instance, in *Phenix City Board of Education* (2009), the arbitrator upheld the district's termination of a teacher who appeared nude on a dating website profile page.[71] The images were graphic.[72] In addition to the public exposure, the pictures impacted the teacher's standing in the community. Indeed, "concerned parents" sent a package with an unsigned note to the superintendent along with images from the website. The Board ultimately terminated her on the grounds that her actions amounted to "immorality and other good and just cause." The arbitrator agreed and also emphasized that a higher standard applied to the teacher's behavior because of her role in the community. Given all of these factors—the link to her job, the nature of the content, and her role as a teacher—the arbitrator sustained the dismissal.

Below are some of the social media controversies that have ensnared teachers. Internet privacy is more of a myth than a fact, which some teachers find difficult to grasp. Teachers who wish to maintain a private life must strive to keep it private. Not everything that happens in a teacher's life needs to be shared over social networking sites.

A teacher in Wisconsin was placed on administrative leave over a Facebook picture depicting her pointing a rifle at the camera.[73] A teacher in Utah, who was also a bikini model and bodybuilding competitor, was challenged by school officials who requested that she remove photos related to these activities from her Facebook and Instagram pages or face termination.[74] In Florida, a teacher lost her job after modeling swimsuits and appearing in some revealing pictures online.[75] Likewise, a student teacher was asked to leave her position after appearing in a newspaper photograph in her bra and a skirt. This teacher was participating in a "SlutWalk," where she was raising awareness of the victims of sexual assault.[76] In 2011, a teacher lost her job after posting a picture on Facebook showing her holding two drinks while vacationing in Europe during the summer.[77] None of these activities is illegal, yet they raised concerns among school officials about the role model the teacher was portraying.

The Apples and the Apple ID: The Inadvertent Sync of Sexually Explicit Material

Wyatt Earling taught second grade for fifteen years in Lincoln County, Utah. Upon being hired in 2004, his school district issued him an Apple computer, and Earling created an Apple ID using his school district email address. Over the years, he had been issued various Apple devices using his original Apple ID. By the 2018–19 school year, he had the following district-issued Apple products: a classroom set of iPads for his students' use, a laptop for personal use, and two outdated iPads (one had a broken screen), which he kept at home. He periodically used the functioning iPad for work emails and allowed his daughters to use it to play games, watch videos, and download apps. In May 2018, he bought his first Apple iPhone using his Apple ID.

The Complaint, the Investigation, and the Administrative Hearing

In March 2019, Earling's ex-wife phoned the superintendent to report that there may be "inappropriate, pornographic, and sexually explicit images" stored on Earling's school-issued iPad.[78] She further noted that Earling's children, who were also students at his school, may have accessed the images. The superintendent drove to Earling's school, conferred with the principal, and removed Earling from the classroom. The superintendent, principal, and Earling then drove to Earling's home, retrieved the iPad, and returned to the district office.

As part of the investigation, the Director of Technology reviewed the phone's images and found approximately 1,000 photos. The superintendent considered fifty of those images "graphic, pornographic, sexually explicit, obscene, and inappropriate for a District device."[79]

At the end of March, the superintendent met with Earling to discuss the initial findings. At the meeting, Earling explained that he had taken his iPhone on a trip to Mexico with his future wife. Pictures taken on the iPhone included nude photos of the two of them and screenshots of text messages that contained sexually suggestive content, "memes" that contained profanity, and sexually explicit jokes. "The photos, text messages, and images were created, downloaded, and shared in the context of their consensual, private relationship."[80]

Mr. Earling explained that the iPad had been at his home as a backup for the 2018–19 school year. He had not used the iPad to teach. He believed the photos and images had been synced through the shared use of his Apple ID. He stated that he had inadvertently stored the pictures and images on his iPad and had not intentionally stored them. The school district's IT employee confirmed that the sync setting was activated on the iPad when the superintendent received it from Earling. He was "remorseful, emotional, and embarrassed."[81]

After the meeting, the superintendent placed Earling on administrative leave. After a full investigation, Earling was served with a notice of termination for violating the District's "Employee Acceptable Use of Technology" procedure. Furthermore, the notice included the following:

1. Mr. Earling caused or allowed graphic pornographic material to be placed or stored on a [District] device, violating other policies and potentially placing students and staff at risk by coming in contact with the harmful material;
2. Mr. Earling's actions constituted immorality, placed students and staff at risk, and were harmful to the educational process[.][82]

The superintendent recommended that Earling be dismissed for "immorality" and "any other good or just cause relating to the educational process."[83] Mr. Earling requested a contested hearing with the Office of Administrative Hearings.

The Hearing, the School Board, and the Courts

How did the objectionable material get placed on the school-district-issued iPad from Earling's personal iPhone? First, it was determined that the pad was not the source of the photos and images. Second, the iPhone images could have been downloaded through a wired connection. Third, the iPhone could have been synced to one or more devices, given that the iPad had already been set up for syncing. No evidence was submitted establishing that the download occurred due to the operationalization of options one or two, leaving option three—the sync—as the most plausible explanation.

The hearing officer concluded that the superintendent had failed to prove actual harm, as no students or staff were exposed to the objectionable photos and images, and had also failed to prove that the allegations had a "sufficient relationship to [Earling's] fitness or capacity to serve as a teacher."[84] The school board rejected the hearing officer's recommendation.

The Board agreed with the superintendent and dismissed Earling for "any other good or just cause relating to the educational process."[85] It did not pursue the charge of immorality. Earling brought a wrongful termination action. The trial court ruled in his favor on all counts, and the Board appealed.

The Wyoming Supreme Court posed two questions regarding the controversy: first, whether the school district's policies provided adequate notice regarding "inadvertent syncing," and second, whether the Board's conclusions about Earling's unfitness to teach were correct.

On the first issue, the Supreme Court found that the school district's technology use policy failed to provide a clear standard of conduct governing Earling's actions. The policy did not prohibit employees from using the same Apple ID for personal and district technology devices. Furthermore, the policy did not inform district employees that they could be disciplined for inadvertent syncing that resulted in inappropriate material being placed on a district device.

The court found that the evidence did not support the Board's conclusion of unfitness to teach. None of Earling's students saw the inappropriate material. Earling had positive evaluations and was well-regarded in the school community. Additionally, he expressed remorse and was embarrassed by the incident. The court found that it was highly unlikely that he would repeat his mistake. Consequently, the Wyoming Supreme Court affirmed the trial court's decision. It concluded that the Board's decision to terminate Earling because he was unfit to teach was "contrary to the overwhelming weight of the evidence."[86]

As the *Earling* decision illustrates, the courts view a teacher's inadvertent, non-planned actions, which are not part of a pattern of aberrant behavior, more favorably than actions taken with conscious disregard for their impact on students. Mr. Earling made an inadvertent error when he stored inappropriate images on his iPhone. He had not intentionally violated school policy.

Teachers, Students, and Their Virtual Contact

When faced with situations that range from mildly unprofessional conduct to serious sexual misconduct, it is no easy task to determine how schools ought to react to employees' social networking. Administrators and policymakers are confronted with the difficult responsibility of balancing protecting school employees' constitutional rights, safeguarding the image of teachers as role models, and preventing inappropriate employee–student relationships.[87]

Another area of technology that poses significant challenges for educators is emailing and communicating with students outside of school. It is an evolving issue that is not just confined to America. For example, an Irish twenty-four-year-old male teacher texted his students—three students aged 14–15—late at night from September 2022 to May 2023. He questioned the students about their sexual orientation.[88]

Concluding Comments

While research has well established that teacher quality makes a significant difference in student learning, a teacher's out-of-school behavior may also be an indicator of fitness to teach. Schools have historically exerted some control over teachers' private lives, but to what degree does the community have a legitimate interest in restricting the private lives of professional teachers?

Law professor of public policy, Jonathan Turley, responded to a question regarding a teacher's private life [see note 59 this chapter for his article], writing,

"We bought their skills and their willingness to meet performance criteria on the job. Firing a teacher for taking a picture with a drink is not advancing any particularly [sic] public policy. Rather, it is using public employment to create a subset of citizens who must not just work according to our demands but then live their lives according to our values."

Alexandra Le Tellier, Should we evaluate teachers outside of the classroom too? Los Angeles Times (April 12, 2012), https://www.latimes.com/opinion/la-xpm-2012-apr-04-la-ol-teachers-private-lives-20120404-story.html.

For over a century, the answer to this question has been a subject of debate and contention. Should the public demand adherence to publicly stated but not necessarily followed moral standards? Should the focus of accountability for educator behavior include scanning a teacher's private behaviors that might negatively impact the learning environment?

Since the founding of America's system of public schools, a teacher's private life has been the subject of community interest. However, in the 1960s and 1970s, the courts gave judicial recognition to an individual's right to privacy, and this trend had a significant impact on teachers. In the schools, individual rights were now being balanced against community interests.

As stated in the previous chapter, the California Supreme Court, in its landmark decision of *Morrison v. State Board of Education*, wrote, "Today's morals may be tomorrow's ancient and absurd customs. And conversely, conduct socially acceptable today may be anathema tomorrow."[89] For example, teachers wearing beards and showing tattoos were once verboten; they are now commonplace. More importantly, a teacher's sexual orientation was once considered a valid criterion for dismissing teachers. Today, a teacher's private sexual life with consenting adults is not the school board's business.

In the second decade of the twenty-first century, social media added a new dimension to questions about a teacher's right to a private life. The ubiquity of social media and the public's ability to monitor a teacher's private life provide parents and community members with a window to judge teacher conduct against the yardstick of a role model. Consequently, a rise in adverse notoriety has impacted teachers' freedom to lead their private lives, similar to the freedom enjoyed by their non-educator neighbors.[90] In the coming years, teachers will continue to be scrutinized about substance abuse, sexual behavior, and off-duty activities that school boards find offensive, and the exemplar model and nexus will both be used to analyze a teacher's private life.

Regardless of which standard applies, the tension over the privacy rights of educators will continue to persist. Teachers would be wise to remember that their private lives become public when they post images or narratives about their off-duty activities on social media.[91]

NEXT: The final chapter concludes the discussion from the previous seven chapters. It explores the relationship of adverse notoriety and its connection to both exemplar and nexus. The impact of adverse notoriety on three cases—marijuana use, viral posts, and domestic battery—is discussed. The chapter concludes with a discussion of the ongoing tension between exemplar and nexus over who decides who shall teach our children.

Notes

1. Suzanne E. Eckes, Todd A. DeMitchell, and Richard Fossey, "Teachers' Career Up in Smoke and Viral: Off-Duty Conduct in Modern Times," *Education Law Reporter* 355 (2018): 633–40, 634.
2. Todd A. DeMitchell and Joseph J. Onosko, "A Parent's Child and the State's Future Citizen: Judicial and Legislative Responses to the Tension Over the Right to Direct an Education," *Southern California Interdisciplinary Law Journal* 22, no. 3 (2013): 591–635, 592.
3. In the early days of the fight to establish the common school, the content of the common curriculum became a matter of great debate and a spark for the Philadelphia Bible Riots of 1844. Bruce Dorsey, "Freedom of Religion: Bibles, Public Schools, and Philadelphia's Bloody Riots of 1844," *Historical Society of Pennsylvania* (May 2008), https://hsp.org/sites/default/files/freedom_of_religion_0.pdf. Furthermore, in 1974, the Great Textbook War in Kenawha County led to violent protests, planting bombs in schools, and shooting school buses. West Virginia Public Broadcasting cast the opposing sides:

   > Textbook opponents believed the books were teaching their children to question their authority, traditional values, and the existence of God.
   >
   > Textbook supporters said children needed to be exposed to a wide variety of beliefs and experiences and taught to make their own decision.

   Author, "Textbook Wars, Cultures Clash Over Education in Appalachia, Then and Now," *West Virginia Public Broadcasting* (October 16, 2015), https://www.wvpublic.org/podcast/inside-appalachia/2015-10-16/textbook-wars-cultures-clash-over-education-in-appalachia-then-and-now. For a discussion of the current controversy over what is taught in the public schools, see Jacob A. Bennett and Todd A. DeMitchell, "Federal District Court Finds Plausible Claims Against 'Divisive Concepts' Law: *Local 8027, AFT-N.H., AFL-CIO v. Edelblut*," *Education Law Reporter* 414, no. 1 (2023): 1–17. See also, Jonathan Friedman and James Tager, "Educational Gag Orders," *PEN AMERICA* (November 8, 2021), https://pen.org/report/educational-gag-orders/ who write,

   > The [divisive concepts] bills' vague and sweeping language means that they will be applied broadly and arbitrarily, threatening to effectively ban a wide swath of literature, curriculum, historical materials, and

other media, and casting a chilling effect over how educators and educational institutions discharge their primary obligations.

Ibid.

4 Kristin D. Shotwell, "Secretly Falling in Love: America's Love Affair with Controlling the Hearts and Minds of Public School Teachers," *Journal of Law & Education* 39, no. 1 (2010): 37–XX, 38.

5 Todd A. DeMitchell, Suzanne Eckes, and Richard Fossey, "Sexual Orientation and the Public School Teacher," *Boston University Public Interest Law Journal* 19, no. 1 (2009): 65–105, 105. The following section is informed by this article and expands the discussion.

6 See *High Tech Gays v. Defense Industry Section Clearance Office*, 895 F.2d 563, 573 (9th Cir. 1990) (recognizing that "homosexuals have suffered a history of discrimination").

7 *McConnell v. Anderson*, 451 F.2d 193, 196 (8th Cir. 1971), *cert denied*, 405 U.S. 1046 (1972).

8 *Rowland v. Mad River School District.*, 470 U.S. 1009, 1014 (1985) (Brennan., J., dissenting from cert. denied).

9 For example, in early 2025, 800 bills were introduced in state legislatures, with 40 already passed that "would negatively impact trans, and gender non-conforming people." Two hundred thirty-five bills target educational settings (site accessed March 22, 2025). Author, "2025 anti-trans bills tracker," *Trans Legislation Tracker*, https://translegislation.com.

10 For an excellent discussion of LGBTQ+ issues in the schools, see Stuart Biegel, *The Right to Be Out: Sexual Orientation and Gender Identity in America's Schools* (Minneapolis: University of Minnesota Press, 2010). Professor Biegel concludes his book with a statement from Judge Donovan W. Frank in the T-shirt case "Straight Pride" writing:

> All students benefit from the respectful and thoughtful exchange of ideas and sharing of beliefs and practices. Schools, in particular, are vital environments that can provide an education of both substance of diversity and the responsible manner with which suchdiversity is approached and expressed."

Ibid., 203.

11 353 F. Supp. 254 (D. Ore. 1973).

12 Ibid., 255 (internal citations omitted).

13 *Burton v. Cascade School District Union High School No.5*, 512 F.2d 850 (9th Cir. 1975).

14 *Weaver v. Nebo School District*, 29 F. Supp. 2d 1279 (C.D. Utah 1998).

15 "Ms. Weaver is entitled to summary judgment on her First Amendment claim." Ibid., 1286.

16 Ibid., 1287.

17 See *Romer v. Evans*, 517 U.S. 620 (1996).

18 *Weaver v. Nebo School District*, 29 F. Supp. 2d., 1279, 1289 (D. Utah 1988), citing *Romer v. Evans.*, 473 U.S. 432 (1985). ("If the constitutional conception of 'equal protection of the laws' means anything, it must at least mean that a bare . . . desire to harm a politically unpopular group cannot constitute a legitimate governmental interest.") Ibid., 1289 (internal citations omitted).
19 Ibid.
20 Ibid.
21 Ibid., 1290.
22 *Citizens for Nebo School District for Moral & Legal Values v. Weaver*, 66 P.3d 592, 594 (Utah 2003).
23 Ibid., 600.
24 Ibid., 600.
25 Janna M. Jackson, *Unmasking Identities: An Exploration of the Lives of Gay and Lesbian Teachers* (Blue Ridge Summit, PA: Lexington Books, 2007), 8.
26 Hillary Rodham Clinton, http://www.hillaryclinton.com/news/speech/view/?id=7903.
27 *Governing Board of Nicasco School District v. Brennan*, 95 Cal. Rptr. 712, (Ct. App. 1971).
28 Claire Hansen, Horus Alas, and Elliott Davis Jr., "Where is Marijuana Legal? A Guide to Marijuana Legalization," *U.S. News & World Report* (March 16, 2023), https://www.usnews.com/news/best-states/articles/where-is-marijuana-legal-a-guide-to-marijuana-legalization. The authors write, "Today, support for marijuana legalization has become mainstream among Democratic politicians, and some Republicans also back the idea," Ibid. The House of Representatives passed a marijuana decriminalization bill on April 1, 2022 and Senate Majority Leader, Chuck Schumer, introduced legislation that would decriminalize marijuana at the federal level.
29 *Texas Education Agency, Educator Leadership and Quality Division v. Maryam Roland*, SOAH Docket No. 701-16-4719.EC, Before the State Office of Administrative Hearings, Proposal for Decision (January 10, 2017): 1, https://s3.documentcloud.org/documents/3386762/PROPOSAL-for-DECISION.pdf. See page *3 for a definition of "unworthy to instruct or to supervise the youth of the state."
30 Ibid., *5. The employee ended her "rambling" email "by reporting that she 'no longer [did] cocaine . . . ecstasy, or marijuana.'" Ibid.
31 Ibid., *6.
32 Ibid., *6–7.
33 Ibid. *10.
34 "Certain conduct or conditions that may demonstrate that an educator lacks good moral character, is a negative role model to students, and does not possess moral fitness necessary to be a certified educator includes, but is not limited to, habitual impairment through drugs." Ibid., *3.

35 *City School District of City of NY v. Campbell*, 798 N.Y.S.D. 54, 56 (N.Y. App. Div. 2005).
36 156 N.E. 2d 1 (Ill. App. 1959).
37 Ibid., 2.
38 Ibid., 3.
39 *Watson v. State Board of Education*, 22 Cal.App.3d 559, 563 (Cal. Ct. App. 1971).
40 Ibid.
41 Ibid., 575 (internal citation omitted). The court continued writing, "A teacher ... in the public school system is regarded by the public and pupils in the light of an exemplar, whose words and actions are likely to be followed by the [students] coming under [his] care and protection." Ibid. (internal citation omitted).
42 *Zelno v. Lincoln Intermediate Unit 12 Board of Directors*, 786 A.2d 1022 (Pa. Cmwlth. 2001).
43 Ibid., 1026.
44 *Moffitt v. Tunkhannock Area School District*, 192 A.3d 1214, 1215 (Pa. Cmwlth. 2018).
45 Ibid., 1216.
46 Ibid., 1217.
47 Ibid., 1218, citing to *Zelno v. Lincoln Intermediate Unit No. 12 Board of Directors*, 786 A.2d 1022, 1025 (Pa. Cmwlth, 2001).
48 Ibid.
49 *Broney v. California Commission on Teacher Credentialing*, 184 Cal. App. 4th 462, 470 (2010). The principal stated: "She works very hard and is passionate about what she does. If anything, her flaw is caring too much about her work." Ibid.
50 Ibid.
51 Ibid., 473.
52 Ibid., 475–6.
53 Ibid., 477.
54 Ibid.
55 *In the Matter of Arbitration Between John Bender and Lancaster Central School District*, 108 N.Y.S. 3d 592, 595 (A.D. 4 Dept. 2019).
56 Ibid., 596.
57 For a discussion of the "shocks the conscience" standard of substantive due process in the discipline of public school teachers for both in-school and out-of-school behavior, see Todd A. DeMitchell and Mark Paige, "Substantive Due Process." 'Shocks the Conscience Standard' Applied to Educator Discipline," *Education Law Reporter* 424, no. 1 (2024): 15–26. The due process standard protects teachers from adverse employment decisions, be they based on exemplar or nexus, that "violations of personal rights so egregious, so disproportionate to the need presented, that government action literally shocked the conscience." Jency Megan Butler,

"Shocking the Eight Amendment's Conscience: Applying a Substantive Due Process Test to the Evolving Cruel and Unusual Punishments Clause," *Hastings Constitutional Law Quarterly* 43, no. 4 (2016): 861–84, 876.
58 Ibid.
59 Jonathan Turley, "Teachers Under the Morality Microscope," *Los Angeles Times* (April 2, 2012), http://articles.latimes.com/2012/apr/02/opinion/la-oe-turley-teachers-under-scrutiny-20120402.
60 Rod Meloni, "Van Buren teacher under investigation for performing for X-rated porn site with husband," (August 22, 2018), https://www.clickondetroit.com/news/2018/08/22/van-buren-teacher-under-investigation-for-operating-performing-for-x-rated-porn-site-with-husband/.
61 Associate Press, "Teacher appeals firing over porn," *SouthCoast Today* (August 12, 1996), https://www.southcoasttoday.com/story/news/state/1996/08/12/teacher-appeals-firing-over-porn/50641830007/.
62 Rachel Zoll, "Porn Maker Teacher Fired," *AP* (January 17, 1996), https://apnews.com/article/761204421aa885151cbfdf0cc02bcd6c.
63 B. MacQuarrie, "Teacher Who Acted in X-Rated Videos faces Faces Investigation," *Boston Globe* (January 16, 1996): 1, 19.
64 Olivia Katrandijan and Sarah Hoberman,*Porn Star Teacher Plans to Fight Dismissal*. ABC NEWS (April 21, 2012), http://abcnews.go.com/blogs/headlines/2012/04/porn-star-teacher-plans-to-fight-dismissal/.
65 *Stacie Halas, Fired Calif. Teacher with Porn Past Loses Appeal*, CBS NEWS (January 16, 2013), http://www.cbsnews.com/news/stacie-halas-fired-calif-teacher-with-porn-past-loses-appeal/.
66 Susan C. Bon, Justin Bathon, and Anne-Marie Balzano, "Social Media (Mis)Use by Teachers: Looking to the Courts for Human Resourced Policy Guidance," *Journal of School Public Relations* 34 (2013): 193–217, 193–4.
67 Kristin D. Shotwell, "Secretly Falling in Love: America's Love Affair with Controlling the Hearts and Minds of Public School Teachers," *Journal of Law & Education* 39, no. 1 (2010): 37–8.
68 *In the Matter of the Tenure Hearing of Jennifer O'Brien,* Superior Court of New Jersey, Appellate Division, No. A-2452-11T4 (January 11, 2013) (slip. op.) at *2.
69 Mark Paige and Todd A. DeMitchell, "Arbitration Litigation Concerning Teacher Discipline for Misuse of Technology: A Preliminary Assessment," *Education Law Reporter* 296 (2013): 22–41, 24.
70 Marlynn M. Griffin and Robert L. Lake, "Social Network Postings: View from the School Principals," *Education Policy Analysis Archives* 20, no. 11 (2012): 1–27, 19, http://epaa.asu.edu/ojs/article/view/862. The researchers concluded, "The data from this study suggest that some information on SNS [social network posts] could influence a principal's hiring decision, and thus, that teachers and future teachers should consider keeping their SNS clean and professional." Ibid.
71 15 LA 1473 (2009).

72 Ibid. They included exposure of her breasts and vagina in compromising positions.
73 Author, "Teacher Placed on Leave for Questionable Facebook Posting," WKOW News (February 3, 2009), http://www.wkow.com/Global/story.asp?S=9781795.
74 Cathy Free, "Utah Teacher who Came under Fire for Posting Body Building Bikini Shots," *People* (October 24, 2015), http://www.people.com/article/utah-teacher-body-building-pictures.
75 *Florida High School Teacher Olivia Sprauer Says She was Asked to Resign over Modeling Photos*, ABC10 NEWS (May 6, 2013), http://www.10news.com/news/watercooler/florida-high-school-teacher-olivia-sprauer-says-she-was-asked-to-resign-over-modeling-photos05062013.
76 Carrie Murphy, *Student Teacher Wears a Bra at a Slut Walk and Gets Fired*, Blisstree.com (May 10, 2013), http://www.blisstree.com/2013/05/10/public-health-2/healthcare/reproductive-rights/student-teacher-slutwalk/.
77 A nontenured Georgia English high school teacher (twenty-four-years old) was on a summer vacation in Europe in 2009. She posted a picture of herself holding a glass of wine and a beer on her Facebook page which was set for high for privacy settings. Her principal summoned her to the office and asked whether she had a Facebook page and whether you have any pictures of you with alcohol. When the teacher responded yes to both questions, the administrator offered her an option to resign or be suspended. He told her that a Professional Standards Commission investigation probably would not end well for her. The school officials also took offence to the use of the B-word on the page (she referred to a bar game called "bitch bingo"). She resigned. A week later she tried to get her job back feeling that she had been bullied into resigning. The board refused to rehire her and did not allow her to have an opportunity to respond to the charges. She filed a lawsuit seeking to be reinstated and back pay. The court denied her suit asserting that it could not enforce a contract which had expired in the spring 2010. The court did not address the issues of breach of contract or a coerced resignation. Sources: Author, "Teacher sacked for posting picture of herself holding a glass of wine and mug of beer on Facebook," *Daily Mail* (February 7, 2011), https://www.dailymail.co.uk/news/article-1354515/Teacher-sacked-posting-picture-holding-glass-wine-mug-beer-Facebook.html#:~:text=The%20picture%20was%20taken%20while,in%20the%20summer%20of%202009.&text=But%20Miss%20Payne%2C%2024%2C%20was,you%20have%20a%20Facebook%20page%3F%22. Merritt Melancon, "Barrow teacher presses forward with Facebook lawsuit," *Onlineathens, Athens Banner Herald* (October 11, 2011), https://www.onlineathens.com/story/news/state/2011/10/11/barrow-teacher-denied-her-old-job-presses-forward-lawsuit/15630646007/#.

78 *Board of Trustees of Lincoln County No. Two v. Earling*, 503 P.3d 629, 632 (Wyo. 2022).
79 Ibid.
80 Ibid.
81 Ibid., 633.
82 Ibid.
83 Ibid.
84 Ibid., 635.
85 Wyo. Stat. Ann. § 21-7-110(a)(ix).
86 *Board of Trustees of Lincoln County*, 503 P.3d at 641.
87 Janet R. Decker, "Facebook Phobia! The Misguided Proliferation of Restrictive Social
Networking Policies for School Employees," *Northwestern Journal of Law & Social Policy* 9, no. 2 (2014): 164–205, 166. Professor Decker cites the following examples of controversial educator posts:
    - A special education teacher in Florida posted on Facebook that he was "super horny"and "an "A++" in bed.
    - A teacher's post read, "I'm fairly convinced that one of my students may be the evolutionary link between orangutans and humans."
    Ibid., 164.
88 Author, "Teacher to be Removed from Register for Private Messages to Students," RTÉ (ridió Teilifís Éireann, Ireland's National Public Service Media (December 10, 2024), https://www.rte.ie/news/educat ion/2024/1210/1485741-teacher-professional-misconduct/#:~:text=Upda ted%20/%20Tuesday%2C%2010%20Dec%202024,students%20aged%20 14%2D15%20years. See *The Teaching Council, Code of Professional Conduct for Teachers* (Updated 2nd Edition 2016) (July 2016) (Ireland), https://www.teachingcouncil.ie/assets/uploads/2023/09/code-of-professio nal-conduct-for-teachers1.pdf.
89 461 P.2d 375, 383 (Cal. 1969).
90 See Paige and DeMitchell, *supra* note 69. They write,

> Social media challenges the concept of privacy for educators; how to keep a social activity meant to be shared, private. The weight of exemplar, while lighter, is still felt. The status of exemplar and the duty to not harm the school, teaching, and students impacts the private online, electronic world of teachers.

Ibid., 41.
91 See Bon, et al., *supra* note 66, 193–217. They write, "Nationwide reports of scandals and abuses involving social media have contributed to increasing concern and public interest in the allegations of unprofessional conduct by teachers, including inappropriate relationships between teachers and students." Ibid., 193–4.

Chapter 8

EXEMPLAR AND NEXUS: THE CONTINUING TENSION OVER WHO SHALL TEACH OUR CHILDREN

Historically, parents and school officials have maintained that a teacher cannot lead two lives—one as a role model in school and another as a private citizen.[1]

In a secular society—America today—There may be a plurality of moralities. Whose morals should be enforced? There is a tendency to say that public morals should be enforced. But that just begs the question. Whose moral are the public morals?[2]

In this volume, we examined the legal constraints on a school district's authority to discipline a teacher for private conduct that occurs outside of duty hours. Many teachers naturally believe that their private lives should not be monitored by their employers and that what they do in their own time is no one's business but their own. School boards, however, have long asserted that they have the legal authority to sanction and even dismiss a teacher for private conduct outside the school day when that conduct offends community values or interferes with the teacher's effectiveness in the classroom.

We assert that the tension between these opposing views is a significant controversy. Teachers are central to the education of our nation's children and youth. It is chiefly through their efforts that educational goals are achieved or thwarted. As Issac M. Opper, and economist and professor of policy with RAND stated, "Teachers matter more to student achievement than any other aspect of schooling."[3]

Indeed, the importance of teachers to a child's learning is indisputable. However, teachers' role as shapers and molders of America's future adult citizens often comes at a personal price to their private lives. Jason

R. Fulmer, writing in 2002, asked whether this price is too high. "Being a role model perhaps is a valid interest during school hours, for which the teacher is paid. But should this interest extend beyond that time? When the teacher signed her contract, did she bargain for an around-the-clock role model job with only eight-to-five pay?"[4]

Must a teacher's private life reflect the community's high ideals for the instructors who teach their children? Must teachers' lives, both inside and outside the classroom, be subject to scrutiny and discipline for any deviation from the community's sometimes arbitrary expectations?

Most Americans agree that teachers must possess the pedagogical skills necessary to educate the nation's youth properly and that these pedagogical skills include serving as role models of ethical behavior. However, this reasonable expectation focuses on the teacher's professional activities in the classroom while respecting the teacher's right to a private life.

The nineteenth-century notion that teachers must be exemplars who model their community's professed values and morals, whether on or off duty, persists, albeit with diminished power in the twenty-first century.[5]

Nevertheless, it is generally acknowledged that some out-of-school behavior can hurt a teacher's effectiveness in the classroom. For example, a teacher who engages in criminal activity, such as theft or drug trafficking, is engaging in behavior that is inconsistent with that teacher's status as a role model for children and youth. A teacher's inappropriate sexual conduct, especially the sexual abuse of a student, comes to the courts with a presumption of harm.[6]

Adverse notoriety is one factor used to determine whether a teacher's out-of-school conduct diminishes that teacher's pedagogical effectiveness. Thus, a teacher's off-duty behavior can provide grounds for dismissal if a court concludes that a teacher's effectiveness in the classroom is impaired by widespread publicity about a teacher's private activities that the community finds objectionable.

Moreover, adverse notoriety arising from criminal charges may sometimes justify a school board's dismissal decision regardless of whether the teacher is found guilty. For example, in a 2023 case, an Illinois school district dismissed Bryan Wagner, a tenured social studies teacher, for domestic battery of his spouse, who was also a teacher in the school district. The Board's bill of particulars determined that the teacher's immoral, criminal, unprofessional, and insubordinate conduct had no legitimate basis in school policy, [was] detrimental to the best interests of the District, [continued] to interfere with [his] ability to teach and with the learning environment, and [had] harmed its students, its staff, and the operations and function[s] of the District.[7]

The school district's deputy superintendent explained her dismissal recommendation, stating that she was "extremely concerned [that] the notoriety of [the teacher's] arrest and the harm he has caused as a role model for students in the District."[8]

The hearing officer found that the teacher's behavior created "significant notoriety surrounding the incident." However, the officer concluded that the teacher's behavior was remediable and recommended reinstatement. The Board disagreed, arguing that his behavior was irremediable in that he could not undo the damage done to his reputation and that he could no longer serve as a role model to his students, and warranted dismissal.

On appeal, the Appellate Court of Illinois affirmed the school board's dismissal decision, stating that the teacher's conduct "was clearly harmful to the reputation of the faculty and the school and harmful to his ability to model positive values for students."[9]

Similarly, a West Virginia court examined whether a school district could dismiss a teacher for off-campus drug use, which the teacher had not publicized. A tenured West Virginia math teacher, Matthew Woo, was arrested and charged with selling marijuana to an undercover police operative. When school officials learned of the arrest, Woo was transferred from Hurricane High School to a position that did not involve regular contact with students.[10]

Woo was acquitted of the criminal charges against him. However, at his trial, he admitted that for a couple of years, he regularly smoked marijuana at home but never during school hours or at school activities. Two newspaper articles about the case were published in early June 1993. The publication was followed by a petition that opposed Woo's return to teaching at Hurricane High School. By August, news stories published correspondence among board members that indicated that the board would likely dismiss Woo. This information was obtained from leaked correspondence. At its August 30 meeting, the board was presented with petitions bearing some 700 signatures opposing Woo's return to teaching at Hurricane.[11]

Woo was terminated for immorality and intemperance. An Administrative Law Judge (ALJ) upheld the dismissal, finding that the "Board had shown that there was a rational nexus between [Woo's] off-duty conduct outside of his job because of the notoriety which had attached to [him]."[12] The ALJ noted that some of the notoriety was linked to communications among board members. Still, an extensive record supported the finding that "substantial notoriety" surrounded Woo's conduct, independent of any school board conduct that might have contributed to the notoriety.

The Circuit Court of Kanawha reversed the ALJ, asserting that the tainted notoriety was significant but requiring the school board to prove that each of the 700 signatures "[was] unaffected by the leaked information."[13] However, on appeal, the Supreme Court of Appeals asserted that the Board could not be required to "*disprove* the possible effect of Board-'tainted' leaked information."[14] The appellate court reversed the circuit court and remanded the case to reinstate the ALJ's decision. After the litigation, the school board's dismissal decision based on adverse notoriety was upheld.

The Tension Between Exemplar and Nexus

> While the school district has a strong interest in protecting the school community, it must recognize that its teachers also have rights that are protected by the Constitution. Because a balancing of interests is required when the government attempts discipline based on a teacher's off-duty conduct, several jurisdictions have proposed a compromise to ensure that both the school board's inquiries are warranted, and the teacher's interests are protected: This is the requirement of nexus.[15]

Exemplar and nexus are two legal concepts that are in tension with each other. Exemplar reflects the philosophy that teachers as role models are expected to adhere to community standards and expectations both in and out of the classroom. Nexus acknowledges that teachers have a reasonable expectation of privacy when they are not on duty. Both concepts are essential and valid considerations when examining how a teacher's private life may affect the teacher's competency in the classroom.

This tension between these two competing standards is found in the two primary aims of education. As one of this volume's authors previously observed, "A dynamic tension exists between these aims, the enculturation of the individual into the existing society and the cultivation of the individual for the good society that does not yet exist."[16]

Bertrand Russell's discussion of the tension between cultivating the individual and producing a proper citizen is helpful to our discussion of exemplar and nexus. Russell wrote:

> [T]here is one great temperamental cleavage which goes deeper than any of the other controversies, and that is the cleavage between those who consider education primarily in relation to the individual psyche, and those who consider it in relation to the community.[17]

Similarly, exemplar expresses the community's expectation that teachers conform to the community's expectations, while nexus recognizes the autonomy of professional practice. Both concepts are valid in determining when teachers' off-duty conduct impairs their effectiveness in the classroom. In sum, the tension between exemplar and nexus is necessary, given the legitimate interests of both viewpoints.

Reflections for Practice

All jurisdictions have established statutory guidelines that specify the types of behavior that provide grounds for dismissing tenured and nontenured teachers. State laws permit school boards to dismiss teachers for committing criminal acts, acts of moral turpitude, insubordination, or incompetence.

Although the terms "nexus" or "exemplar" may not be explicitly stated in statutory language, courts often look to these concepts when determining whether a school board's dismissal decision based on the teacher's off-duty conduct is in accordance with state law. Thus, all educators should be aware of these two concepts and how they are defined by the courts in their respective jurisdictions.

In recent years, courts have become increasingly sympathetic to the argument that teachers have a broad right to a private life, one that is not subject to their employers' supervision or control. Nevertheless, no court has ruled that a school board is entirely without authority to terminate a teacher for off-duty conduct. Instead, as this volume explained, the courts generally examine a teacher's private conduct under either the exemplar standard or the nexus standard to determine whether that conduct provides just cause for dismissal.

As explained in Chapter 6, the nexus standard, as articulated by the California Supreme Court in the *Morrison* decision, has become the prevailing standard that courts utilize when reviewing a school board's decision to terminate a teacher's employment due to off-duty conduct. Courts across the United States have relied on the nexus standard because it, unlike the exemplar standard, recognizes that a teacher has a right to a private life. But how private is that life when there is an ongoing tension over the ownership of who shall teach our children? As Joseph C. McElhannon almost 100 years ago sagely wrote, "If education is a social enterprise, then the civilization of the future will bear a close resemblance to the teachers of the present."[18] And Harold Punke in 1971, at the cusp of the nexus movement, wrote, "An efficient school system, in a complex industrial democracy, necessitates protection for competent and devoted teachers."[19]

Our earlier statement with our colleague Suzanne Eckes sums up our conclusion. As we wrote in 2021:

> Adverse notoriety and exemplar placed upon educators, at times unfairly, the watchful burden of community expectations, while easing that burden has been the establishment of the counterbalance to the excesses of nexus, which requires a link between the questioned behavior and harm to the school. Exemplar without nexus allows the community to be oppressive in its control of who shall teach its children. Nexus without exemplar subordinates the community to the profession and may leave the public out of the public school. In seeking a balance between the two, where to place the fulcrum is the question.[20]

Our public schools are probably the nation's most accessible of public institutions. The community must not be left out of its public schools. Yet, we must always seek a reasonable and rational balance between a teacher being held to the standard of an exemplar in their private life and the impact on their professional life.

LAST: We assert that both exemplar and nexus are essential factors in determining who shall be permitted to teach in the nation's schools. The contours, boundaries, and expectations for the private lives of teachers are part of the calculus for determining who to hire and who to retain. Four aspects of a teacher's private life have come to the courts, which could also serve as a guide for administrators investigating out-of-school behavior.

1. A teacher's felony conviction comes to the courts with a heavy presumption of unfitness. On the other hand, an arrest or indictment by itself may not justify dismissal.

2. A teacher's past misconduct without a current negative response from the community may not be sufficient grounds for terminating the teacher's employment.
3. Sexual misconduct involving minors, whether a student or not, is always grounds for termination.
4. Adverse notoriety that arises within the community is a significant factor in determining whether a teacher's off-duty behavior constitutes grounds for termination, regardless of whether a court applies the exemplar or nexus standard. A teacher's private conduct is more likely to provide grounds for dismissal if it provokes a strong negative reaction by parents and the larger community. The destructive effect of notoriety weighs heavily in issues of out-of-school conduct.

As we have stated above, our system of education is crucial for the well-being and future of society and all its individuals—it is a public good of paramount importance. And, central to supporting this public good are the educators who staff those schools and educate our children. There is a pressing need to attract, hire, and retain professional educators. Teaching is more than a job; it is a profession. Its practitioners, like those in other occupations, appropriately seek and expect to balance their professional life with their personal life. We hope that our discussion on the balance between public and private life contributes to this critical conversation.

Notes

1 Tammy Summerville, An Examination of Court Cases Relating to the Dismissal of K-12 Teacher for Immorality (1977–2007), Unpublished doctoral dissertation, University of Alabama, Tuscaloosa, Alabama (2010), 23, https://ir-api.ua.edu/api/core/bitstreams/03c36 92b-f62d-48d7-bb09-7769343bb077/content.
2 Morrison v. State Board of Education, 461 P. 2d 375, 384 (Cal. 1969).
3 Isaac M. Opper, *Teachers Matter: Understanding Teachers' Impact on Student Achievement*, RAND (December 4, 2019), https://www.rand.org/education-and-labor/projects/measuring-teacher-effectiveness/teachers-matter.html.
4 Jason R. Fulmer, "Dismissing the 'Immoral' Teacher for Conduct Outside the Workplace—Do Current Laws Protect the Interests of both School Authorities and Teachers," *Journal of Law & Education* 31, no. 1 (2002): 271–86, 277.

5 "It is just that the vast majority of courts, when faced with a choice between evaluating teacher off-duty conduct under a role model standard derived from statutory morals provision or under a nexus standard, has opted for the nexus standard." John E. Rumel, "Beyond Nexus: A Framework for Evaluating K-12 Teacher Off-Duty Conduct and Speech in Adverse Employment and Licensure Proceedings," *University of Cincinnati Law Review* 83 (2015): 685–746, 698.
6 For a discussion of the sexual abuse of a student, see Chapter 4, The Sexual Abuse of Students Perpetrated by Educators: A Trust Betrayed.
7 *Wagner v. Board of Education of North Shore School District 112*, 228 N.E.3d 996, 1001 (Ill.App. 2 Dist. 2023).
8 Ibid. at 1002.
9 Ibid. at 1010. The court cited *Board of Education of Argo-Summit School District No. 104 v. State Board of Education*, 138 Ill. App. 3d 947, 952 (1985) writing, "Teachers occupy a special position of trust in our society. As leaders and role models, it is the teacher's responsibility to instill basic societal values and qualities of good citizenship in the students."
10 *Woo v. Putnam County Board of Education*, 202 W.Va. 410, 410 (1998).
11 Ibid., 410–11.
12 Ibid., 412.
13 Ibid., 413.
14 Ibid.
15 Fulmer, *supra* note 4, 282.
16 Todd A. DeMitchell, "Utopia or Dystopia? A Philosophical/Policy Perspective on Educational Reform," *International Journal of Educational Reform* 5, no. 3 (1996): 356–66, 357.
17 Bertrand Russell, *Education and the Social Order* (London: George Allen & Unwin, 1932), 9.
18 Joseph C. McElhannon, "The Social Failure of the Teacher," *The Journal of Educational Sociology* 2 (1929): 535–44, 535.
19 Harold H. Punke, *The Teacher and the Courts* (Danville, IL: The Interstate Printers and Publishers, 1971), 620.
20 Todd A. DeMitchell, Suzanne Eckes, and Richard Fossey, "Adverse Notoriety, the Student Protest, & the Viral Facebook Posts: Immoral Conduct and Evident Unfitness to Serve. *Crawford v. Commission on Professional Competence*," *Education Law Reporter* 391 (2021): 426–35, 435.

Appendix A

RULES FOR TEACHERS IN THREE ERAS

These representative sets of rules for teacher employment over a half a century during the formative years of the Nation's system of public schools target female teachers and circumscribe the private lives of both female and male teachers. A number of these rules seem more directed to adolescents than to employed adults.

1872 Rules for Teachers

1. Teachers each day will fill lamps, clean chimneys.
2. Each teacher will bring a bucket of water and a scuttle of coal for the day's session.
3. Make your pens carefully. You may whittle nibs to the individual taste of the pupils.
4. Men teachers may take one evening each week for courting purposes, or two evenings a week if they go to church regularly.
5. After 10 hours in school, teachers may spend the remaining time reading the Bible or other good books.
6. Women teachers who marry or engage in unseemly conduct will be dismissed.
7. Every teacher should lay aside from each day's pay a goodly sum of his earning for his benefit during his declining years so that he will not become a burden on society.
8. Any teacher who smokes, uses liquor in any form, frequents pool or public halls, or gets shaved in a barber shop will give good reason to suspect his worth, intention, integrity and honesty.
9. The teacher who performs his labor faithfully and without fault for five years will be given an increase of twenty-five cents per week in his pay, providing the Board of Education approves.

Appendix A

1915 Rules for Teachers

1. You will not marry during the term of your contract.
2. You are not to keep company with men.
3. You must be home between the hours of 8 p.m. and 6 a.m. unless attending a school function.
4. You may not loiter downtown in ice cream stores.
5. You may not travel beyond the city limits unless you have the permission of the chairman of the board.
6. You may not ride in a carriage or automobile with any man unless he is your father or brother.
7. You may not smoke cigarettes.
8. You may not dress in bright colors.
9. You may under no circumstances dye your hair.
10. You must wear at least two petticoats.
11. Your dresses must not be any shorter than 2 inches above the ankle.
12. To keep the school room neat and clean, you must sweep the floor at least once daily, scrub the floor at least once a week with hot, soapy water, clean the blackboards at least once a day and start the fire at 7 a.m. so the room will be warm by 8 a.m.

Susan Marquardt Blyston, "Rules for one-room schoolhouse teachers," *Illinois State University (News)* (February 17, 2014), https://news.illinoisstate.edu/2014/02/rules-one-room-schoolhouse-teachers/.

Circa 1936 North Carolina Contract

I promise:

- to take a vital interest in all phases of Sunday-school work, donating of my time, service, and money without stint for the uplift and benefit of the community.
- to abstain from all dancing, immodest dressing, and any other conduct unbecoming a teacher and a lady.
- not to go out with any young men except in so far as it may be necessary to support Sunday-school work.
- not to fall in love, to become engaged or secretly married.

- to remain in the dormitory or on school grounds when not actively engaged in school or church work elsewhere.
- not to encourage or tolerate the least familiarity on the part of my boy pupils.
- to sleep at least eight hours a night, to eat carefully, and to take every precaution to keep in the best of health and spirits in order that I may be better able to render efficient service to my pupils.
- to remember that I owe a duty to the townspeople who are paying me my wages, that I owe respect to the school board and the superintendent that hired me, and that I shall at all times be the willing servant of the school board and the townspeople and that I shall cooperate with them to the limit of my ability in any movement aimed at the betterment of the town, the pupils, or the schools.

For this the school board promised to the teacher $637.50 for the school year.

Howard K. Beale, *Are American Teachers Free?* (New York: Charles Scribner's Sons, 1936), 395–6.

Appendix B

EFFICIENCY REPORTS ON TEACHERS FROM 1923 TO 1928

Joseph C. McElhannon studied the efficiency reports of 893 teachers. The following is a summary of the reasons for teachers who were not reelected to their positions.

- Of the 893 teachers he reviewed, 343 (34 percent) were not reelected.
- "They were not identified with the community (191 teachers)."
- "They were more interested in the town sheiks (126 teachers)."
- "They frowned upon church and Sunday school (79 teachers)."
- "They left Friday and returned on Monday to work (53 teachers)."
- "They were grossly immoral (22 teachers)."

Clearly, it was expected that the teacher would identify with the community. The teacher was expected to uphold and adhere to the standards the community espoused. They were expected to participate in all things but to determine none.

McElhannon wrote, "If education is a social enterprise, then the civilization of the future will bear a close resemblance to the teachers of the present."

Joseph C. McElhannon, "The Social Failure of the Teacher," *The Journal of Educational Sociology* 2, no. 9 (May 1929): 535–44, 535.

Appendix C

TABLE OF COURT CASES

FEDERAL CASES

Cases	Chapters
US Supreme Court	
Adler v. Board of Education of City of New York	3, 5
Ambach v. Norwick	3
Baggett v. Bullitt	4
Beilan v. Board of Education	5
Board of Regents v. Roth	1
Brown v. Board of Education	3
Cafeteria Workers v. McElroy	4
City of Cleburne, Texas v. Cleburne Living Center, Inc.	7
City of San Diego v. Roe	4, 6
Cleveland Board of Education v. Loudermill	6
County of Sacramento v. Lewis	4, 8
Dobbs v. Jackson Women's Health Organization	1
FCC v. Fox Television Stations, Inc.	4
Gebser v. Lago Vista Independent School District	4
Grannis v. Ordean	4
Grayned v. City of Rockford	4
Joint Anti-Fascist Committee v. McGrath	4
Mahanoy Area School District v. B.L. ex rel. Levy	4
Morrissey v. Brewer	4
Olmstead v. United States	1
Palmore v. Sodoti	5
Pierce v. Society of Sisters	2
Planned Parenthood v. Casey	1, 8
Plyler v. Doe	3
Prince v. Massachusetts	2
Romer v. Evans	7
Rowland v. Mad River School District	7
Sessions v. Dimaya	4
Shelton v. Tucker	6
Tinker v. Des Moines Independent School District	4
United States v. Williams	4
Vernonia School District 47J v. Acton	1
Wolff v. McDonnell	4, 8

FEDERAL CASES

Cases	Chapters
Federal Court of Appeals (Circuit)	
First Circuit	
Timothy W. v. Rochester School District	4
Ward v. Hickey	5
Wishart v. McDonald	5, 8
Fourth Circuit	
Stroman v. Colleton County School District	6
Fifth Circuit	
Andrews v. Drew Municipal Separate School District	3, 5
Avery v. Homewood City Board of Education	3
Gonzalez v. Ysleta Independent School District	4
Sixth Circuit	
Doe v. University of Cincinnati	4
Littlejohn v. Rose	5
Seventh Circuit	
Doe v. St Francis School District	7
Doe-2 v. McLean County Unit District 5 Board of Directors	4
Hansen v. Board. of Trustees of Hamilton Southeastern School Corp.	4
Zellner v. Herrick	7
Eighth Circuit	
Fischer v Snyder	6
McConnell v. Anderson	7
Stephenson v. Davenport Community School District	4
Ninth Circuit	
Burton v. Cascade School District Union High School No. 5	1
High Tech Gays v. Defense Industry Section Clearance Office	7
Federal District by State	
Alabama	
Drake v. Covington County Board of Education	5
Nebraska	
Brown v. Bathke	5
Nevada	
Jane Doe A. v. Green	4
New Hampshire	
Local 8027, AFT-NH, AFL-CIO v. Edelblut	4
New York	
Immediato by Immediato v. Rye Neck School District	1
Oregon	
Burton v. Cascade School District Union High School District, No.5	7

Appendix C

FEDERAL CASES

Cases	Chapters
Pennsylvania	
Munroe v. Central Bucks School District	1
Texas	
Doe v. Beaumont Independent School District	4
Utah	
Weaver v. Nebo School District	7
Virginia	
Murmer v. Chesterfield County School Board No. 3	3
Ponton v. Newport News School Board	6
District of Columbia	
Swift v. United States	5

STATE COURTS

Cases by State	Chapters
California	
Board of Education v. Jack M.	8
Board of Education of the City of Los Angeles v. Swan	6
Broney v. California Commission on Teacher Credentialing	7, 8
Crawford v. Commission on Professional Competence	7, 8
Daly v. Derrick	4
Goldsmith v. Board of Education	5
Governing Board of Nicasco School District v. Brennan	7
McLaughlin v. Board of Medical Examiners	1, 5
Morrison v. State Board. of Education	1, 3, 4, 6, 7, 8
Pettit v. State Board. of Education	1 5, 6, 8
San Diego Unified School District v. Commission on Professional Competence	6
Watson v. State Board of Education	7
Florida	
Clark v. School Board of Lake County	1
Nodar v. Galbreadth	8
State Ex Rel. Schweitzer v. Turner	5
Illinois	
Board of Education of Argo-Summit School District No. 104 v. State Board of Education	8
Chicago Board of Education v. Payne	3, 5
Fallon v. Indian Trail Sch. Addison Township School District No. 4	4
People ex rel. Odel v. Flaniingan	5
Scott v. Board of Education	7
Tingley v. Vaughn	1, 5
Trustees of School Board v. People ex rel. Van Allen	2
Wagner v. Board of Education of North Shore School District 112	8

FEDERAL CASES

Cases	Chapters
Indiana	
State v. Bailey	1
Iowa	
Erb v. Iowa State Board of Public Instruction	6
Kansas	
Hainline v. Bond	1
Kentucky	
Board of Education of Hopkins County v. Wood	3, 6
Gover v. Stovall	1, 5, 6
Williams v. Stanton Common School District	2
Louisiana	
Desselle v. Guillory	5, 8
Massachusetts	
Dupree v. School Committee of Boston	6
Freeman v. Bourne	3
Michigan	
Beebee v. Haslett Public Schools	8
Land v. L'Anse Creuse Public School Board of Education	5, 8
Satterfield v. Board of Education of Grand Rapids Public Schools	6
Minnesota	
Backie v. Cromwell Consolidated School District No. 133	5
Missouri	
In Re Thomas	6
McLellan v. Board. of Presidents, etc. of Public Schools. of St. Louis	5
Nebraska	
Fisher v. Snyder	6
Kelley v. Ferguson	2
State ex rel. Sheibley v. School District No.1	1
New Hampshire	
Fogg v. Board of Education	2
New Jersey	
In the Matter of Tenure Hearing of Jennifer O'Brien	7
New York	
Ansorian v. Zimmerman	8
C.M. v. City of New York	4
City School District of City of New York v. Campbell	5, 7
City School District of the City of New York v. Colleen McGraham	7
Community School Board District 25 v. Drew	1
Denicolo v. Board of Education of City of New York	4
Doe v. Hauppauge Union Free School District	4

FEDERAL CASES

Cases	Chapters
In the Matter of Arbitration Between John Bender & Lancaster Central Sch. Dist.	7
Mercein v. People ex rel. Barr	2

North Carolina

In Re Freeman	4

Ohio

Chardon Local School District v. Chardon Education Association/OEA/NEA	4
Hoffman v. State Board of Education	6
Jarvella v. Willoughby-Eastlake City School District Board of Education	6
Prude v. Ohio State Board of Education	5

Pennsylvania

Community School Board. District 25 v. Ronald Drew	1
Horosko v. School District of Mount Pleasant Township	5
In Batrus Appeal	5
Moffitt v. Tunkhannock Area School District	7
Reitmeyer v. Unemployment Comp. Board of Education	1
Zelno v. Lincoln Interm. Unit 12 Board of Directors	7

Tennessee

Crosby v. Holt	4

Texas

Galveston Independent School District v. Boothe	4
Texas Education. Agency, Educator Leadership and Quality Division v. Roland	7

Utah

Citizens for Nebo Sch. Dist. for Moral& Legal Values v. Weaver & Utah St. Bd.	7
Weaver v. Nebo School District	7

Virginia

Murmer v. Chesterfield County School Board No. 3	3

Washington

Cronin v. Central Valley School District	4
Gaylord v. Tacoma School District No. 10	5

West Virginia

Golden v. Board of Education	5, 8
Powell v. Paine	1
Rogliano v. Fayette County Board of Education	3, 5, 8
Woo v. Putnam County Board of Education	8

Wisconsin

Soglin v. Kauffman	4

Appendix C

FEDERAL CASES

Cases	Chapters
Wyoming	
<u>Board of Trustees of Lincoln County No. Two v. Earling</u>	7

International Courts

Canada

John Shewan and Lize Shewan v. The Board of School Trustees School District	1
New Zealand	
CAC v. Teacher	1
Collie v. Nursing Council of New Zealand	1

INDEX

adult bookstore 161–3
adultery 156–8
Adverse Notoriety 9, 121–3, 124, 131–2, 155, 180, 186, 206, 210, 211
alcohol 102 n.41, 183–4
   DUIs 184–8
Australia 85, 108 n.94

Beale, Howard K. 39, 65, 114, 115

Canada 10, 11, 13, 20 n.14, 24 n.53, 45, 85
Catholic School System 40–4
   Philadelphia Bible Riots (1844) 43
colonial education 28, 29–31, 33, 35
   Dame Schools 30
   Middle Colonies 31
   Old Deluder Satan Act (1647) 29
   petty schools 29
   Southern colonies 31
common school movement 1, 5, 13, 16–18, 33–7, 39, 47, 49, 64, 175
   access, lack of 45
   bureaucracy, rise of 44–6, 47
   challenges for schools 35
   reform measures 36
Communist Party 118–20, 146
Craigslist 164–8
   application of *Morrison* 166–7, 186–7, 190
Cremin, Lawrence A. 27, 45–6, 62
criminal activity 8, 104 n.53, 107, n.93, 125–7, 134, 137, 138, 149, 153–4, 155, 158, 160, 170 n.20, 176, 182–7, 206, 207, 209

drag queen 13–16
due process 66, 88–90
   procedural due process 88–90
   substantive due process 89–90

educational practice 80–2
Ellsbree, Willard 1, 16, 37, 137
equal protection 66, 179
exemplar 4, 5–7, 8–10, 13, 16, 17–18, 64–6, 70, 84, 111–15, 169, 175, 176, 182, 184, 206, 209, 210
   role model 4, 39, 47, 63, 64, 65, 67, 68, 71, 83, 112–15, 132, 133–4, 137, 138, 161, 165, 167, 190, 206

feminization of teaching 37–40, 54 n.53
Fourteenth Amendment 2, 88, 89, 120, 145

Goldstein, Dana 35
Gusfield Model 17, 68–71
   causation 69, 70, 71
   ownership 68–9, 70, 71
   political responsibility 68, 69

immorality 2, 4, 5, 8, 65–6, 112, 113, 116–18, 122, 124, 133, 134, 136, 137, 147, 149, 150, 161, 167, 177, 184–6, 189, 191, 193–4, 207

Kaestle, Carl F. 35, 40, 42, 52 n.39

"last chance agreement" 187–8
Lortie, Dan C. 3, 82

Mann, Horace 31–3, 36–7
mannequins 122–3, 128–9
marijuana 125–8, 180–3, 207
moral panic 16, 46, 97

negligence 93–5
New Zealand 11–13
Nexus 3, 7–10, 12, 13, 66–8, 70, 84, 146–7, 148, 159, 180, 182, 184, 209, 210
  Morrison and Nexus 18, 121, 123, 124, 128, 130–1, 134, 148–52, 155, 157, 158, 159, 166–7
  Morrison standards 151

parental rights 18, 48, 49, 58–9 n.108
pregnancy 65–6, 135–7, 139 n.15
privacy, rise of a teacher's right to 145–7
profession 36, 75–8, 100 n.23, 111, 112
  code of ethics 85–8
  educators' voice on professionalism 82–5
  semi-profession 79–80
  standards 77–8
public conduct 121, 122, 137, 142 n.91, 184

Rumel, John Front Piece, 17, 67

school climate/environment 95–6, 97, 101 n.28
Scotland 135
sexual abuse of students 90–5, 206
  Alida Starr Gebser 91–3
  grooming 95, 108 n.94
sexual behavior, prior 188–90
sexual orientation 132, 134, 176–80
shaking dice 117–18, 148
shoplifting 123–4
Shotwell, Kristin D. 10, 47, 176
subversive organizations 118–20
swingers party 152–6

technology 129–31, 190–5
  Facebook posts 6–7, 129–31
  virtual/internet contact 194–5
Tyack, David 17, 18, 34, 47
Tyack, David & Elizabeth Hansot 37, 65, 113

United Kingdom 12–13, 85, 135
unprofessional conduct, 14, 84, 86, 91, 149, 150, 154, 170 n.20, 186, 189, 190, 194, 203 n.89, 206

ABOUT THE AUTHORS

Todd A. DeMitchell (B.A., M.A.T., University of La Verne; M.A., University of California, Davis; Ed.D., University of Southern California; Post-Doctorate, Harvard Graduate School of Education) is Professor Emeritus of Education Law & Labor at the University of New Hampshire. He previously held the John & H. Irene Peters Endowed Professor of Education and the Lamberton Endowed Professor of Justice Studies positions. In addition, he was named Distinguished Professor at the University of New Hampshire. He also received the Excellence in Teaching Award from the College of Liberal Arts and the University Graduate Student Mentor Award. Prior to joining the faculty at the University of New Hampshire, he spent eighteen years in the public schools holding such positions as teacher, principal, director of personnel & labor relations, and superintendent.

Richard Fossey (B.A., Oklahoma State University; M.A., University of Texas; J.D., University of Texas; Ed.D., Harvard Graduate School of Education) is Professor Emeritus of Education Law & Policy at the University of Louisiana at Lafayette, where he was the Paul Burdin Endowed Professor of Education. Previously, he held the Mike Moses Chair of Education at the University of North Texas. From 2011 until 2021, he was Editor of Catholic Southwest and is a Fellow of the Texas Catholic Historical Society. Prior to entering higher education, he practiced law in Alaska, where he represented school districts in Aleut, Athabaskan, and Inuit communities.